'64

P9-DTJ-227

DE

PS1541
Z5
G7

49107

TERTELING LIBRARY
THE COLLEGE OF IDAHO
CALDWELL, IDAHO

THE LONG SHADOW

Emily Dickinson's Tragic Poetry

THE
LONG
SHADOW

Emily Dickinson's Tragic Poetry

Presentiment—is that long Shadow—on the Lawn—
Indicative that Suns go down—

The notice to the startled Grass
That Darkness—is about to pass—

BY CLARK GRIFFITH

PRINCETON UNIVERSITY PRESS · PRINCETON · N.J.

1964

PS1541
Z 5
G7

COPYRIGHT © 1964 BY PRINCETON UNIVERSITY PRESS
ALL RIGHTS RESERVED
L.C. CARD: 63-16234

✠

PRINTED IN THE UNITED STATES OF AMERICA
BY THE VAIL-BALLOU PRESS, BINGHAMTON, NEW YORK

49107

For Kathy Griffith

STRAHORN LIBRARY
THE COLLEGE OF IDAHO
Caldwell, Idaho

Acknowledgments

▄▄▄

M Y CHIEF DEBT is to four readers who watched the manuscript develop: Christopher Drummond, Peter Everwine, Audrey Griffith, and Claire Rosenfield. It is only fair to say that I have insisted on points with which none of the four would agree. On the other hand, they kept me at it; their sensitive and varied understandings of Emily Dickinson have greatly contributed to my own understanding.

I have also had the encouragement of colleagues at the University of Iowa, particularly of John C. Gerber, W. R. Irwin, and Alexander C. Kern, mentors and friends of long standing. And, in more than just the coventional sense, I owe much to the staff and readers of the Princeton University Press. By challenging some of the ideas they found in it, Miss R. Miriam Brokaw, Professor Roy Harvey Pearce, and an anonymous third reader for the Press have made this a better book than it was when they saw it initially.

An early, briefer version of Chapter V appeared in *University of Kansas City Review*, Winter 1960; in virtually its present form the same chapter appeared in *Iowa English Yearbook*, 1961. The material is used here with the permission of the editors. I also acknowledge these other permissions: that of the Belknap Press of the Harvard University Press and the Trustees of Amherst College from Thomas H. Johnson, editor, to quote from *The Poems of Emily Dickinson*, © 1951, 1955; that of Little, Brown and Co., to quote from *The Complete Poems of Emily Dickinson*, © 1960; that of Har-

ACKNOWLEDGMENTS

court, Brace & World, Inc., to quote from *Collected Poems of T. S. Eliot*, © 1936 and from T. S. Eliot, *Four Quartets*, © 1943; that of Alfred A. Knopf, Inc., to quote from Wallace Stevens, "Sunday Morning"; and that of Alan Swallow, Publisher, to quote from Yvor Winters, *In Defense of Reason*, © 1947, 1960.

C.G.

Contents

THE LONG SHADOW

Emily Dickinson's Tragic Poetry

Introduction

···

THE TITLE AND TITLE POEM of this book suggest its
scope and emphasis. The need for such a title can
perhaps be illustrated through a comparison of the two
following poems:

> I never saw a Moor—
> I never saw the Sea—
> Yet know I how the Heather looks
> And what a Billow be.
>
> I never spoke with God
> Nor visited in Heaven—
> Yet certain am I of the spot
> As if the Checks were given—

· · ·

> I know that He exists.
> Somewhere—in Silence—
> He has hid His rare life
> From our gross eyes.
>
> 'Tis an instant's play
> 'Tis a fond Ambush—
> Just to make Bliss
> Earn her own surprise!
>
> But—should the play
> Prove piercing earnest—
> Should the glee—glaze—
> In Death's—stiff—stare—

> Would not the fun
> Look too expensive!
> Would not the jest—
> Have crawled too far!

The superiority of the second example is, one would suppose, quite indisputable. For all its chipperness and air of serenity, the first carries little real conviction. Its analogies are trite and excessively facile; its reasoning seems shallow, especially when we contrast it with the sense of struggle which gives so much power and dramatic interest to the other text. Nor does this judgment merely reflect a critic's preference for skepticism over affirmations. On technical grounds alone, the difference between the two poems is surely self-evident. There is, among the images of the first, not one which will compare with that figure of the glazed and staring eyes. Nothing in the pretty melodiousness of the first can begin to match the way in which the theme of the second is underscored by a deliberately harsh diction, the repeated use of spondees, and the severe absence of rhyme.

One might also suppose, then, that the second poem would have achieved a certain distinction in the Emily Dickinson canon. But this is so far from being true that it is actually the first piece—the tinkling little credo —which has become a classic: a kind of Emily Dickinson trademark. Not only is it widely known and almost unfailingly anthologized; the frequency with which it is reproduced would suggest that, by many readers at least, it has been accepted as perfectly typical of Miss Dickinson's basic viewpoint. Concerning its counterpart, however, next to nothing is ever heard. My survey of a good many anthologies has failed to locate more than one or two in which this enormously complex poem is reprinted. Nor do I find that it is generally familiar to Miss Dickinson's readers, not even to those who have looked with some depth into her work.

Why is it that Emily Dickinson often seems best known by her most trifling poems? The responsibility, I am convinced, does not lie solely with the anthologists' poor selections or with critical sophistries. Miss Dickinson's worst is frequently confounded with her best because of a widespread failure to come to terms with her true intellectual position. Her poetry is misread for the simple reason that her intelligence is slighted and the view of life she maintained has been persistently oversimplified.

In those rare moments when they have dwelt as long on her work as on her life, the critics have somehow produced an Emily Dickinson who was, in attitude, a smiling cosmic optimist and, in technique, a writer closely akin to the English Victorian gentlewoman. Upon the topic of Miss Dickinson's blighted romance, interpretation has, to be sure, expended a vast deal of energy. The effects of this episode on her poetry stand fully— not to say lovingly—"researched" in a dozen different places. But aside from the romance and the suffering it is presumed to have caused, Emily Dickinson continues to be a figure around whom there cluster adjectives like "exultant" and "playful," "mystical" and "ecstatic"; her work continues to attract such labels as "comic" and "sentimental," "transcendental" and "serene." When the poetry was first published, it seemed to many to combine the spirit of Whitman, in miniature, with the easy, empty grace of Elizabeth Barrett Browning. And even now, over a half century later, there is scant rea-

5

son to believe that these initial impressions have changed much. One suspects that the favorite public images of Miss Dickinson are still those of an American Mrs. Browning, with a shade less preciousness and minus of course the husband, or of a feminine Walt Whitman, with the "yawp" tuned down somewhat, and minus of course the whiskers.

Such images could hardly be more false, or more pernicious in their falsity. The truth is that Emily Dickinson was a tragic poet, endowed with great tragic insight and a great tragic sensibility. Her finest poems have to do with man's lot in a world that is tragically "other" than himself; developing this theme, they anticipate the tragic sense of life as it has been reformulated for our time by Unamuno and the existentialists. Whether Miss Dickinson's outlook derived from her blighted romance—or whether, even, such an experience occurred—are, it seems to me, very open questions. But about the nature of her outlook, one finds it possible to speak with force and certainty. It was, in the sense with which existentialism now defines these terms, an outlook suffused with *Angst*, dread, and terror. It was uniquely responsive to the brutalities which life imposes on the individual, and acutely aware of the nothingness with which individual existence appears surrounded. Born, in some fashion or other, of personal frustration, the outlook passed the supreme test which art demands of suffering. It transcended the personal to become concerned with suffering and frustration as universal themes.

If one wishes to discover among her contemporaries the mind which most resembled Emily Dickinson's, one should look not to Whitman or the Victorian ladies, but to Herman Melville. Together with Melville, Miss Dickinson was plagued by philosophical uncertainties, and bedevilled by a world which struck her as a place of mystery, ambiguity, and obscure horrors. She shared with Melville essentially the same view of man's predicament, seeing him as a finite creature, craving order and infinity, but set down in a "multiverse" that thwarts his cravings and remains deaf to his appeals. More often than Melville, Miss Dickinson sought to resist her tragic vision: her poetry—indeed her whole way of life—show her trying to devise means of escape which would never have occurred to him. In her most meaningful poems, however, the tragic vision prevails. And the themes of the most meaningful poems are not basically different from those explored in *Moby Dick* or *Pierre*.

This conception of Miss Dickinson's work has been the starting point for my study, and it will color all that is to come. The central intention here is to reclaim Miss Dickinson for the tragic tradition to which she properly belongs. The aim is to spell out the sources of her tragic awareness, and to show how those sources were transmuted into art. I wish—in sum—to demonstrate that the frozen horror of "I know that He exists" is not restricted to one remarkable poem, but that it represents, as well, the characteristic stance in much of Emily Dickinson's writing.

II ✛

With the overt circumstances of her life, I am not greatly concerned. Numerous biographies are already available; and while I have from time to time questioned the assumptions in some of them, I have no new background information to contribute. On the other hand,

I am vitally concerned with Miss Dickinson's inner life
—the life persistently revealed in her poetry. There is
a sense, I suppose, in which this study becomes, at certain points, a psychological biography. It has seemed to
me that the inner can be made more approachable if we
begin with the barest summary of the outer. From this
handful of factual details, two preliminary inferences
will be drawn. Then, in subsequent chapters, the inferences will gradually be expanded into a theory meant
to illuminate both Miss Dickinson's art and certain aspects of her personal behavior.

Emily Dickinson was born, in 1830, in Amherst, Mas-
sachusetts, then as now a small college community located within a hundred miles of Boston and Concord.
Her father was a prominent citizen, an intellectual,
and, if not an absolutely ruthless, at least a stern and
domineering, parent. The mother, according to Miss
Dickinson's own estimate, was a complete nonentity.
There were two other children: a brother Austin, who
eventually married one of Emily's school friends and
took up residence in the house next door, and Lavinia,
a sister, who, like Emily, remained a spinster, living
at home. Except for a term at Mt. Holyoke College in
1846, and a brief stay in Washington while her father
served in Congress, Miss Dickinson dwelt almost continuously within the confines of Amherst. She died there
in 1886.

The most dramatic event in her external life—and it
is dramatic in a rather negative way—started occurring
in 1858 and 1859. These were the years when she began, definitely and noticeably, to seclude herself from
the outside world. Her decision was still not irrevocable,
for she was twice in Boston for medical care in the

1860's. Nor was it as yet accompanied by the peculiar mannerisms that would emerge later: her dressing all in white for furtive strolls through the garden at nightfall; her habit of speaking to callers from behind a screen, or while remaining hidden in an adjoining room; her refusal to address in her own hand the letters which were her only ties to the world without. But if her reclusion was gradual, still, following 1858–1859, there could be little doubt about the way of life that Emily Dickinson had chosen. She had begun a process of withdrawal that would be consummated within a decade, when she wrote that "I do not cross my Father's ground to any House or Town."

Simultaneously with this came the drama of her *inner* life. Prior to 1858, she had written a little light verse, and a few other surviving poems which can most charitably be described as the work of a sentimental schoolgirl. In 1858, however, her creative energies were released: suddenly, fully, even frighteningly released. Composing them, apparently, over the space of three and a half years, Emily Dickinson had on hand no fewer than four hundred separate poems when, in 1862, she addressed her famous appeal to Thomas Wentworth Higginson, the editor of *The Atlantic Monthly:* "Mr. Higginson,—Are you too deeply occupied to say if my verse is alive? . . . The mind is so near itself it cannot see distinctly, and I have none to ask." Hence one clear fact from Miss Dickinson's life is this: that seclusion was a necessary condition for creativity, that experience had to be retreated from before it could be written about. If her personal behavior was mad—and in some respects it no doubt was—then the madness was at least a productive aberration, very close to genius.

The first point with which this context supplies us is a firm sense of Emily Dickinson's cultural and literary connections. We note that both chronology and geography relate her to the Transcendentalist phase of the American Romantic era. Her formative years coincide exactly with the publication of the great Transcendental texts: Emerson's essays and poetry, *Walden*, the *Dial*, the early versions of *Leaves of Grass*. Moreover, the nearness of Amherst to Concord suggests the ease with which Miss Dickinson would have been imbued with the general spirit of Transcendentalism. There is no need to ask when—or even if—she read Emerson. It is enough to see that the atmosphere around her was literally pervaded by Emersonian doctrines. Inevitably, these doctrines were engrained into her thinking and became major parts of her intellectual equipment.

At the same time, however, it is equally evident that her place is on the outer fringes of Transcendentalism rather than at its vital center. By the late 1850's, when her first poetry was written, the crest of the Transcendentalist movement—the ebullient mood of thirty or even ten years earlier—had, in large measure, commenced to wane. Hastening this historical deterioration was Emily Dickinson's own temperament, a temperament which made her skeptical of all ebullience, and, in particular, led her to question the brighter side of Transcendentalist thinking. The result is that Miss Dickinson is best conceived of as a post-Emersonian, or, still more accurately perhaps, as a sort of Emersonian-in-reverse. Inheriting all the basic expectations of Transcendentalism, she found they could give rise to pain and disillusionment quite as readily as to the bland assurances of Concord. Possessing the "knife in the brain"—

the will to know, the passionate desire for certitude—which Emerson bequeathed to New England youth, she found the knife had an edge and a power to mutilate that were far more dangerous than anything Emerson himself had ever visualized. Probably the term which will most effectively describe Emily Dickinson is the term "marginal writer." It is meant to imply an artist who still belongs to a specific literary tradition, yet who is prevented by time, by circumstance, and by disposition from sharing the convictions by which that tradition had once been characterized.

With her retreat indoors, we come at once to the so-called "riddle of Emily Dickinson." It is a subject which has fascinated novelists and playwrights, critics, biographers, and scholars alike—and which, down through the years, has set them to ransacking the poet's biography for the key to her strange and exotic conduct. The overall effect, as Allen Tate once remarked, has only been that of making the riddle seem more riddlesome, or of spicing it up a trifle with the invention of something suggestively nasty. My surmise has been, therefore, that the explanation for Miss Dickinson's self-exile is simply not to be found in biographical data alone. Instead, remembering the traditional kinship between art and neurosis (and noting how her poetry began at almost the same moment as her seclusion), I have guessed that we must look directly to the poetry if we hope to fathom the last thirty years of Emily Dickinson's life and the increasingly neurotic behavior to which those years were given over.

The guess has proved well-founded, I think. When it is read closely, the poetry turns out to contain not one but several reasons both for the retreat itself and also for the mannerisms Miss Dickinson adopted, once her isolation was complete. Indeed, the reasons are rather insisted upon. Either as plain statements or in a thinly disguised form, they stand squarely in the foreground of much that Miss Dickinson wrote. One concludes, eventually, that if poems were Emily Dickinson's letters to the world, they likewise constituted her explanation. They were her way of telling the world why it had to be addressed from behind the protective screen.

Thus it is that of the eight chapters to come, at least five will arrive ultimately at the upstairs bedroom-study, where, after 1858, Emily Dickinson lived and worked. We are led there naturally by poetry in which a uniquely private poet found it possible to speak about herself with candor. The seclusion motif, the motives for and the consequences of withdrawal, the images and the idea of self-isolation—all these matters are so deeply imbedded in Emily Dickinson's recurrent themes that an account of the poetry apart from an account of the room upstairs would be unthinkable. It would be like a study of Dostoyevski which made no mention of the epileptic, or a reading of Melville from which all references to the sea had been left out.

III ✛

The poetry must speak for itself, then; but its manner of speaking requires a word or two of comment. I have had the inestimable advantage of writing since the publication of the variorum edition by Mr. Thomas Johnson. This excellent piece of scholarship seeks to date the individual poems, using for evidence such things as shifts in handwriting, differing qualities of paper, and Emily Dickinson's habits of binding her manuscripts into collections of little booklets. What, for my purposes, has been of decisive importance is the way the new compilation suggests that there were no set periods in the development either of Miss Dickinson's style or of her attitudes. The years of her greatest productivity can easily be isolated; they ran from 1858–1859 to 1869– 1870, with almost no poetry before, and a marked decline in output directly afterward. But within the span itself one finds little evidence of continuous growth, and there are few marked year-to-year variations in technique or idea. Instead, some of the most mature poems come early, while the later years have their fair share of the trivial and the inane. As it happens, the two texts which I quoted at the outset were written about three years apart. Yet the whole drift of Emily Dickinson's career indicates that, for all their radical difference in value and viewpoint, the two could have been composed in the same period, and even, for that matter, on successive days of the same week.*

This fact will illuminate the organization of my material. In the earlier stages of what follows, I have stressed Emily Dickinson's dependence upon irony, and her use of various kinds of ironic stratagem. Later chapters then turn to a poetry in which the ironic defenses have collapsed, giving way to a full and unqualified sense of commitment. At no point, however, do I mean to imply that this change can be charted chronologically. Like the brilliant writing and the abominable in her poetry, Miss Dickinson's examples of the ironic view of life and the non-ironic stand side by side. Her transi-

* It bears upon my point to notice that "I know that He exists" came early (1862), while the business about "the Moor" was apparently not composed until 1865.

13

tions from detachment to tragic involvement occur very rapidly, and take place from one poem or one topic to another, not from year to year or period to period. On some pages of Mr. Johnson's edition, one can watch her donning and doffing the "ironical mask" on as many as three separate occasions.

At first glance, in fact, these sudden changes may seem to convict her of a certain willful inconsistency. But that charge would be grossly unfair and inexact. In all her serious poetry, Emily Dickinson returns again and again to the same hard core of issues. Toward all these issues she counsels the ironic response; toward some, she is actually able to follow her counsellings. Other of the problems, however, prove far too knotty and too terrifying to be turned aside by irony. Miss Dickinson is forced to take a firm emotional and psychological stand concerning *their* significance, because their very character leaves her with no other choice. In a way, my study is divided between the enigmas which she could hold off with ironic defenses and those which she could not.

Finally, a remark concerning my method of choosing poems for discussion. Emily Dickinson composed well over a thousand texts. Many are intrinsically worthless —yet not really very many. When one considers her enormous volume, the level of excellence she maintained was astonishingly high. Hence the critic is easily tempted to deal very extensively with her material, so that no part of its richness will have to be sacrificed. The extensive treatment, however, is precisely what I have attempted to avoid. I have taken my cue in this matter from several earlier studies, whose authors apparently felt obliged to quote from or to paraphase—or at all events to mention—some half of what Miss Dickinson wrote. The consequence, it seemed to me, was not only a vast medley of awkwardness and confusion; it amounted to tabulation or mere description rather than to serious literary criticism.

My policy, therefore, has been to select relatively few poems, to quote most of them in full, to analyze them intensively, and to hope that they will seem representative of the best qualities in the poetry as a whole. Naturally, there are risks this way. Some areas of Miss Dickinson's work may be inadequately treated; others will appear to be simplified. But, if they have been chosen wisely, the texts should provide a comprehensive view of Emily Dickinson's art and attitudes, of her psychological make-up, and of her relationships with Romantic thought. Comprehensiveness has, at least, been my constant and conscious purpose.

CHAPTER I

The Post-Romantic Child

✢ Mirth is the mail of anguish

EMILY DICKINSON'S POETRY surveys a world that is fraught with perils and profoundly contemptuous of human needs. Much of the poetry is constructed around one or the other of two possible responses to that world. One is an attitude involving submission to tragic realities. The second countenances what might be thought of as a strategic retreat from the circumstances of tragedy. It is the second possibility—the principle of the astute withdrawal—which I wish to develop initially.

For that purpose there is no better starting place than a scattering of Miss Dickinson's lyrics which have, as their distinguishing feature, the dramatization of childhood. Sometimes the child will appear directly, to act as the speaker of a text. Again, the child is a figure whose activities the text portrays. On still other occasions, the child remains a kind of implied presence, only suggested by the images and diminutives of which the text has been composed. No reader of the poetry can be wholly unaware of the child poems, for they are relatively numerous. But perhaps because of their simplicity, their seeming childishness, the pieces have rarely received much critical attention. Interpreters have been prone to ignore them as a group—or, treating them at all, to link them to the trifling vein of Stevenson and A. A. Milne.

Yet we can hardly afford to minimize their significance. Beneath deceptively charming surfaces, these child poems have a way of broadening suddenly into malice and sly mockery. Out of their winsomeness, invective is likely to emerge, and not infrequently a touch of pure blasphemy. Of the various sides to Emily Dickinson's writing, none does more than the child poems to reveal the sardonic twists in her imagination or the deep and devious undertones of which she was capable. By commencing with her uses of childhood, we shall have located at once one of the basic strategies in Miss Dickinson's work. And we shall have avoided the blunder which comes from associating Emily's little maids with the nursery, the playpen, or the idyllic garden.

II ✧

An example will be helpful to start with. "By the Sea," which is altogether typical of the child poems, has the added advantage of being somewhat better known than most:

> I started early—Took my Dog—
> And visited the Sea—
> The Mermaids in the Basement
> Came out to look at me—
>
> And Frigates—in the Upper Floor
> Extended Hempen Hands—
> Presuming Me to be a Mouse—
> Aground—upon the Sands—
>
> But no Man moved Me—till the Tide
> Went past my simple Shoe—
> And past my Apron—and my Belt—
> And past my Boddice—too—

And made as He would eat me up—
As wholly as a Dew
Upon a Dandelion's Sleeve—
And then—I started—too—

And He—He followed—close behind—
I felt His Silver Heel
Upon my Ancle—Then my Shoes
Would overflow with Pearl—

Until We met the Solid Town—
No One He seemed to know—
And bowing—with a Mighty look—
At me—The Sea withdrew—

The intriguing thing about "By the Sea" is the way it
has of appealing to certain set expectations, which it
promptly goes on to defy. At the beginning, we seem
headed in a direction that is going to be conventional,
almost to the point of triteness. Then, abruptly, this
movement is arrested, for the poem veers off on a surprisingly different tack. Even now, however, the full
implications in the text are easy to miss. They become
fully evident only when, from the standpoint of the
total poem, we look backward to a few crucial details,
note their position in the narrative, and observe how
they suggest that a lovely and seemingly innocuous
situation must actually be understood as an ugly and
a highly complex moral problem.

One's first impulse is to consider "By the Sea" a characteristically Romantic celebration of childhood. The
two figures in the poem are the speaker and the sea:
a child and Nature. The incident recounted is one in
which the child undertakes a trip to Nature's house.

19

Neither these particular characters nor this particular episode are exactly an invention of Emily Dickinson. For three-quarters of a century before she wrote, the game of going to Nature's house had been a familiar theme in Romantic poetry. Elfin pilgrims were sent piping down the valleys wild; or they were shown to have discovered a special rapport with "Meadows, Hills and Groves"; or they were seen as sallying forth daily into a world as innocent as themselves, and one which they always and perfectly comprehended. Throughout the opening two stanzas of "By the Sea," Emily Dickinson appears to have imposed upon her material the same happy alliance between Nature and childhood which had begun with Blake, continued into Wordsworth, and reached its apogee in Whitman. Setting off to visit Nature, arriving easily and safely, received with apparent hospitality by sands and mermaids and sunken frigates —in all these roles Miss Dickinson's little maid seems to conform exactly to the Romantic conception of childhood. Indeed, she strikes us as just one more romanticized urchin, who is claiming her rightful status in the natural world, and for whom, in another moment, the complexities of existence will commence to dissolve.

But the moment never comes. Instead of the acceptance we had anticipated, there begins in line nine a drama of rejection which continues to the end of the poem. Going to Nature's house involves difficulties, after all; for despite an early welcome, the sea now shows a hostile face to the little maid, and menaces and pursues her. And yet, read casually at least, even this development contributes little to the text that could be called genuinely ominous. For one thing, there is no sharp break in tone between the second and third stanzas, no interruption of a gay and rather rollicking pace. Though *we* may be surprised by Nature's pursuit, the child, whose voice we are hearing, betrays neither astonishment nor alarm. For another, the images which describe pursuit are decidedly *not* the images of a dangerous situation. The sea, we are reminded, is no more harmful than a dew upon a dandelion. If the sea rejects, still he seems to make partial amends by giving the child the lovely gift of pearl. Both these details establish a context in which nothing very frightening would be likely to occur. They make the rebuff of the little maid seem totally unimportant, her whole adventure only an amusing *jeu de spirit*.

Can it, however, be dismissed quite so lightly? The more we ponder the relationship in "By the Sea," the more those details, which seemed so innocent the first time around, come to take on shadings of the unpleasant —and even of the downright horrifying. Consider, for instance, the characterization of the sea. Almost invariably in Romantic poetry, we would expect the ocean to be personified (if at all) in a *feminine* form. Here, by contrast, the usual personification has been reversed. It is a *masculine* ocean which accosts the little maid: it is a "he"—a "man"—who turns on her, attacks her, and sends her scurrying for safety. Nor, having put the child in the clutches of an adult male, does Emily Dickinson permit so enormously suggestive a relationship to drop. Instead, she immediately goes on to magnify its suggestiveness by presenting the attack itself in terms that are distinctively and even baldly licentious. The description in the third stanza will bear particular scrutiny; for the "man's" gestures—his reaching from shoe to waist to bosom—all strongly imply sexual molesta-

21

tion. In the ensuing chase, it increasingly appears that the male ocean has followed the little maid by way of corrupting her purity. (Note, in this regard, how the imposition of water upon the dandelion can now be taken to indicate defloration—or how the filling of the shoe with pearl, ostensibly the loveliest of images, now becomes a further mark of the sea's lasciviousness.) At the end of the poem, there can no longer be much doubt. As the sea withdraws from her, "he" displays a kind of fine insolence, a completely brazen quality, which graphically re-enforces his role as the seducer.

If this reading is at all correct, then, "By the Sea" constitutes, at bottom, a savage and a terrifying indictment of Nature. There is, to be sure, very little in the poem which points *overtly* to this theme. *Overtly*, all we have is the game, a harmless morning's frolic. But as we linger over the participants in this game—and attend to the terms through which their frolic is related—the sinister and unlovely undertones become progressively more difficult to deny. It grows ever clearer that in picturing the child's flight from Nature, Emily Dickinson has done far more than simply undermine the Romantic tradition of childhood. With subtle insistence, she has likewise forced us to think of Nature as the violator of human sanctities. She has made us glimpse in the motives and actions of the natural order the behavior of the most perverted type of criminal.

Her intentions were entirely deliberate, I believe. Moreover, it is my belief that the same intentions, or very closely related ones, are repeated virtually every time Miss Dickinson makes use of the child. But before proceeding to other examples, I wish to re-emphasize the method of "By the Sea." I wish, that is, to draw attention to the essentially *double* function which childhood has served in the poem.

In one sense, of course, it is the child's presence which invests "By the Sea" with its peculiar air of menace. Precisely because a child has been victimized, we are compelled to feel Nature's hostility the more deeply, and to have a sharper sense of Nature's wanton disregard for human welfare. But this is the case only *after* we have grasped the full consequences of what the poem says. And until (or unless) those consequences are seen, the child has a totally opposite effect. Far from heightening the menace, she actually negates it, simply by lending to the narrative an air of charming innocence. Because an ingenuous little maid is the speaker, the imagery can remain so delicate and the tone so light and playful that we easily overlook the serious moral critique which has been presented. In short, technique in "By the Sea" derives from a curious contradiction. The very device which ultimately evokes the full force of horror in the poem also acts, in the short run, to soften the horror and even to blur it completely.

Obviously much care has gone into an exercise such as this. More than care, there is cunning: a kind of cunning which seems born of the realization that certain things can be attacked with impunity only when one has concealed the attack and given every indication of not really attacking at all. Probably, then, it is the underlying principle of the child poems—the curious use of a *persona* on which they turn—that we should come to next. From "By the Sea" and other similar texts, we can readily discover *how* Emily Dickinson utilized the child. But what we need to know in addition is *why:*

why she resorted to this stratagem, why she thought it necessary to hide malice behind the mask of dimpled simplicity.

The answers, if they can be found, promise to take us directly into the workings of Emily Dickinson's mind and to disclose psychological drives that affected not just the child poems, but were responsible, as well, for the main patterns in every important thing she wrote.

III ✛

The *Weltanschauung* which Emily Dickinson inherited may be loosely described as Transcendentalist or, better yet, as Emersonian. It included views more extensive than those of Ralph Waldo Emerson, reaching as they did into the work of Whitman, Thoreau, and certain of the English Romantics. But the views crystallized around an elaborate and widespread theory of man's relations with God and Nature. What, in general, they said was this: Nature is benevolent, compassionate, kindly disposed toward the individual. With a right good will, she snuggles up to man, permitting him to use her for his profit and instruction, allowing him to read with ease her deepest and inmost meanings. Furthermore, Nature is laden with a spiritual significance, which, again, she gladly yields up to the perceptive human observer. Starting with the visible facts of experience, the observer discovers that the phenomena overlay symbolic clues. Pursuing the clues, he is free to rise above them until, in a moment of supreme ecstasy, he stands face to face with Nature's Cause, who may be God, or the Oversoul, or the Great Camerado, or simply the Creative Fountain.

Emily Dickinson matured under the influence of this

outlook, and it is a mistake to assume that she ever wholly discarded it. Had she done so—had she successfully wiped from her mind all the vestiges of Transcendentalism—Miss Dickinson's life and attitudes would have been very different, and quite possibly she would have written no poetry. The trouble was, however, that she could dismiss, as blithe and facile, Emerson's conclusions, yet still find herself drawn irresistibly to many of his basic premises. Or, to put the case more specifically, she could perceive a lamentable want of realism in the way Emerson theorized about man's kinship with the cosmos; yet she was much preoccupied with the same elemental kinship, and continued to think of it in fundamentally Emersonian terms. Accordingly, Miss Dickinson could not—and did not—abandon Emersonian principles. Much more complexly, she inverted them.

Where the Emersonian held Nature to be deliberately benevolent, Emily Dickinson agrees that Natural processes are indeed deliberate—but deliberately treacherous and unpredictable. In her poetry, Nature is capable of conferring moments of great ecstasy. But the moments prove fleeting and transitory. They tantalize the observer, lull her into feelings of false security. Suddenly they pass, to be followed by periods when Nature glares back with a chilling hostility. With the Emersonian contention that Nature is rich with symbolic significance, Emily Dickinson again concurs: she never doubts for one moment that all Natural phenomena are intensely meaningful. The difference is that, for her, the meanings are ambiguous at best, and at their worst they become openly terrifying. As her poetry records them, the symbolic gestures in Nature suggest that Nature is actively antagonistic toward the individual. They imply a cleavage, broad and irreconcilable, between the human being and his non-human surroundings. Above all, they point to the animosity of God; for to the extent that Nature reveals God to Miss Dickinson, she reveals a Creator who harbors toward creation some bitter resentment, whose attitude toward the human race is grounded in a deep and abiding ill-will.

These views recur everywhere in Emily Dickinson's poetry. They are, indeed, the substance of her tragic vision, the prime sources of the grimness and the terror in her writing. At the moment, however, it is enough to see that they are perfectly exemplified in the following magnificent poem—and that the poem illustrates as well a decidedly Emersonian cast to the poet's thinking:

> There's a certain Slant of light,
> Winter Afternoons—
> That oppresses, like the Heft
> Of Cathedral Tunes—
>
> Heavenly Hurt, it gives us—
> We can find no scar,
> But internal difference
> Where the Meanings, are—
>
> None may teach it—Any—
> 'Tis the Seal Despair
> An imperial affliction
> Sent us of the Air—
>
> When it comes, the Landscape listens—
> Shadows—hold their breath—
> When it goes, 'tis like the Distance
> On the look of Death—

Certainly, there is no trace of Transcendentalist optimism here. The situation is one in which the speaker, contemplating the dying day and the death-like season, is reminded by both of her own ultimate extinction. At first glance one will be tempted to assert that a theme this bleak can scarcely be thought of as Emersonian in any respect. Nevertheless, a tendency central to Emersonianism has been perpetuated. In Emerson's scheme, it is obviously quite impossible ever to conceive of Nature as merely a clod of matter. Given the Emersonian outlook, Natural phenomena will inevitably have to be endowed with an anthropomorphic status, will have to be provided with intelligences and personalities distinctively their own. This is precisely the conception which Emily Dickinson has retained. Seeing Nature in a way that Emerson never would—as the source of pain rather than pleasure, as the bearer of bad news rather than of benevolent tidings—Miss Dickinson still manages to stay well within the Transcendentalist tradition. Like Emerson, she declines to treat her subject as a "thing," but she imputes to the Natural environment the motives, the impulses, and the temperamental qualities of a human (or, really, a super-human) being.

For in the poem, Nature acts, while the human observer is acted upon. Syntax, symbolism, and description all conspire to suggest that the actions of the nonhuman must be interpreted as parts of a deliberate plot against the human observer. Thus the light *gives* her an injury, and the air has *sent* her the *Seal Despair*. Furthermore, both light and air are portrayed as symbolic of God, so that they become agents through whom God imposes His *Heavenly Hurt* upon the speaker, or maims her with His *imperial affliction*. Finally, air and light remain aloof and mysterious because they seem to wish to elude the human mind. *None may teach [them]—Any* (that is, no human being can hope to master them intellectually), for the simple reason that these Natural forces do not permit themselves to be understood. The non-human, in brief, has been made to possess human desires, human cunning. As Nature (and by symbolic extension, God) bring their great weight of pain to bear on the speaker, they are shown to have injured and oppressed with a conscious will.

There is, one supposes, something terribly primitive and childlike about attitudes like these. It is even possible to question the value of the poem, by saying that it presents activities which do not really occur in Nature. To make such a statement, however, would be to deny the influence upon Emily Dickinson of her literary heritage. Her views of Nature are neither more absurd nor more simplistic than the views which they have clearly supplanted. Since the birth of the Emersonian perspective, poets had grown accustomed to thinking of Nature as a cuddly companion; they had been pleased to glimpse in their Natural surroundings a friendly pet, always eager to lick their hand and to set about their bidding. Emily Dickinson's Nature is no less personal or dynamic than this—and no less a Nature read by the light of the pathetic fallacy. It is simply that she sees as tigers what others have mistaken for pets.

Which is to say that the effect of Miss Dickinson's kind of thinking is to make the world uniquely hazardous, a place given over to strange powers and to extraordinarily dangerous adversaries. All around the individual, there are intelligent and unfriendly forces that lurk and listen: creation, as one of the poems says, is a perpetually watchful sentinel.* And as they listen, these forces are likely to tolerate no nonsense from mere human beings. Unstable at best, they will be quick to strike back if someone insults or questions them. Always potentially destructive, they are domineering masters who can harm and cripple, once they have been sufficiently aroused. It is, therefore, extremely unwise to affront Nature; in fact, it is indiscreet even to draw the notice of the Natural to one's self. The hushed expectancy of Emily Dickinson's writing derives, in large measure, from just this crucial recognition. Miss Dickinson was the poet of dread—the recorder of nervous fears—for the excellent reason that there were few aspects of her experience which, in her own mind, did not represent something to be feared and dreaded.

Creation listens, then, and listening brooks no back talk. But for Emily Dickinson, this difficult conception of reality was complicated by one further problem: an

---

* The text deserves to be quoted in full:

> To my quick ear the Leaves—conferred—
> The Bushes—they were Bells—
> I could not find a Privacy
> From Nature's sentinels—
>
> In Cave if I presumed to hide
> The Walls—begun to tell—
> Creation seemed a mighty Crack
> To make me visible—

What the text demonstrates, of course, is the acute self-consciousness, the sense of being constantly exposed and habitually preyed upon, which living in Nature's house evoked from Emily Dickinson. It thus sets forth the attitudes of both "By the Sea" and "Slant of light," though it expresses them somewhat more directly.

absolute compulsion for talking back. Such a compulsion, it seems to me, is totally inseparable from Miss Dickinson's poetic practice. She wrote, to a considerable degree, out of an urge to assert herself in the face of a hostile universe. Fearing Nature and the God whom Nature disclosed, she likewise assumed that sanity, dignity, and personal integrity could be maintained only if she somehow made reply to what she feared. In spite of her awe of the sinister forces about her, she yearned sometimes to mock their power, to berate and belittle them—in a word to show them up for what they really were. Thus what Emily Dickinson needed was a method, a method involving the sort of dramatic or verbal indirection which would allow her to say one thing while implying another. Specifically, she required a way whereby she could express her resentments, but express them in the language of sweet submissiveness. She required the means of unleashing vituperation and blasphemy, but of preserving, all the while, a pious and proper tone. She needed, in sum, to remain wholly detached from the world—but to convert detachment itself into a frontal attack upon the world's abuses.

In a succeeding chapter, many such methods will be isolated; for Miss Dickinson's mastery of innuendo was all but boundless. But within the present context only one of her subterfuges is really relevant. That, as I hope is by now self-evident, is the ruse practiced in "By the Sea": the ruse of the simple child.

For when we return to "By the Sea," is it not to discover that the child has been almost perfectly suited to Emily Dickinson's purposes? The little maid is small and unobtrusive; no one notices a little maid. Still more to the point, she is shy and prim and demure; and no one suspects a little maid. So, she is ideally fitted to serve as the instrument for an adult attack, made against enemies of imponderable power. What the child supplies are two defensive weapons: a mask that will betray next to nothing, and a voice so simple and innocent that it will scarcely be overheard. Standing securely behind the mask, losing her own identity in the voice of seeming innocence, Emily Dickinson, the mature poet, is at liberty to encompass both her ends. She makes herself completely safe from reprisal; whereupon she is free to cope with—to castigate, or to put on trial, or to laugh up her sleeve at—a universe that is contaminated to the core.

IV ✛

This, by and large, is the situation we encounter most often in the child poetry. There are times, true enough, when a particular poem will acquire a rather different shading, times when the delineation of childhood becomes, for Emily Dickinson, an excuse for nostalgia and sentimentality. In the main, however, the voice and the mask and the resultant point of view utilized in "By the Sea" tend to persist as basic gambits, and "By the Sea" is in no sense the finest single example of how effective they can be. Other and more mordant texts are discoverable, including, for instance, this bit of unqualified blasphemy:

> I meant to have but modest needs—
> Such as Content—and Heaven—
> Within my income—these could lie
> And Life and I—keep even—

31

But since the last—included both—
It would suffice my Prayer
But just for One—to stipulate—
And Grace would grant the Pair—

And so—upon this wise—I prayed—
Great Spirit—Give to me
A Heaven not so large as Your's,
But large enough—for me—

A Smile suffused Jehovah's face—
The Cherubim—withdrew—
Grave Saints stole out to look at me—
And showed their dimples—too—

I left the Place, with all my might—
I threw my Prayer away—
The Quiet Ages picked it up—
And Judgment—twinkled—too—
That one so honest—be extant—
It take the Tale for true—
That "Whatsoever Ye shall ask—
Itself be given You"—

But I, grown shrewder—scan the Skies
With a suspicious Air—
As Children—swindled for the first
All Swindlers—be—infer—

Once again, everything on the surface conspires to
make the poem appear all cheerfulness and unremitting
gaiety. We commence with a statement of needs, which

is promptly translated into the little prayer of the third stanza. The prayer, we notice, involves only modest requests; and it is, in all respects, the prayer of an unusually precocious and well-mannered child. Both in terms of how it asks and what it asks for, then, this petition is bound to strike us as a model of grace and simple dignity. But now an interesting ambiguity occurs. From the long and complicated fourth and fifth stanzas, we are not able to determine exactly what the disposition of the prayer has been. Is it granted or denied?—the point is never made explicitly. And yet, on the basis of the activities in these twelve lines, the possibility of its being granted would seem much the better bet. After all, love and generosity must certainly pervade a cosmos in which Judgment twinkles, in which divine beings are as sprightly and jocular as the ones pictured here, and in which even God is wreathed in glowing and genial smiles. Surely, Jehovah is laughing with pleasure at His one child who is honest enough to believe Christian precepts—and forthright enough to make belief the grounds for prayer. Surely, the naïve child, so pleasant in demeanor and so earnestly faithful, could not have been denied.

But a close rereading of the text will gradually force us to concede that denial has, in fact, been her fate. To begin with, the happy interpretation of her prayer has all along been contradicted by the verb-forms in the opening stanzas. Unfailingly past tense—

I meant to have . . .

It would suffice . . .

. . . upon this wise—I prayed—

33

—the verbs create an atmosphere in which the speaker is saying: once I had hope and faith and the will to pray, but actual experience has dashed these impulses. Beyond that, there are the odd gestures of lines seventeen and eighteen: if the child has communed successfully with God, why should she throw her *Prayer away* and leave *the Place, with all [her] might?* Most decisively of all, we find in the final references to swindling—

> As Children—swindled for the first
> All Swindlers—be—infer—

—clear evidence of what has befallen the little pilgrim and her little petition. Despite earlier indications to the contrary, her plea for a minor share of Heaven has obviously been rejected.

But more than a simple process of rejection is involved. If the child has not found fulfillment in God's throne room, then we must take a radically different view of those seemingly pleasant details in the two middle stanzas. What—we now have to ask ourselves— what is God laughing at so jovially, if it is not with delight at the child's candor? According to the more realistic reading of the poem, three things occasion His mirth. He is enormously amused by people who are so honest that they take prayer seriously. He mocks those foolish and simple-minded enough to believe in the Christian doctrine of "Ask and it shall be given." And, most especially, He repudiates, just by laughing it down, the Christian promise of "Suffer the little children to come unto me." For not only does Jehovah, once we have reconsidered His role, effectively violate every traditional tenet of Christianity; His particular bar-

barousness lies in His withholding compassion from the child, in His having corrupted the simple faith of the simple, trusting maid.

When applied to this poem, "blasphemous" seems scarcely too strong a word. At least the poem manages to present God in the worst possible light. Nowhere has Deity been directly maligned, of course. Indeed, except for the term *swindler,* from which the sting is very nearly removed by its context, divine duplicity has not even been named. Yet we pause over "A Prayer," watch its good spirits drop away, and find within it vituperation that is so studied and so cleverly planted as to be almost breathtaking. The same childish demeanor which originally blinded us to Emily Dickinson's intentions now, as we read and re-examine, serves to disclose her purpose with a double vengeance. As in "By the Sea," we have watched Miss Dickinson take refuge in dimples and diminutives, while, at the same time and never ceasing to smile, she has set forth a bitterly serious theme—one in which God the Father is branded charlatan, thief, hypocrite, the demonic betrayer of His children.

There is a sense, clearly, in which *we—we* thought of now as adult readers of the poetry—are as likely to be taken in by the child poems as either God or Nature. Both "By the Sea" and, particularly, "A Prayer" have a way of seeming to confirm our cherished values, only to reduce the values (and thereby ourselves, who believe in them) to absurdities, as we grow accustomed to what is actually being said. Thus, like the non-human aspects of creation, which constitute Emily Dickinson's principal targets, *we* too are duped: we mistake simplicity for sweetness, and listen in rapt delight while sly assaults are made on the most pious and sentimental commitments we have. Upon occasion, furthermore, this clash between *our* adult gullibility and *their* childish wisdom turns out to be the principal subject of a child poem. As the last example which it seems necessary to cite, "After the Storm" will illustrate the conflict admirably:

Glee—the great storm is over—
Four—have recovered the Land—
Forty—gone down together—
Into the boiling Sand—

Ring—for the Scant Salvation—
Toll—for the bonnie Souls—
Neighbor—and friend—and Bridegroom—
Spinning upon the Shoals—

How they will tell the Story—
When Winter shake the Door—
Till the Children urge—
But the Forty—
Did they—come back no more?

Then a softness—suffuse the Story—
And a silence—the Teller's eye—
And the Children—no further question—
And only the Sea—reply—

As the imperatives, the tone, and the strident, bumptious meters indicate, this is surely to be a hymn of rejoicing. *We* are going to roll forth loud hosannahs, are going to pound them relentlessly out in the name of the four survivors. God's in His Heaven; glad tidings pour in from every quarter; ours is a splendid world, where miraculous deliverances are quite the commonplace. In our enthusiasm for these propositions—these handsomely orthodox affirmations—mere statistics are made to seem wholly unimportant. The storm's forty victims grow dim and very remote. Virtually drowned out by our loud paeans, they almost manage to slip our minds entirely.

But then the children raise their crucial question. Now they raise it inadvertently, of course. Children— which of us will doubt it?—are dewy-eyed little darlings who never act in any fashion except with the best and purest of motives. Nevertheless, the question is raised; and once it stands before us, *our* noisy shouts of triumph come to sound exceedingly hollow. Here, as in a poem quoted earlier, the glee suddenly glazes in death's stiff stare. *Our* enthusiasm for this best of all possible worlds lapses into a strained and somewhat embarrassed silence. The children have spoken. If we are perceptive enough to comprehend at all, it takes only *their* simple utterance to recall *us* to what a brutal and thoroughly indifferent place the universe really is.

During the last half of the nineteenth century there began to appear in both English and American literature a figure who might be thought of as the "post-Romantic child." Like his Wordsworthian-Emersonian predecessors, this child was also a pilgrim of sorts—a wanderer through his native environment. For him, however, the environment no longer bothered to put on its best or friendliest features. Instead, the little traveller set out with great expectations—and promptly encountered horror and corruption wherever he turned. Sometimes he was actively betrayed by his surroundings. But more generally, he functioned as a figure in irony: it was his fate to be the guileless observer, reporting on a spectacle of evil which he did not invariably or altogether fathom, but which he made the more horrendous, simply because of his own naïveté. The post-Romantic child would of course be Huckleberry Finn, recording the cruelties of life along the river. Or the child would be Henry James's Maisie, perceiving her parents in frequent and frantic adulteries. Or the child would be Alice, discovering that among the properties of Wonderland not the least important are vulgarity and degradation. Naturally, there is no question of influences. The post-Romantic child was the spontaneous creation of a number of writers, each of whom used childhood for different reasons and to achieve a rather different effect. Yet if, in "After the Storm," Emily Dickinson did not invent the post-Romantic child, she at least established herself as an early and distinguished practitioner in the new tradition of childhood.

V ✚

It is her particular version of the child which fascinates; and to it we must briefly return. Perhaps at this point a comment on the ironic poseur will be helpful. For irony *is* a pose, in some sense or other; and, as the classicist J. A. K. Thomson reminds us, the pose has not always been identifiable with sophistication or detachment. Quite the contrary: irony, in its earliest manifestations, was the result of something more pitiful and grotesque. It derived from the superstitions of primitive man and, in particular, from his fears of the world he occupied.

There came the time when man learned to see his non-human surroundings as similar to himself but utterly more potent, the time when he beheld Nature and the Gods as extensions of his own personality, but extensions infinitely magnified, so that they were willing, and even eager, to destroy his very being. Confronted with this awful vision, the primitive had a choice between two modes of conduct. He could placate the powers around him, which was the way of prayer and supplication. Or he could choose to deal with the powers more rationally, and through tactics of indirection. Electing the latter course, man donned the mask of a conscious ironist. He made a great show of being small and trivial and exceedingly humble. But he engaged in the pretense, as Thomson puts it, so that he could lie low in the presence of his cosmic enemies, and simultaneously have a bit of fun at their expense.

To lie low in order to gain the freedom for striking back—here, surely, is the essence of the child poetry, precisely the spirit from which Emily Dickinson's little maidens must have emerged. Partly, as we have seen, the outlook was a condition of Miss Dickinson's time and place. Born to the Emersonian habit of personifying all experience, she continued to behold the nonhuman cloaked in a human form. But in the process she came to recognize her surroundings as hazardous and not friendly, as forces to be dreaded rather than cherished. Accordingly, her world was a place in which the wise lay low and remained thoroughly meek. For the rest, Miss Dickinson's outlook was the product of her own special temperament. Though experience could arouse her to acute anxieties, she was not one to truckle before the enemy. Complete submission was not, for her, a way of life to be endured. Hence fear and irreverence for the things feared struggled together in Emily Dickinson's imagination, and the contradiction was resolved through irony. Thrusting backward to primitive roots—as each in his own way, Emerson had done, and Wordsworth—Emily Dickinson recovered in the nineteenth century a way of dealing with a hostile world which was as old as human cunning itself.

Do not the deceptions practiced in the child poems have a rather obvious corollary in what might be termed the masquerade of Emily Dickinson's life? The possibility is worth lingering over. When, in her late twenties, Miss Dickinson turned indoors, it was no single motive that sent her, but her response to a complex variety of issues. Underlying them all, however, we sense what seems to have been a strong urge for concealment. The impulse to hide; the desire to immolate one's self and so to keep one's self completely out of sight; the quest to shed a public identity—these must have been predominant in the poet's need for seclusion. And then, having made good her defenses, Emily Dickinson commenced to write. As if it were necessary for her to assume a pose first—as if, in a way, it had first been necessary for her to revert to childhood (for recall the little white dress, the prim little mannerisms)— she now became free to assert herself, and in a manner that had hitherto been impossible.

It seems fair, consequently, to argue for a symbolic kinship between the actions within the child poetry and those that were taking place in the upstairs bedroom at Amherst. To hide, in both instances, is a matter of achieving liberation. To become the child is to gain a latitude for speaking openly and with candor. A mask is set in place; and once it has been securely adjusted, the criticism of life proceeds without constraint or inhibition.

40

CHAPTER II

The Uses of Irony

✛ Superiority to Fate
Is difficult to gain
'Tis not conferred of Any
But possible to earn

IN THE CHILD POEMS, the dominant motive is that of
self-preservation. Emily Dickinson creates and uti-
lizes the child out of a keenly conscious instinct to protect herself. She wishes to strike out at certain of the
least amiable features in creation, without running the
risk that they, who are so much the more powerful, will
strike out at her in return. The child, a small and deferential figure, is the perfect *persona* for anonymity, the
perfect mask for a mature poet whose aim is to retreat
from tragedy, by escaping the notice of tragic realities.

But the strategy of the child leads on to the more
general proposition that vast stretches of Emily Dickinson's poetry are likely to be ironic in both tone and
argument. More than that of any other major American
writer save Melville, Miss Dickinson's world was a place
of the sudden and unpleasant surprise, a place where
terror lurked around the nearest corner and where experience was forever bursting in with some new and
ingeniously contrived horror. The poetry, more often
than not, seems a search for ways in which to counteract the surprises, to negate the terror, and to ward off
the blows that come raining in from without. In this
connection, the child poems represent a special case,

41

though an exceedingly important one. These texts point *outward*, in the sense that they utter sly comments about aspects of experience which everyone, except those involved in the aspects discussed, is meant to overhear and appreciate. For the most part, however, the poetry is more subjectively directed. It tends, indeed, to read somewhat like a personal diary: a diary in which the speaker addresses only herself and keeps counselling herself on how best to resist the wounds and the outrages, the frustrations and disillusionments, which life is always terrifyingly eager to impose.

Perhaps my point will be clarified if I quote together a trio of Miss Dickinson's poems, which, while they are not defensive in themselves, do suggest the urgent necessity for constructing defensive bulwarks. This is the first:

> I many times thought Peace had come
> When Peace was far away—
> As Wrecked Men—deem they sight the Land—
> At Centre of the Sea—
>
> And struggle slacker—but to prove
> As hopelessly as I—
> How many the fictitious Shores—
> Before the Harbor be—

The second:

> For each exstatic instant
> We must an anguish pay
> In keen and quivering ratio
> To the exstasy.

42

For each beloved hour
Sharp pittances of years—
Bitter contested farthings—
And Coffers heaped with Tears!

And the last:

The first Day's Night had come—
And grateful that a thing
So terrible—had been endured—
I told my Soul to sing—

She said her Strings were snapt—
Her Bow—to Atoms blown—
And so to mend her—gave me work
Until another Morn—

And then—a Day as huge
As Yesterdays in pairs,
Unrolled its horror in my face—
Until it blocked my eyes—*

Despite significant differences in technique (only the third example could lay claim to being interesting or distinguished poetry), all three of these texts are variations upon a single theme. Among them, they assert that human experience is capricious and untrustworthy, that it is characterized by cruel ambiguities, by an unremitting mysteriousness, and by an appalling lack of the

---

* I have taken the liberty of printing this poem as it has always appeared in the anthologies. The Johnson edition has turned up two additional stanzas. These will be printed in Chapter III, and discussed there in a different connection.

predictable or the certain. Peace, when it seems near enough to touch, suddenly becomes a delusion. Suffering is somehow the price we are compelled to pay for ecstasy. The agony recedes, but then, after a brief respite, emerges again with devastating consequences. Nothing is dependable. No part of experience consents to hold firm. All values are unreliable; and there is no hope or outcome, no wish or promise, which can be counted upon with assurance. Everywhere the human being turns, he risks betrayal, for it is the nature of his world to wear the double-face of chicanery and deceit.

This, obviously, is a view to be borne only if one has mustered psychological defenses against it. The defense most frequently advanced by Emily Dickinson is that of the scrupulously ironical outlook. She argues that since the actions of the world itself are uncontrollable, the best the inhabitant of the world can do is to cultivate, from within, the ironist's rigidly controlled responses. Reacting ironically to experience, one will learn to look with equal favor upon the contradictions and the clashing possibilities which surround him. But more than that, one can achieve detachment from them all. The ironist eschews commitments; consequently, he has no values to lose, no expectations to be violated, and no hopes to be confounded. The ironist thrives on contrariety; accordingly, he will rarely expose himself to disappointment or surprise. His way, in brief, is a way that Emily Dickinson associates with the maximum in poise. Irony, as an attitude toward life, represents to Miss Dickinson the sort of steadfast composure which declines involvements, presupposes ambiguity, spurns all firm expectations—and, therefore, cushions the

ironist from the tricks and wry jokes that life delights
in playing.

For Emily Dickinson, the ironist has an opposite number, who is the sentimentalist: the affirmer, the credu-
lous yea-sayer. The virtues of irony grow plainer still
when, as in the following poem, we note how sentimentality, with its preference for the stock response, is
often the prelude to disaster:

> The *Sun—just touched* the Morning—
> The *Morning*—Happy thing—
> Supposed that He had come to *dwell*—
> And Life would all be *Spring!*
>
> She felt herself *supremer*—
> A *Raised—Etherial Thing!*
> Henceforth—for her—*What Holiday!*
> Meanwhile—Her wheeling King—
> Trailed—slow—along the Orchards—
> His *haughty—spangled* Hems—
> Leaving a *new necessity!*
> The *want* of *Diadems!*
>
> The Morning—*fluttered—staggered*—
> Felt *feebly*—for Her *Crown*—
> Her *unannointed forehead*
> *Henceforth*—Her *only* One!

The blunder here is unmistakable. Touched by the
sun—and, we observe, *just touched*, at that—morning
engaged in a sentimental response: that is to say, a one-
sided and excessive response. She assumed that her
ecstasy would be permanent; she actively depended

45

upon the sun's remaining, and even, as the mock-heroic tone, the exclamation points and the underlinings (italics here) imply, began to take herself seriously. By contrast, a confirmed ironist would have known better. In the same act which brought ecstasy, the ironical mind would have glimpsed the distinct possibility of ecstasy's withdrawal. Aloof and thoroughly neutral, the ironist would have appraised the splendor of the moment; he might even have permitted himself to luxuriate in its dazzle. But he would have retained, all the while, the lively awareness that a moment *is* a moment, and not necessarily a lifetime. This basically double attitude toward experience amounts to something far more complex than the sentimentalist's response, and to something immensely more difficult to maintain. It has, however, one clear and unarguable advantage. So long as one can keep it up, one is provided with a measure of protection. There can be none of the disillusionment which paralyzes morning, when, to her infinite astonishment, the world parts company from her own naïvely elaborate plans.

So, in Emily Dickinson's world, sentimental commitments are a form of self-indulgence, not gladly tolerated. The very texture of experience cries out against them, saying, in effect, never come too close, never hope for too much, beware of the involvement that is too deep. On the other hand, irony, with its carefully noncommittal bias, *will* work in such a world. It will allow one to cope with life, pretty much on life's own capricious and difficult terms. In poem after poem, Emily Dickinson seeks to lay hold of the ironist's sense of balance. In much the same spirit which prompted her to retreat behind the child, she struggles to wall out experience with the bland mask of imperturbability. Her aim is to be prepared for all possibilities, and to learn to care for none of them. She hopes to remain completely detached from the world—and, thereby, to spare herself from the foolish vulnerabilities of the foolish morning.

II ✠

One of her persistent themes involves the unexpected conferment of a precious gift. Typically, the poems which develop this idea commence with a picture of grim privations. The speaker "had been hungry all the years"; or, in the past, she was banished from home, or denied access to some other earnestly sought privilege. Now, however, her luck has suddenly turned. Not only does the benefit come; it is bestowed with a kind of ceremonial generosity, quite as though, today, experience were making up for the niggardlinesses of yesterday.

Yet in the midst of the new satiety a curious reserve always exists. There is a reluctance to seem too pleased or too grateful. Emily Dickinson's speakers can rejoice in their good fortune; but they do so with such an air of sober watchfulness that the jubilation they feel seems sharply qualified. It is of course possible to read this theme as no more than a reworking of the familiar idea that expectations will always outrun fulfillment. But to press the point no further would result in a serious cheapening of Miss Dickinson's intentions. Underlying the theme of the "unexpected gift" we may discover three closely related views of reality. Taken together, these views define anew the full scope of Emily Dickinson's tragic vision. And they add a new substance to the poems in question, stripping them of any traces of banality and converting them into powerful statements of the poet's tragic insight.

First of all, then, the unexpected gift is suspect because the mere act of receiving it necessarily entails the prospect of a future loss. This point takes us back to "The sun just touched the morning," and reminds us that, in that poem, the morning's folly lay in conceiving of only one possibility, when, as matters turned out, a simultaneous vision of two mutually opposed outcomes would have been far sounder and more realistic. Beyond that, however, the unexpected gift is suspect because even as it seems to behave benevolently, the world that gives continues to retain a number of malevolent characteristics. The powers responsible for the gift have already denied far too long, and then they bestow far too abruptly. The powers were altogether too willing to torture Emily Dickinson's speaker—to tantalize her, engage her in a war of nerves—before they unaccountably ended the game and introduced her to contentment. Her gift has ultimately come, true enough. But in coming, it emerges from a background so obscure and mysterious that its value has been greatly diminished. To paraphrase another and later ironist, the craving is half famished by confusions; the pleasure of receiving is more than half negated by seemingly deliberate terrorizations on the part of the giver.*

Finally, the gift is suspect because, with it in hand, one will find any subsequent deprivations doubly hard to bear. This is, in fact, the last turn of the screw, the somber reflection which adds the greatest poignance to

---

* The later ironist is Eliot's Gerontion:

> Think now
> She gives when our attention is distracted
> And what she gives, gives with such supple confusions
> That the giving famishes the craving.

what Emily Dickinson is saying. So long as one was a beggar, she implies, one could at least be accustomed to the ways of beggardom; riches were glimpsed at a distance then, and their sheer remoteness helped to minimize one's need. Once those riches have been possessed, though, the hazards must become correspondingly greater. If a loss occurs now, it will divest the speaker not merely of what she desires, but of that which she has actively and intimately known. Just here, the poetry keeps insisting, lies the quintessence of pure horror: it is the pain that comes after pleasure, the suffering which succeeds ecstasy, the sudden blow that descends to reduce one from pomp to poverty. Thus even at what appears the height of good fortune, Emily Dickinson still argues for the suspension of all final judgments. Her speakers, if they have wisdom, perceive that no blessing ever comes unmixed or is ever securely possessed. They frankly distrust a world which has given too freely. Ironic detachment, preserved in the moment of great and unexpected plenty, is the measure of their skepticism.

At the other extreme, and usually with somewhat less success, Miss Dickinson undertakes to make the same ironical analysis of impending doom. Feelings of dread, she attempts to persuade herself, may just possibly be more gruelling than the events which are dreaded. There is certainly no known method for preventing disaster; indeed, the chances that the disaster *will* come always seem rather better than even. Yet one should still refrain from definite expectations since even the horrible may occasionally be remitted. Inquisitors, as the poetry shows from time to time, have been known to change their minds.

What both these attitudes demonstrate is the degree to

49

which, in Emily Dickinson's scheme, man is the absolute pawn of circumstance. There is no sense in which it can be said of the individual that he has made things happen. Rather, he is portrayed as the passive observer, who can merely look on while things happen to him. The human being has no power to create pleasure or pain, and no facility for assuring himself profit or loss. These conditions impinge upon him from without, in a fashion that is altogether arbitrary and as tokens of some insuperable power. In certain quarters, I believe, it is still fashionable to decry the "littleness" of Emily Dickinson's poetry, as if her tastes for the small and fragile were the marks of a defective intelligence or of a contemptible eccentricity. The fact is, however, that her stress upon the tiny, the abject, and the helpless is completely consistent with her general view of life. Weighing man against the gigantic forces that control his destiny, Emily Dickinson does, necessarily, see him as at once paltry and trivial, and pathetic in his finitude. She scales human actions down in size in order to catch the full force of the human predicament.

The corollary to his "littleness" is, of course, that man avoid all stock responses. When the human being assents to *or* denies his non-human surroundings; when he confronts them with hope *or* despair, joy *or* anguish; when he believes that they are interested in his welfare, *or* openly assumes that they are not—when he yields to any one of these inclinations without also taking cognizance of its opposite, he merely attracts notice to himself and is exposed to grave and perhaps fatal dangers. Experience, being both arbitrary and fickle, is a poor risk on which to place the absolute bet. Hence what little security the individual can find, he finds in treading a strictly middle ground. Intelligence for Emily Dickinson consists of the capacity for taking all possibilities into account, and for fusing all oppositions into a coherent world view. In a justly famous poem, she praises the flowers for responding, "apparently with no surprise," to the onset of frost. Her point, when read symbolically, is that human beings, too, must withdraw into this same shell of studied indifference if they hope to inhabit their world with anything like serenity.

At this point the force of a detailed example is required. We need to see the "unexpected gift" in action. And nowhere is it portrayed more effectively than in "The Final Inch," where Emily Dickinson has transformed theme and ironic tensions alike into the materials of great and enduring poetry:

> 'Twas like a maelstrom, with a notch,
> That nearer, every day,
> Kept narrowing it's boiling wheel
> Until the Agony
>
> Toyed coolly with the final inch
> Of your delirious Hem—
> And you dropt, lost,
> When something broke—
> And let you from a Dream—
>
> As if a Goblin with a Gauge—
> Kept measuring the hours—
> Until you felt your Second
> Weigh, helpless, in his Paws—
>
> And not a sinew—stirred—could help,
> And sense was setting numb—

51

When God remembered—and the Fiend
Let go, then, Overcome—

As if your Sentence stood—pronounced—
And you were frozen led
From Dungeon's luxury of Doubt
To Gibbets and the Dead—

And when the Film had stitched your eyes
A Creature gasped "Reprieve!"
Which Anguish was the utterest—then—
To perish, or to live?

Considered on any grounds, this is a lyric of extraordinary power. It is, indeed, so spare of style and yet so
connotatively rich, so simply designed and yet so terrifying in implication—withal so perfect a blending of
sound, sense, and image—that one scarcely knows where
an analysis should commence. Perhaps, however, we
should turn first to the speaker's three assailants. Let
us see what can be made of the maelstrom, the goblin,
and the sentence.

For Emily Dickinson, as for Melville and Poe, the
maelstrom—the bottomless, eternally spinning whirlpool—symbolizes both moral and physical dissolution.
It is a cruelly destructive force—dark, primordial, pop-
ulated by those shapes and spectres which are most appalling to the human sensibility. *Goblins* are a recurrent metaphor of Miss Dickinson's, standing for madness or, more especially, for the coming of madness.
The generalized *sentence* acts to provide "The Final
Inch" with a peculiarly excruciating climax. Deliberately
left vague, sentence may be thought of as subsuming the

qualities of maelstrom and goblin, but also as extending beyond them to horrors of an even worse and more grotesque kind. The effect magnifies our sense of shock; for through the ambiguity we are allowed to raise the speaker's suffering to the most intense pitch, and to visualize the causes of her agony in virtually any form we please.

But her ordeal is finished, of course. That fact is immediately established by the past-tense verbs and then still further explained by the gradual introduction of *something, God,* and *creature.* The speaker's misery, when she underwent it, was almost incredibly great: note simply how the frequent *b* and *p* sounds create, in this context, an atmosphere of throbbing, incessant brutality; or note how the presence of the foully subhuman is suggested through terms like *Paws* and *Fiend;* or how *numb* and *Film* indicate the absolute limits of endurance. On the other hand, rescuers did come. At the last moment they brought the unexpected gift of peace; and because of their intervention the speaker has managed to survive. However close the assailants came to destroying her, they had relinquished their grasp, had been made to abandon their assault, even before the poem began.

It is in the light of their remission that the last two lines acquire a special sort of terror: call it, possibly, the terror of irresolution. Given the turn of events that has been dramatized, we might well have looked for hyperbole at the end of "The Final Inch." Grateful for relief, the speaker could have concluded with loud affirmations, meant to glorify life and to praise its essential fitness. Or, exhausted by pain, she could, understandably, have lost the will to live, and so concluded (no less hyperbolically) by invoking death. But steadily declining either commitment, Emily Dickinson strikes a note which is infinitely less hopeful than the first and, in its own way, immeasurably more dreadful than the last. She poises us finally upon the sharp edge of an ironical attitude. There are no statements in the end; there is only a question. As the poem in its earlier stages had hovered between goblin and God, between doom and reprieve, so, at the last, we are left with the harrowing uncertainty of

> Which Anguish was the utterest—then—
> To perish, or to live?

One recognizes that interpreting a poem in terms of an analogy is not, on the whole, a very satisfactory practice. Not only are the correspondences likely to seem forced; the substitution of one context for another often obscures both more than it really clarifies either. And yet in the case of "The Final Inch" there are, it seems to me, compelling reasons for citing a parallel. For what Emily Dickinson has captured in this poem is the spirit of another text—and it, in many respects, the greatest tragic document which human intelligence has framed. Both in specific details and unstated suggestions, "The Final Inch" will bear a point-for-point comparison with the Book of Job.

Consider, in bare outline, Job's history and the nature of his predicament. Day before yesterday (let us say) he had five thousand cattle and his health. Yesterday he was bankrupt, and a leper. Today, however, his goods are doubly restored. An unexpected gift arrived, so that he finds himself in possession of ten thousand animals, and, presumably, twice as much vitality. But what about tomorrow? This time things turned out happily.

But what of tomorrow? Will it be a day of continued prosperity? Or will Job's anguish, so unaccountably begun and ended, as unaccountably be resumed?

These are the overriding questions to which any thoughtful reading of Job must eventually lead us. There is, strictly speaking, very little in the text that can help us to come to grips with the issues involved. In the series of events that Job has just passed through, his world has lost all semblance of order, has been stripped of all the signs and portents upon which predictions are customarily based. For a frightening instant, man has looked into the abyss and discerned not pattern but merely sequence—not the logical distribution of woe or bliss, but the haphazard imposing of now woe and now bliss. And more: man has glimpsed the clear proof of his own utter impotence. He has discovered, as Job says, that he is "hedged in": that he can neither earn good nor counteract evil, but that good and evil alike are dependent upon the whims of a Higher Power.

Obviously, actions and perceptions like these have consequences. They mean that never again can the individual presume to judge experience rationally. They mean that he can never hope to spell out his own destiny by the light of human ethics. They mean, above all, that ever afterward he must recognize himself as limited, helpless, the pawn of circumstance. At the close of Job, there is absolutely nothing which guarantees that, come tomorrow, the protagonist's sufferings will not reappear. Though the book does not make the point explicitly, we are left with the presumption that man's only hope for the future lies in preparing himself for multiple possibilities and in steeling himself, so far as he can, to a stern indifference toward them all.

Emily Dickinson, as if writing an epilogue to Job's dilemmas, restates the problem, and then lets it guide "The Final Inch" to an inexorably ironic conclusion. In her poem the torturers are gone, yes. Nevertheless, they exist *in posse*. And who can know when they may strike again? Help arrived, true. But it arrived not because of anything the speaker could do:

> And not a sinew—stirred—could help

Hence who can say why there was remission, or how long it may prevail? In the face of these imponderables, the only adequate recourse would seem to be the wisdom not to care. Emily Dickinson has demonstrated two points: first, that the world, by its every act, is a place of continuous and unbearable suspense; second, that the individual, whether the recipient of good fortune or bad, is always dominated by the mysteries around him. Her concluding inference is the outgrowth of both perceptions. Between living helplessly in such a world or dying out of it, Emily Dickinson says, the choice seems frankly negligible.

III ✙

The idea of the completely ironic life fascinated Emily Dickinson. It partly motivated her seclusion—her quest for a hiding place in which neither contacts nor commitments would any longer be necessary. In her poetry, as we have seen, irony functions as a constant and pervasive theme, and, inevitably, the ironic outlook came to affect Miss Dickinson's poetic style, to influence not just what she said but also her manner of expression.

Commonly, one hears that irony is not really entitled to a style. The argument goes that the ironist, like the skeptic, has so undercut his privilege of speaking openly that he ought, by all rights, to preserve a complete silence. But this is nonsense, surely. Irony is as psychologically valid as any other approach to experience, and quite as capable of being communicated. On strictly practical grounds, moreover, there are excellent reasons why the ironist may choose to be heard from. For one thing, ironical modes of seeing are seldom maintained without a struggle; hence the ironist may resort to expression simply to instruct himself on how to keep breaches from showing in his armor of detachment. Or, since the ironist, like the skeptic, attaches a kind of therapeutic value to his outlook, he may seek to state his position for the edification of others. For Emily Dickinson, irony never acted as a deterrent to creativity, but rather as a positive and compelling spur. Always anxious to keep her guard in place, Miss Dickinson adapted method to attitude and developed what might appropriately be termed an ironical aesthetic. It is out of this aesthetic that there evolve the language and structure, the tone and wit, which are the hallmarks in much of her most interesting poetry.

Sometimes, for instance, Miss Dickinson achieves ironic effects through a calculatedly ambiguous image, or through the use of descriptive touches which seem to invite one sort of interpretation but then turn out to resist it vigorously. This technique, though easily managed, actually serves a two-fold purpose. It makes the poem ironic at its own expense: that is, it adds unexpected richness and density to a given context. It likewise provokes wariness in the reader, thus guarding against the "heresy of inattention," which, in her own way, Emily Dickinson would have found fully as objectionable as did that other supreme ironist, Henry James. Let me illustrate through citation:

> When Night is almost done—
> And sunrise draws so near
> That we can touch the Spaces—
> It's time to smooth the Hair—
>
> And get the Dimples ready—
> And wonder we could care
> For that old—faded Midnight—
> That frightened—but an Hour—

Here, to the unwary, is a perfectly straightforward poem. It says simple things, and says them simply: night and night's terrors have waned; the time is now come for renewed hope, renewed cheerfulness. The points are made without any apparent qualification, and, as far as that goes, with a bow or two in the direction of the platitudinous. Yet the wary will nonetheless wish to qualify —will question the poem, in part, because of the laborious way in which the speaker has to discipline herself before she can become cheerful. Is there not something desperately mechanical about the smoothing of that hair, a note of something strained and stilted in the arrangement of those dimples? Do not both gestures somehow debase the speaker's optimism, suggesting that she has had to cover real fears beneath a made-up, a wholly artificial state of mind?

Then, augmenting these equivocal details, there are the diurnal images around which the text has been organized. As a symbol for some form of regeneration, the shift from night to day is not only trite; it is perhaps the most ancient of all clichés, just the sort of vapid and overworked metaphor that can be encountered everywhere in bad poetry. On the other hand, where irony is present, clichés have a way of being strangely refurbished, so that even as conventional a trope as this one is perhaps susceptible to a reversed reading. We might profitably remember that if day ends night, then day must, perforce, prepare for a new night all over again. At the end of the poem, consequently, we are headed quite literally back into darkness. Before us stretch that *old—faded Midnight,* now curiously revivified, and the frightening hour, from which escape has after all been impossible.

Through meticulously selected details, Emily Dickinson has created a double effect where only a single, pat theme seemed possible. Her poem asserts one thing, but promptly supplies a number of good reasons for negating, or at least qualifying, the assertion. Point becomes counterpoint as the images undermine themselves to deny their own validity. What we initially took for straight lines—the easy movements from dark to light, from fear to peace—become circles, as the poem returns us to the very states which it appeared to have abolished. Therein lies the fineness of Emily Dickinson's ironic style.

Another of her strategies is used with similar intent, although in design it is often rather more sophisticated. It consists of choosing key terms which will be ever so slightly out of keeping with the context where they appear. One's response at first reading is a mild shock— a sense of annoyance at the seeming inappropriateness. But thereafter the lapse grows purposeful, for one sees that Miss Dickinson has utilized her "mistake" as the means of cleverly demolishing some idea—some concept or attitude—which she purports to sanctify. She writes:

> Prayer is the little Implement
> Through which Men reach
> Where Presence—is denied them.

This seems a definition guaranteed to gladden the hearts of the pious, or will seem so at any rate until the full force of *little Implement* has registered. If *little* diminishes, shrinking prayer to something trivial and inefficacious, then *Implement* (tool, utensil, instrument, etc.) surely degrades, investing prayer with an aura of the hard and metallic, the strictly business-like, the strangely unspiritual. We can hardly be surprised, therefore, when the poem proceeds:

> They fling their speech
>
> By means of it—in God's ear—
> If then He hear—
> This sums the Apparatus
> Comprised in Prayer—

Nor, in the end, is irony evoked solely by that highly problematical *If.* Throughout the five last lines, a painstakingly controlled diction is at work, and clustered around the *If* are other word choices which contribute to the same ambiguous effect. *Fling,* for example, which hints that prayer is nothing more than the aimless, empty mouthing of words. Or *sums, means,* and *comprised:* all of them counting-house terms, which continue to emphasize prayer as a kind of commercial venture. Or, above all, *Apparatus,* which reaches backward to pick up *Implement* and completes the incongruity that *Im-*

60

plement had begun. To think of prayer as *Apparatus* and *Implement* is obviously to place sacred ritual in a very doubtful light. Is prayer really a meaningful link between the human and the divine? Or is it, as Emily Dickinson's language slyly implies, a hopeless routine —an enterprise that is futile, unheard, and so utterly devoid of point or significance?

In both the foregoing examples, the irony has been dependent upon subtle tricks of rhetoric. But it is in connection with her ironical aesthetic that we can possibly come to terms with the most distinguishing quality of Emily Dickinson's style, which is her deliberate suppression of rhetorical forms: her preference for the austere, laconic, carefully guarded utterances that can be descibed only as "non-rhetorical." Or better than merely explaining it, perhaps we can defend this tendency in her work, since among Miss Dickinson's detractors it is the one that excites the greatest amount of adverse comment. The case against her in this respect is notorious. Her poetry suffers, the critics have often insisted, because it is too terse, too threadbare, too inveterately lacking in the niceties of adornment and refinement. Even in her most powerful lyrics, they claim, these deficiencies make themselves felt, resulting in a certain monotony of expression, a spareness and want of polish that are usually objectionable. At their worst, the same faults are responsible for crudities and lapses from taste which are grave enough and frequent enough to impose severe limitations on Emily Dickinson's stature as a poet.

That such strictures at least succeed in isolating the essential character of her style, no one would care to deny. On nearly every page, Emily Dickinson presents the short, cramped line, the crabbed and cryptic phrase, the equivocal question, the flat and the unembellished statement. Plainness in diction, a hesitant and hence involuted syntax, a studious avoidance of ornamentation, a cautiously subdued tone: these are the recurring features in her poetry. At times, unquestionably, they do grow tedious through sheer repetition, and they do give rise to an atmosphere which, for lyric poetry, seems grim and rather forbidding. But whether they must invariably be thought of as defects is, it seems to me, a very different matter. The fact is that just the reverse position could be argued. Given Emily Dickinson's particular outlook, her distaste for the conventions of rhetoric was inescapable. The relative absence from her work of rhetorical flourishes is a testament to her complete honesty, as, in the final analysis, it may constitute one mark of her greatness as an artist.

For in lyric poetry, where the speaking voice is likely to be that of the poet himself, rhetoric is the language of involvement. It is the substance of panegyrics and amorous avowals; it bears the weight of the personal credo; it enters into bald declarations of affirmation or denial. Naturally there are times when Emily Dickinson's own lyric themes will necessitate rhetorical flights. Suffering invokes them, as we shall presently discover, and also the occasional bursts of exaltation that do seem genuine. On the whole, however, Miss Dickinson shied away from rhetorical devices because most forms of the rhetorical were totally at odds with her ironic pattern of thought. Trapped in a world which declined to be committed, she saw that any avowal suggesting her commitment to it would be a confession of naïveté and, much more seriously, a jeopardizing of the poise and security that indifference alone could afford. Hence just as Emily Dickinson, the composer of ironic themes, remonstrated against overly grand expectations (or overly grand denials), so Emily Dickinson, the ironic stylist, remained chary of making statements that were likely to seem overly sweeping, overly passionate, or merely overwrought. Miss Dickinson's drab and narrow language was not, as has been asserted, the product of an insensitive ear or of a constitutional awkwardness with words. Her language sprang, instead, from her conviction that in a world characterized by manifold uncertainties, the only viable speech would be a terse and astringent speech—the speech of careful, quiet inconclusiveness.

This point needs the fullest possible emphasis, I believe; and it can perhaps be sharpened up a bit if we think of another so-called "problem style": a style very different from Emily Dickinson's, but one that has to be approached in much the same terms that have been applied to hers. In our time we have been attuned, as the two previous centuries normally were not, to the poetry of John Donne, and to the harshness, the verbal incongruities, the strained and convoluted syntax which are its chief stylistic components. We have seen, moreover, that Donne's peculiarities of style served as the exact reflectors of his philosophical position. We have come to understand that, far from being personal idiosyncrasies, his stylistic mannerisms registered the profound sense he had of the disorder and the incoherency in the world around him. And with Emily Dickinson, the background for a style is remarkably similar. To expect that she would, or could, write prettily; to assume that she might remain within the bounds of a conventional, nineteenth-century lyric eloquence—this is to presume for

Miss Dickinson a view of experience which she was never prepared to muster. It is on the basis of what she did see that her writing has to be comprehended, and on that basis the principal stylistic modes open to her can be defined rather readily.

They involved a sort of studied ugliness: an attempt to record the treacheries of experience by the blunt antithesis, the guttural expression, the abrupt break in meaning, the barbarous lapse from rhyme. They involved the logical contradiction and the apparently inept word: qualities which reflected Miss Dickinson's sense of a tangled and indecipherable reality. And they involved dryness, reticence, and understatement: qualities that satisfied her need to be uncommitted and inconspicuous. One and all, these were the mannerisms best suited to Emily Dickinson's vision of man's difficult place in a difficult world. If, as poetic technique, her way of writing can offend the eye or rasp angrily in the ear, the way was nonetheless essential to the poet. The reader must accept it as he accepts Emily Dickinson's themes, seeing that in her work style is the measure of content and that both were of prime importance to the way of life which she adopted.

To the extent that Miss Dickinson did regularly resort to rhetorical forms, she drew upon devices which, again, would embody her ironical perspective. Like Donne, for example, she was inordinately fond of the paradox, which she used, as he did, to express the fundamental disharmonies of life. Observe, in isolation, a half dozen of her paradoxical utterances:

> Success—is counted sweetest
> By those who ne'er succeed . . .

A *Wounded* Deer—leaps highest—
I've heard the Hunter tell—

To learn the Transport—by the Pain—
As Blind Men learn the Sun . . .

Just lost—when I was saved . . .

We lose—because we win—

Tell all the Truth—but tell it slant—
Success in Circuit lies—

In each instance, paradox derives from the way in which antithetical concepts or experiences have been yoked together into a meaningful, if bitter, perception. The ideas stated are basically tragic; from the standpoint of a sentimentalist they would seem unnerving and therefore repellent. Yet they catch precisely the spirit of irony, for they have enunciated with force and lucidity the ironist's recognition of how disparity and contradiction rule human experience. And when Emily Dickinson extends paradox through an entire poem, the tensions of thought which she begets can frequently be astonishing. Thus in the full text from which the first quotation was taken, complexity is the result of a deft steering between two extreme views. Avoiding the purely logical proposition, which says that success is best comprehended by the successful, Miss Dickinson likewise remains aloof from the sentimental truism: "success in failure" or "sweet are the uses of adversity." The point she makes is that the *idea* of success will be most poignantly real to those who have been denied the actuality.

It is a bleak, complicated, and paradoxical truth—one which none save the ironical intelligence could possibly have formulated.

It is, then, largely through a wry poetic diction that Emily Dickinson's ironies are conveyed: through the single off-key word, or through a series of such words, joined together into the equivocal passage. It remains, however, to speak of how her ironical sensibility is also manifested in certain of the strictly formal features of her poetry. Perhaps the chief of these would be the short, epigrammatic line. What a short poetic line tends to preclude, of course, are the expansiveness and looseness which we associate with the rhetorician. The short line is ordinarily not an ideal vehicle for grandiose assertions; tense and pithy, it is admirably suited for holding in balance the contrarieties and dissonances which are aspects of an ironical style. The incidence of this type of line in her work reminds one of Emily Dickinson's fondness for the hymn form, and of the way in which it too could become a part of her ironic strategy. This, to be sure, was not always the case; Miss Dickinson doted on hymn measures, which she adapted to fit a wide range of different subjects. Yet she did at times devise the cruelest kind of irony, simply by grafting hymn rhymes, hymn meters, and the hymn tone onto themes or statements that were profoundly at variance with those in the hymnal. A fine example would be "After the Storm"

> Glee—the great storm is over—
> Four—have recovered the land—

where the irreverent content, which we noticed earlier, is rendered more intense by the hymn-like structure of the poem and by the fact that heresies must be read with all the thumping vehemence of a camp-meeting paean.*

Finally, one suspects that her determination to be ironic will, in some measure, explain the strange habits of punctuation that Emily Dickinson employed. Largely expurgated by the early editors, her irregularities along this line have come to light only with the publication of Thomas Johnson's variorum text. They persist through all the poetry, the ironic and the non-ironic equally, so that elsewhere certain of them will have to be dealt with

---

* Because it does so much resemble a hymn, "After the Storm" is, in one way, a highly rhetorical poem. But its rhetorical flourishes are used mockingly, of course. What the text demonstrates is that the grandiloquent responses in which it abounds are certain to be false, since nothing in life ever warrants or sustains this kind of grandiloquence.

Note a similar situation:

> At least—to pray—is left—is left—
> Oh Jesus—in the Air—
> I know not which thy chamber is—
> I'm knocking—everywhere
>
> Thou settest Earthquake in the South—
> And Maelstrom, in the Sea—
> Say, Jesus Christ of Nazareth—
> Hast thou no Arm for me?

Partly, irony results from the fact that Christ, about whom there should be nothing ambiguous, is here portrayed as being at least as destructive as He is benign, and at least as callously indifferent to man's needs as He is attentive. But irony is also to be found in the tone and structure of the poem. We miss the point unless we see that the same rhetorical sweeps—the same hymn-like bumptiousness—which normally praise Christ for His power and love have now been brought to a context where they suggest Christ's ambiguousness.

in a different fashion. But a cursory reading will indicate that Miss Dickinson's favorite marking was the dash, which she used copiously as a substitute for commas, semicolons, and periods, and that her standard practice was to leave the final line of the poem dash-stopped or completely open-ended. About the kinship to an ironic style of both these practices, little real doubt can exist.

What the dash alone accomplishes is a keen sharpening of Emily Dickinson's antitheses. It points up the paradoxical quality in her writing, sets off and thereby dramatizes the ambiguous word, acts to underscore the doubleness that is latent in many of her themes. In conjunction with the dash-stopped or unstopped last line, furthermore, the dash creates in the poetry a certain fragmentary effect, a sense of the broken and unfinished —in brief, just that air of sustained and intentional inconclusiveness which Emily Dickinson's viewpoint required. When taken together, these markings do either or both of two things. They help to set forth a world that is far too erratic and disordered to permit deep human engagements. Or they become integral parts of the only prudent and feasible response to that world, which, as they help to demonstrate, is the open, the suspended, the carefully divided response. For all their lack of conventionality, the markings are usually functional rather than mere oddities. Like every other device discussed here, they tend to be the highly conscious contrivances of a highly self-conscious ironic artist.*

---

* Since this passage was written, my views of Emily Dickinson's punctuation seem to have been confirmed by Edith Perry Stamm, in her paper "Emily Dickinson: Poetry and Punctuation," which appeared in *The Saturday Review of Literature* for March 30, 1963. Mrs. Stamm detects *four* unconventional

IV ✠

Irony, at least the variant of irony used by Emily Dickinson, must be conceived of as a protective measure. It is a carefully composed mask which one slips between one's self and the external world. Thereupon, the world and all its powers to aggrieve are kept at bay. One may employ the mask in order to forsake one's true identity, and so become free to upbraid enemies "out there," as would be the case in Emily Dickinson's child poems. Or, as in the poetry we have just been examining, one may find solace in the steadfast indifference to "out there" which a wearing of the mask ensures. Either way, there is a dissipation—a simplification— of the forces without. Viewed through the mask and held at a distance by the mask, experience is blunted, and loses its full capacity for striking back. Life is not easily able to penetrate ironic features. Hence it cannot af-

pointings in the poetry: the slash ($/$), the reversed slash ($\setminus$), and the circumflex ($\smile$), as well as the dash. These she relates back to Noah Porter's *Rhetorical Reader*, where the marks were associated with public speech, so that the slash stood for rising inflection, the reversed slash for falling inflection, the circumflex for a rise and fall in combination, and the dash for a monotone delivery. The chief consequence of this discovery is to make Emily Dickinson more than ever a poet of her age: a writer who, quite like Emerson and Whitman, conceived of poetry as something to be recited orally. But the identification of the dash with monotone opens up other possibilities. It suggests, again, the presence in the poetry of the guarded voice: of a speaker whose tone is often expressionless because, through the carefully flattened monotone, she can avoid the indiscreet assertion, the sense of an imprudent commitment.

flict so directly, nor can it annoy with such vindictive-
ness.

But the mask of irony—to generalize for a moment
about its behavior—inevitably goes awry. Perhaps this
is so because irony is basically artificial in the first
place: a "prepared" view, so to speak, that is "put on"
by way of concealing true emotions. At all events, sooner
or later the time comes when the painstakingly imposed
masquerade weakens, cracks, and falls into disrepair.
In the *Apology*, a hitherto ironical Socrates is suddenly
transfigured. Despite his earlier pretensions to the contrary, despite his seeming non-commitment when he questioned Euthyphro—Socrates *does* care, he cares deeply
enough, indeed, to be willing to die for his involvements.
With hardly less suddenness, the hero in Hemingway's
fiction undergoes a kindred change. Dignity and cour-
age, he discovers, are not really matters to be taken or
left alone. Rather, they constitute positive values: values
that captivate and must be accepted wholeheartedly. The
Hemingway hero makes the acceptance, and passes from
the rigorous self-restraint of "In Another Country" to
the rather mawkish sentimentality of *Across the River
and into the Trees*.

In moments of great stress, then, the ironical mask always disintegrates. The special pose practiced by Emily
Dickinson proves to be no exception. For her, as we have
seen, irony was the means of circumventing tragic realities. In much of the poetry, she faced outward with
perfectly blank features, hoping thereby to gain detachment from the fearful risks of living in a fearful world.
But the very urgency with which she sought for this escape is, of course, a clear indication of Miss Dickinson's
actual involvements. Beneath her surface equanimity

—her cautiously cultivated self-effacements—she obviously existed as an acutely self-conscious personality and as a mass of seething anxieties.-Her determination never to be betrayed by life is, in turn, a betrayal of how thoroughly susceptible she was to life's ambuscades. - Eventually, therefore, her ironic self-control had to be relaxed. A point had to come, beyond which she could carry the strategic retreat no further. There had to be certain tragic realities which declined to be stared down by the mask, but which broke in upon Emily Dickinson, to take full advantage of her real susceptibilities.

When this breaking point is, in fact, reached, Emily Dickinson's vulnerability becomes painfully, overwhelmingly evident. The "mirth" departs from her writing, leaving behind only the "anguish" which, in other places, mirth had been designed to hide. Indifference recedes, to be supplanted by a terrifying commitment, an enormous capacity for being hurt, a despair and sense of dread that are altogether genuine. In a way, probably, the failure of the mask constitutes the ultimate irony about Emily Dickinson. No longer the mistress of her responses, she now becomes the victim of an irony—not one that she has created, but one which exists at her expense. From the standpoint of the reader, however, the failure opens up a rich new vein in the poet's imagination. As the mask goes to pieces, Emily Dickinson's tragic view of life is exposed in bold relief, and we are brought face to face with the most dramatic configurations in her poetry.

CHAPTER III

The Poet of Dread

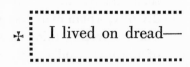

✢ I lived on dread—

At the beginning, it was claimed that in the following poem one can find an excellent index to the depth and intensity of Emily Dickinson's tragic awareness:

> I know that He exists.
> Somewhere—in Silence—
> He has hid his rare life
> From our gross eyes.
>
> 'Tis an instant's play,
> 'Tis a fond Ambush—
> Just to make Bliss
> Earn her own surprise!
>
> But—should the play
> Prove piercing earnest—
> Should the glee—glaze—
> In Death's—stiff—stare—
>
> Would not the fun
> Look too expensive!
> Would not the jest—
> Have crawled too far!

Now I wish to return to this extraordinary text, and to give it the sort of detailed analysis which it deserves.

73

Its subject is the remoteness of God. Through a series of speculations concerning His conduct, Deity is made to seem elusive and wholly mysterious—a will-o'-the-wisp divinity, whom man may neither clutch nor comprehend. The interesting thing to notice is how, within the body of the text, God's remoteness is developed in terms of two widely divergent attitudes. In the first two stanzas, His ephemeral qualities are spoken of lightly and even with a certain flippancy. They are not, we are led to presume, matters of very much concern. If God stays out of sight and out of hearing, this is so only because He plays a harmless version of hide-and-go-seek. The terminology of the game clearly defines His motives, and the playful, lighthearted tone suggests that man's pleasure in the sport ought to be equally as keen. Throughout these eight opening lines, the speaker has seemed to laugh a bit at God for preferring obscurity, and then has chuckled casually at herself for being in any way disturbed by a problem that is so trivial—or so susceptible to ultimate solution.

But then comes the change to a radically new viewpoint which pervades the two last stanzas. Where the speaker had commenced in the indicative mood, and with a simple declaration of faith—

I know that He exists

—she now switches to the subjunctive—

But—should the play

Once in the realm of uncertainty, she utters a series of increasingly grim hypotheses. It first occurs to her that the search for God is really too difficult and frustrating to be conceived of as a delightful pastime. One seeks,

and never finds—a fact that so kills one's pleasure in
the sport that the play proves piercing, the glee glazes,
the fun comes to look too expensive. Next, however, a
still more terrifying possibility is broached. In hide-and-
go-seek, there ought always to be two players. But suppose, in the present situation, that only one exists. This
would mean that the speaker is engaged not only in a
game that she can never hope to win, but in perpetuating
a gigantic self-delusion. No one is hidden from her;
hence she has nothing to look for. It is a thought that
gives rise to the two concluding lines, lines which turn
from the pain of playing to the possible fraudulence of
the game itself:

> Would not the jest—
> Have crawled too far!

[handwritten marginalia: If she has nothing to look for that perhaps this is a reason for seclusion]

No matter how much she struggles to resist the implications of God's behavior, His elusiveness does sincerely
trouble the speaker. In the midst of bland reassurances,
she is struck by the idea that this is no game she plays,
but a desperate search for the unobtainable; she is overwhelmed by the notion that the silence of Deity may
never be broken, because there is, in fact, no Voice to
break it. Obviously admissions such as these are no
longer compatible with the double-edged attitude of
irony. In irony, alternative possibilities (God may exist,
or He may not) are poised on either side of a fulcrum,
which is the point of total indifference. Here, by contrast, the poem only begins ironically, with its basically
comic approach to a serious theme. Then, as we arrive
at the center of the text, the ironic method collapses,
giving way to an expression of forthright concern. Faced
by an enormity like God's non-existence, the speaker is

stripped of her detachment. Her aplomb, so cool and comforting while it lasted, yields in the end to a sense of involvement that is both complete and overpowering.

What the poem has dramatized, therefore, is the deterioration of an ironical mask. Before our very eyes, as it were, the façade of unconcern goes to pieces, exposing beneath its set features a residue of pure fear. The strain of maintaining a sharply divided response has grown intolerable; whether or not the ironist approves, the underlying emotion—the feeling which irony was intended to repress—has burst through. On the basis of the irruption, we are now in a position to deal fully and directly with Emily Dickinson's deeply rooted sense of dread. From the fears disclosed by this text and from their particular source, it is no great distance to the fears which resulted in the crisis of Emily Dickinson's life and which aroused within her a trepidation that no amount of irony could ever wholly quell.

II ✝

Emily Dickinson's creative life began in crisis; and over the years interpreters have explained the upheaval with varying degrees of plausibility, but always against the background of the same general situation. We are asked to believe that sometime in 1858 or 1859, when Miss Dickinson was in her late twenties, she met and fell in love with a married man. Probably he was the Reverend Charles Wadsworth, a distinguished Philadelphia minister; certainly, whatever his identity, the man's marital status is indisputable. Then, presumably made desperate by the problem and perhaps terrified by the removal of Wadsworth (if it was he) from Philadelphia to San Francisco, Emily Dickinson turned inward. From a predicament so hopeless, she sought refuge in her upstairs bedroom, and found consolation in the poetry which commenced almost simultaneously with her seclusion. As Thomas Johnson, whose version of the episode is among the sanest, has put it, Wadsworth precipitated a "volcanic commotion" in Miss Dickinson, and, "as muse, made her a poet."

This, beyond doubt, is an extremely fetching story. It retains a certain glamour even after the more sensational elements have been trimmed away. And when, as has often happened, those elements are emphasized, one can be titillated by secret meetings, proposed elopements, an irate father, tearful family conferences, and all the other fine trappings that belong to melodrama. There is, however, one detail that makes the whole account seem questionable. No matter how cogently or conveniently the forbidden affair may explain the *fact* of Emily Dickinson's exile, it fails utterly to square with much of what she wrote, once her seclusion got underway. When Miss Dickinson went upstairs, she did not, in any ostensible fashion, go to memorialize the Reverend Mr. Wadsworth. Nor, as we shall discover presently, did she retire to write love lyrics, at least not in any conventional sense of the term. And yet, very frequently during the years between 1859 and the end of her life, she was at some pains to record her reasons for flight. These reasons figure prominently in her writing: become, indeed, the chief themes of her poetry, when the poetry is likely to be most impressive. Far from suggesting a thwarted romance, the reasons point to a crisis that was otherwise directed. They indicate that Emily Dickinson's problem was not a frustrated personal relationship, but a metaphysical quandary; they imply that, in seclusion, her

77

struggle was not against temptations of the flesh, but against a religious skepticism, of the severest and most gripping kind.

In putting the case this way, I have no wish to create a philosophical temperament where none existed, or to translate psychological realities into vague gnawings of the spirit. At bottom, unquestionably, Emily Dickinson was a highly eccentric personality. She was obsessively, almost morbidly self-centered, a figure who went out of her way to court suffering, and so was tormented by all the hobgoblins which customarily afflict her kind. All I would argue is that when the hobgoblins attacked most fiercely, the shape and form they took were those of a specifically metaphysical dilemma. It is entirely possible that contact with Wadsworth, or with someone like him, served as the immediate cause for Miss Dickinson's crisis. If so, however, the occasion was little more than incidental, and it merely prodded into full wakefulness a set of issues that had long been slumbering. One can—as Mr. Johnson concedes—find only "circumstantial evidence" to support the view that Emily Dickinson was ever in love with a man. But for the view that she fell fervently in love with God and was convinced God spurned her—for this, the proof is overwhelming.

There is no way of determining when her spiritual trauma commenced. As with many situations of this type, the true origin probably lies buried in child-parent relationships, so that before we could plot out the entire sequence we would need to know more than can fully be known about the nature of Emily's associations with her cold and forbidding father.* One also notes, in pass-

---

* We can, of course, *speculate* about the early relationship between Emily and Edward Dickinson; and such a conjecture will be attempted in the Epilogue of the present study.

ing, that while she was still a student at Mt. Holyoke, Emily apparently underwent some severe test of faith; this, however, seems to have left few overt scars, and to all outward purposes was soon forgotten. About the form the trauma took once it had commenced, there needs to be much less doubt. On this point at least, the poetry is clear—admirably and abundantly clear. What the poetry consistently reveals is that, in temperament and outlook, Emily Dickinson was amazingly akin to her great (though undoubtedly unknown) contemporary, Herman Melville.

Like Melville, Miss Dickinson was endowed with the sort of religious sensibility which can be satisfied with nothing less than absolute certitude. She needed to *know*, in the fullest and profoundest sense of knowing. She could have accepted life as being fit and orderly, provided she possessed the unqualified assurance that God exists, and provided she had full and valid insights into the workings of God's mind. But, again like Melville, she brought her spiritual requirements into an age and cultural climate which had little to offer her in the way of doctrine, theology, or institutionalized guidance. Born two centuries earlier in the New England theocracy, Emily Dickinson would not have been burnt for a witch, as Allen Tate once conjectured; quite the contrary, she would have derived complete peace of soul from the certainties inherent in Calvinistic theology. Set down at a different time or in a different geographical region, furthermore, she might actually have been the convert to Roman Catholicism which, with a good deal of obtuseness, Sr. Mary Power James has made her out to be, in name, if not in fact. As matters stood, however, the dogmas of Calvinism lay dead beyond recovery; conversion to Catholicism was, from the standpoint of the old

Yankee aristocracy, still socially unthinkable. In consequence, Miss Dickinson had no place to turn for solace or for ultimate answers except to the watered-down Protestantism of nineteenth-century New England. This, given the nature of her spiritual cravings, was like asking for help from nothing at all.

The religion of her time had become the urbane and preeminently civilized study of man's relations with man. To the larger question of man's kinship with God, the church in New England was no longer much in the habit of addressing itself. It found such questionings quite uninteresting, and probably regarded them as not quite respectable. If the individual hungered for the security and stability of a metaphysic, he had to construct that metaphysic out of the fabric of a personal belief—doing it, as Emerson did, after first resigning from a pulpit, or, in the manner of Whitman, after first renouncing all the priests. Within the religious institution, as Emily Dickinson knew it, dogma had been displaced by humanism and the "pale negations." Spanning the gulf from creature to Creator was, by now, strictly a problem for the private sensibility to resolve. For Miss Dickinson—as for Melville; that parallel will still illuminate—the problem proved insuperable. Between her will to believe and her capacity for establishing the grounds of belief, there yawned a vast void of doubts, a void which, alone and unaided, Emily Dickinson was powerless to cross.

The specific issue which she confronted may be described in some such fashion as this. Emily Dickinson yearned to assume that, despite any evidence to the contrary, there was an underlying pattern in human experiences, which gave to the experiences both coherence and meaning. The "modest needs" to which she refers in one of her poems were, fundamentally, the needs for conviction: conviction that life was somehow purposive; that suffering and death could be justified; above all, that death itself was no more than the prelude to personal immortality. In order to fulfill these needs, Miss Dickinson had to have a vision of things, much like the vision set forth in Emerson's essay, "Illusions": "There is no chance and no anarchy in the universe. All is system and gradation. Every god is sitting there in his sphere. The young mortal enters the hall of the firmament; there is he alone with them alone, they pouring on him benedictions and gifts, and beckoning him up to their thrones." In other words, she had to have the sense that the universe before her was all order and firmness. She had to have a sense of watching while the Eternal operated upon the actual. She could come to terms with experience only if she achieved the level of transcendent understanding, from whence experience might be contemplated as the work of a benign and immutable God.

Experience, unfortunately, declined to accommodate. When Emily Dickinson looked to the actual, tangible world around her, it was to discover that the pattern which she craved was forever dissolving into a ceaseless flow of time and change. When she surveyed life, as life could be known, she found no system and no gradation—and no trace of God in his benevolent majesty. She was greeted instead by whirl and mutability, by the uninterrupted scattering and steady vanishing away of all experiences. In terms of *what* she saw, naturally, Miss Dickinson's perception of reality was no different from anyone else's. Even Emerson acknowledges that the "young mortal" sees Eternity only after he has somehow gazed through a "blinding, incessant snowstorm of time." Short of certain variants of Oriental mysticism, no philosophy or religious system has ever denied that time and change are among the prime realities in the world men know. But time and change proved peculiarly disturbing to Emily Dickinson because she regarded them as autonomous processes which belied— or at least concealed—every fixed principle except their own autonomy. In the sheer, relentless flowing of details, Miss Dickinson saw a denial to her devout wish for harmony and stasis. Her sense of helplessness lay in the fact that she was everywhere surrounded by motion—and could find nothing *beyond* or *above* or even *within* the motion which might be said to elucidate its whirl, or to invest the whirling with a moral point and purpose.

Stated thus abstractly, her dilemma will seem akin to one that is fairly traditional in philosophy. Certainly the crux of the matter was not new. The difficulties of reconciling Divine Constancy with empirical temporality have been both ancient and continuing, as the long history of the problem, from Heraclitus to the poetry of T. S. Eliot, will indicate. For Emily Dickinson, however, the traditional problem of time was complicated by a still further feature: a feature very possibly unique with her, but one which, in any case, became the darkest component in her tragic view of life. Where the typical Heraclitian sees time only as a negative quality, sees it as a distraction or confusion that man is hard-pressed to overcome—Emily Dickinson placed temporality and mutability in a rather more sinister light. She glimpsed in each the workings of a positive and dynamic evil.

Hemmed in by these forces and loathing them, Miss Dickinson could only imagine them to be deadly personal enemies; she could only portray them as if they were actors in a conspiracy, planned against herself. In her universe, either time and change seem to be absolute masters, who delight in baffling, whose aim it is to blot out the basis for ultimate understanding. Or, still more dreadfully, they seem the instruments of a malign God—a Deity who cloaks Himself with the time process, which He uses to withhold answers from his creatures. Cast in either role, time prevents knowledge of the Timeless. The terror of the situation is that, whichever role time plays, the preventions seem conscious and willful and maliciously contrived.

This, then, is the issue upon which Emily Dickinson floundered: her desire for stability, in conflict with her realization that all seems chaos; her quest for the orderly and the intelligible, in conflict with her suspicion that order and intelligibility have been deliberately denied her. Once the issue has been defined, much that has always been obscure about Miss Dickinson becomes crystal-clear. For one thing, we now possess the likeliest key to her seclusion, seeing that it was not a married man who compelled her to flight, but rather fear of change and a desire to keep her door closed on the troublesome and time-ridden world outside. Still more to the point, we can proceed from her obsessions with time to the starkest of Emily Dickinson's poetic themes. It is when what she calls "Time's wily chargers" accost her that Miss Dickinson writes most powerfully, most openly, and, therefore, with the least reliance upon ironic indirection. As in the poem with which this chapter commenced, her defenses are easily overrun; falling

before an unresolved metaphysical problem, they collapse for substantially the same reasons.

III ✠

Out of her aversion to time and change, there emerge
the darkest moments in Emily Dickinson's poetry: her
portraits of death, her doubts concerning immortality,
her analyses of pain and love and evil, her delineations
of the dreaded invasion and of the periodic molestations
which the self undergoes. It is the fact of the aversion
that needs to be demonstrated first. To that end, let us
consider three poems, chosen from among literally
dozens of possibilities. The texts obviously share a common attitude toward a single subject, and I shall print
them consecutively. But since a certain number of cross-
references will be necessary in the ensuing commen-
tary, the designations "A," "B," and "C" will probably prove useful:

[A]

Presentiment—is that long Shadow—on the Lawn—
Indicative that Suns go down—

The notice to the startled Grass
That Darkness—is about to pass—

[B]

Further in Summer than the Birds
Pathetic from the Grass
A minor Nation celebrates
It's unobtrusive Mass.

No Ordinance be seen
So gradual the Grace

A pensive Custom it becomes
Enlarging Loneliness.

Antiquest felt at Noon
When August burning low
Arouse this spectral Canticle
Repose to typify

Remit as yet no Grace
No Furrow on the Glow
Yet a Druidic Difference
Enhances Nature now.

[C]

A Light exists in Spring
Not present on the Year
At any other period—
When March is scarcely here

A Color stands abroad
On Solitary Fields
That Science cannot overtake
But Human Nature feels.

It waits upon the Lawn,
It shows the furthest Tree
Upon the furthest slope you know
It almost speaks to you.

Then as Horizons step
Or Noons report away
Without the Formula of Sound
It passes and we stay—

A quality of loss
Affecting our Content
As Trade had suddenly encroached
Upon a Sacrament.

Compressing it to a phrase, one might say that the theme of all three poems is that of "the momentous transition." In each case, we are in the midst of change —change which is a product of time's machinations and which, as we watch, is gradually being imposed by time upon the images in the landscape. The overall effect of the poetry is to enlarge beyond the particular shift, until change, and the temporal processes which wrought it, are made to seem a relentless ritual, a kind of slipperiness and evanescence which must be felt as universal qualities. This effect is evident even in "A," the least memorable poem, but one where the specific incident —the particular lapse from light to darkness—clearly possesses the most generalized of implications. In "B" and "C," the intense dramatic impact is largely a result of our perception that the death of the insects and the passing of light are portrayed here merely as symptoms: as small signs of the still larger impermanence which exists always and everywhere and on a cosmic scale. As Yvor Winters has said, in commenting on "B" and "C," both poems present change as inherently terrifying, because mutability is at once "an inexplicable fact" and yet the basic and essential component of every human experience.

It is typical of Winters that while he possesses the greatest possible insight into Emily Dickinson's preoccupations, he nevertheless interprets the time-and-change theme in her work as being primarily "naturalistic" in viewpoint, rather than philosophical. The truth is of course that Winters abhors unresolved metaphysical riddles, which he sees as running counter to his classicism and preference for decorum. Moreover, he holds such riddles to be especially obnoxious in poetry, since, by his own definition, the good poem will automatically banish ambiguity and bring order and resolution to whatever subject it touches. The result is that in Miss Dickinson's time poems, which he deeply admires, Winters declines to find any hint of metaphysical overtones. He orients the texts specifically in *this* world, reads them, indeed, as if they amounted to no more than an orderly description of the disorders in Nature. Thereby, he limits far too severely what the poetry itself conveys.

For the real problem of the momentous transition lies, precisely, in the metaphysical uncertainties which time and change are constantly occasioning. The combination of bafflement and despair that permeates the writing does not spring exclusively from the poet's vision of the changing world as an observable fact, a series of strictly natural phenomena. It derives, mainly, from the way in which this shifting, changing world seems intent on harassing the poet, on blocking her off from understanding, on separating her from any fixed point outside its own mobility. That reading will seem the least warranted probably in the case of poem "A," though even there, as we shall find in a moment, it is bound up with Emily Dickinson's tone and images. In "B" and "C," however, phrase upon important phrase indicates the philosophical drift of the poetry—and suggests that just as the particular movement is made to symbolize movement-in-general, so movement-in-general becomes a horrifying spectacle by epitomizing for the poet everything that is ambiguous and unaccountable in the universe which confronts her.

Note, to begin with, the circumstances recounted in poem "C." Here, as the last word implies, a change on the landscape must be associated with the speaker's loss of spiritual fulfillment. When the light goes out, the speaker is deprived of a *Sacrament*—is robbed, in other words, of the joy which might have come through some sort of spiritual communion. Not only are time and change seen as being directly responsible for her loss; in the conduct of these two forces, we are made to feel them as deliberately malevolent, as treacherous forces which express, through their every action, a profound contempt for the human observer's needs. The verb *encroach* shows this. Implying trespass or infringement, it points up the extent to which temporal experiences gladly, and even eagerly, impose themselves between the speaker and her quest for communion. When the light is taken away without the *Formula* (that is, without the remedy or the alleviation) *of Sound*, this fact emphasizes, in another way, the cruelties of experience. It draws attention to the intense mystery of time's behavior, and so begets in the speaker a sense of something unfathomably strange in what has happened to her and to her landscape. Taken together, then, the ideas of an *encroachment* and of *silence* get exactly at the attitude toward time which Emily Dickinson will regularly develop. They describe a Power which first robs the human observer of contentment, then goes on to compound the injury by providing her with no clues through which the deprivation might be understood.

This notion that time is a Power—a Power at once

ponderous and yet terrifyingly impalpable—is still further magnified by the stress, in all three texts, upon the sheer inexorability of temporal sequence. In poem "A" the arrogance of time is suggested by the lofty *notice* that darkness gives. The same air of relentlessness is introduced into poem "B" through the use of ceremonial words—words like *Custom* and *Mass* and *Druidic*—to convey the facts of change. In poem "C" the steady, inflexible passage of time—the stepping of Horizons or the brisk reporting away of Noons—contributes, once again, to an identical mood. The consequence of this sort of language is one of investing temporality with a distinctively ceremonial guise. Emily Dickinson shows time and change beating down upon the human observer in the form of a grim, remorseless, and overbearing ritual.

In part, no doubt, this was her chief intention. She wished to emphasize the oppressiveness of temporality, to depict it as a process which no act of the human will could curb and against which all human exertions would prove futile. And yet, in poems "B" and "C" at least, one finds an added implication. It is that change could hardly come this ceremoniously or time behave this oppressively, unless a Power existed to direct temporal movements. The very least the ceremonial gestures do is convert Time and Change into monstrous personifications, a pair of forces that have set out intentionally to persecute the human observer. At the very worst, furthermore, the gestures hint that somewhere behind the time ceremony there is its Master, the "approving God" who has invented change as a "Heavenly hurt," and who imposes the hurt on humanity as one mark of His supreme disdain. From the poetry, the final complication to be inferred is this: that the human observer, caught as she is in the midst of the time ritual, can only *suspect* its motions to be meaningful, without having any clear idea of what the meanings really signify. It is her plight, *as* a human observer, to be exposed unwillingly to the dance of time, and to recognize that by the ambiguity of the dance she has been effectively cut off from ever comprehending its source.

Her predicament is poignantly revealed in the emotional point of view which the poetry establishes. As the poet beholds her world in a process of transfiguration, she finds in the spectacle a cause for her most somber feelings. Particularly in poem "B," her reactions extend well beyond the overt circumstances in the text— well beyond a lament for the insects or grief for the dying season—to become identified with a cosmic riddle, of which the overt circumstances supply only a single, concrete instance.

Thus the funeral mass of the insects is a *pensive Custom,* because the poet glimpses, in the alteration before her, a symbol of the saddest and the most solemn engima that humankind must face. Similarly, the feelings aroused by the death of Summer are *Antiquest* feelings, because this specific manifestation of time passing appeals to an old and instinctive dread; it begets a primordial fear, which is the speaker's fear of everything in experience that is ineffable and unknown. The enlarged *Loneliness* which the poet experiences in the presence of change does not come, as Mr. Winters would have it, from a recognition of the "essential cleavage between [herself] . . . and nature." (Actually just the reverse is true: in the perishing of the crickets the poet perceives, with painful clarity, her *kinship* with the natural processes of death and decay.) But *loneliness* is the result of her failure to grasp the reasons for change. It embodies her sense of being, like the cricket, a member of a *minor Nation*—minor not because she is physically small as the cricket is, but because she shares with the insects the plight of being cast adrift in an indifferent and thoroughly unintelligible world.*

The tendency of the time poetry is to conceive of time as a veil, one drawn tightly and firmly between the human observer and the stability for which she craves. Where the observer asks for intuitions of Eternity, time and change show her only beginnings and ends. Where she yearns to feel at home in the universe, time poses a problem that leaves her the perpetual outsider, involved in temporal processes but with no understanding of what they mean. The further implication is that a kind of demonic strategy underlies time's behavior, so that time's blotting out of ultimate values is an entirely self-

* Note, in this regard, a valid distinction between the crickets who are observed and the human observer. The insects are destroyed by time; but they have no real knowledge of the destructive processes, to which they respond instinctively, and hence no reason to struggle against them. Accordingly, their situation is one of pathos; and their funeral arises

Pathetic from the Grass.

By contrast, the human observer sees herself as being destroyed by the same temporal forces, but she recognizes them as enemies, and her quest for understanding is the mark of her struggle against them. This difference in awareness elevates pathos to tragedy. A situation that is merely pathetic, when it is thought of with reference to the cricket, becomes, when the speaker involves herself in it, the basis for a tragic vision of her own plight and the plight of all mankind.

conscious activity. And this implication becomes undeniable when we look, finally, at the two sets of images around which the time poems are habitually organized.

A casual glance at "A," "B," and "C" will suffice to point up the images: images that time bears away on the one hand, and on the other a category of details that time is portrayed as bringing. At one end of the momentous transition, there are such things as *day, light,* and *Summer;* and reading from other time poems, we may add to this group *sun, Spring,* and *flowers.* These are light images that disappear under the pressures of time. For Emily Dickinson, the light images possess a special significance. They are her supreme values, exalting and reassuring her, filling her with momentary ecstasy, adding to her contentment and her spiritual stature. As symbols, they stand for life, for immortality, and for the nearest approach that man can make toward Godhead. If they endured, the poet's faith could easily remain unshaken and unshakeable. But they do not endure. Set off against them are their symbolic counterparts: *night, darkness,* and *Fall,* and from other places *Winter, chill,* and *frost.* These are negative emblems, representing pain and death, bespeaking the malignity or the outright absence of God, suggesting all the limitations on human knowledge. They remind one of one's physical corruptibility. They hold out the threat of a total annihilation after death. They stand, in sum, as Emily Dickinson's thresholds to despair and to the dark night of the soul.

In the time poetry, the movement of the momentous transition is always toward the negative: toward darkness in "A," toward Fall in "B," toward the dissipation of light in "C," toward some similar condition in virtu-

ally every time poem that Emily Dickinson ever wrote.
Very occasionally, time will appear to have reversed
its direction:

> These are the days when Birds come back—
> A very few—a Bird or two—
> To take a backward look.
>
> These are the days when skies resume
> The old—old sophistries of June—
> A blue and gold mistake. . . .

Since this poem is about Indian Summer, however, the
reversal is a fraud, and the poet treats it as a cruel and
apparently malicious jest on time's part. For, in the
main, it seems the business of temporality and mutability to undermine the foundations of human faith. All
the human observer must do is raise her eyes to see the
impending future swooping down upon her, ready to
destroy the light images, to leave in their place some
one of the several forms of darkness, and to render her
destitute of either hope or belief.

IV ✚

As with her attitudes toward God and Nature, Emily
Dickinson's conception of Time may, at first glance,
seem too primitive to be altogether credible. We are
likely to feel that the practice of personifying temporal
experience into a deadly enemy could hardly have existed in nineteenth-century America, or that if it did
exist, the outlook was too childishly silly to deserve our
serious attention. But perhaps such a feeling can be
forestalled—and the outlook itself made more plausible

—if we contrast Emily Dickinson's time sense with the view of time that was cultivated by one of her distinguished contemporaries.

The point was made earlier that Emily Dickinson and Walt Whitman appear to have been opposites, in the sense that he easily developed the sort of private metaphysic which she, though hungering for it quite as avidly, found unobtainable. But surely no creative intelligence could have been more immersed in a time-and-change motif than was Walt Whitman's. If the world slips and slides in the poems we have just examined, then the oscillations of experience are no less dominant and no less a repetitive feature in the poetry of *Leaves of Grass*. Wherein, then, is the crucial difference that permitted one writer to assimilate time and change into his philosophy, yet made of these same qualities a persistent stumbling-block on which the other poet tripped and faltered?

The answer lies in the diametrically opposed views of time-future which the two writers took. In *Leaves of Grass*, the future is normally thought of as a state into which the individual projects himself. It lies before him, as a realm of infinite possibilities. As he forges through it, man is constantly engaged in a fresh and decisive act of double discovery: the discovery of his own potentialities and the renewed understanding of his physical surroundings. The traveller is not really borne along by time, but, active and resourceful, he can divert the flow to fulfill his own special ends. Thus the narrator of "Song of Myself" exerts dominion over time, until, at a key point in the text, he throws off the "ballasts" of temporality—

My ties and ballasts leave me, my elbows rest
  in sea-gaps,
I skirt sierras, my palms cover continents,
I am afoot with my vision

—and is transformed from the role of detached spectator to that of the spiritualized seer, the unencumbered
wanderer who is completely at one with every item in
his environment. In the poem "To Think of Time,"
futurity and immortality are equated, so that the perpetual unfolding of earthly time is the best clue man
can obtain to the existence of Eternity. Like much else
in his thinking, Whitman's attitude toward the temporal
reaches a shrill climax in "Passage to India," where
time is shown to gather disparate experiences into a
coherent unity, and where the human soul, with the
future as its ever-so-willing conveyor, makes passage to
"more than India," arriving eventually in "all the seas
of God."

What obviously sustained Whitman's time views was
his sense of the universe as an "emergent" or a "becoming" place. In this conception of experience—one
which makes common cause of Platonism, Romanticism,
and the still more recent theories of Henri Bergson—
time is regarded as an evolutionary force, which the individual mounts and, having mounted, rides through
ever higher stages of progress. The worm, in Emerson's
well-known epigram, moves upward along the time
scale to become man. Today man has achieved approxi-
mately the same heights where God camped yesterday.
God, in turn, manages to stay a jump or so ahead of the
pack, though He too is a fully evolving Deity. From top

95

to bottom, every detail in the hierarchy of existence is forever on the move. Each new movement, each new moment, each fresh change: these constitute another dynamic step forward. The future is both purposeful and alive with promise, since it spirals toward improvement and points to a faraway Ultimate that is gradually being realized in the here and now.

This happy version of temporality was perfectly consistent with Whitman's general optimism. It reinforced his faith in progress, gave him yet another excuse for keeping the poem immense and open-ended, and is in fact a prime explanation for the clutter and fluidity of which his work is characteristically composed. But for Emily Dickinson—even supposing that she was familiar with them—the niceties of a "becoming universe" would have provided no consolations whatsoever. Her need, it will do no harm to re-emphasize, was for belief in a fixed and unalterable Absolute. If she was to satisfy her tastes for order and intelligibility, she had to *begin* with a clear notion of what the Absolute was, and then proceed *downward* to experience. Hence the same unceasing novelty, the same multiplicity and endless proliferation which served as starting points for Whitman's metaphysic became, in her view, disastrous qualities which led away from the Absolute and left the world a shambles, as ravaged as it was impenetrable. The temporal flow was simply not designed to carry Emily Dickinson across "all the seas of God." In her poetry, the flowing of the future has just the opposite effect. It separates one from Godhead, and it attests to a universe which is—and the full force of the pun is intended—profoundly "unbecoming."

Yet is it not clear that even as she rejected the evolutionary-utopian ideals of her contemporaries, Miss Dickinson continued to scrutinize time through the same all-personifying glasses which her contemporaries were likewise wearing? If she thought of the future as a ruthless and intransigent master, this view seems not fundamentally different from that of Whitman, who found in the well-oiled conveyor belt of futurity the features of the meek and willing servant. If she pictured time as an ominous threat and an appalling actuality, if she saw it as scattering human values or as dissolving the rapport between humankind and Eternity— these associations are really of a kind with Whitman's, for they reflect, no less than do his, the conviction that Natural forces have a definite personality and that the universe never deals with the individual except in ways that are deliberate and intensely meaningful. The truth is that Emily Dickinson's affinities with Transcendentalist thought are nowhere more evident than in the bleakest sections of her time poetry. Her attitude toward temporality is credible, because it retains the basic assumptions of Transcendentalism, though it pushes those assumptions to new and radically more pessimistic conclusions.

Against the background of Emersonian lore, let us reinvestigate "A Light exists in Spring," emphasizing, this time, the organization of the poem. Into the three opening stanzas, the expectations of an age appear to have been concentrated:

> A Light exists in Spring
> Not present on the Year
> At any other period—
> When March is scarcely here

A Color stands abroad
On Solitary Fields
That Science cannot overtake
But Human Nature feels.

It waits upon the Lawn,
It shows the furthest Tree
Upon the furthest slope you know
It almost speaks to you.

Consider the properties of the *Light*. It hovers on the landscape as a unique Natural phenomenon, and, apparently, as one swollen with significance. It is not subject to rational analysis, for *Science* cannot overtake it; but it does appeal to the intuition, so that *Human Nature* feels it to be important. Finally, it clarifies the speaker's immediate surroundings, bringing into bold relief *the furthest Tree/Upon the furthest slope you know;* and it seems to promise a still greater enlargement of the understanding, since *It almost speaks to you.* In each of its roles, therefore, the light is typically —indeed, almost classically—Emersonian: it is an aspect of Nature that knows, and that seems anxious to communicate its information to the human being. Another moment, the text seems to suggest, another slight increase in this growing radiation, and the poet's mind will be completely enlightened. Her horizons will be so greatly extended that everything now remaining dark and inscrutable in the cosmos will suddenly become plain. Reading these twelve lines, we sense that the speaker stands on the verge of the same sort of mystical experience which Emerson describes in *Nature*. Or we are reminded of Whitman's assertion that "truths wait in all things," from whence they are forever ready to be plucked forth by the human observer.

With the coming of the next new moment, however, the Emersonian situation, as we are accustomed to think of it, abruptly disintegrates:

> Then as Horizons step
> Or Noons report away
> Without the Formula of Sound
> It passes and we stay—
>
> A quality of loss
> Affecting our Content
> As Trade had suddenly encroached
> Upon a Sacrament.

The light recedes; and whatever truth it might have imparted when it almost spoke, the message is lost now, overtaken by temporality and borne silently off into the darkness, which is at once that of the landscape and of the dark confusions within. Time-future has not, after all, brought the poet nearer to the Ultimate; the future, instead, has acted as a divisive force, pushing off a promised revelation when the disclosure and all it signified seemed scarcely outside the poet's grasp. The contrast of the sixteenth line makes her plight unbearably poignant. The light *passes,* carried away by exacerbating temporal processes. But *we stay.* As bewildered human beings, we have been robbed by time of an opportunity to gain increased comprehension, and we have no choice except to be deprived and to endure the deprivation.

One may feel that "A Light exists in Spring" involves a cruel inversion of the traditional mystical experience.

Certainly, the structure of the poem implies this, beginning as it does on the very brink of insight, only to lapse backward into the dark night of the soul. It seems to me, though, that a still more fruitful approach to the poem lies through a comparable episode that is presented in *Moby Dick*. The episode occurs when the *Pequod*, its voyage just underway, encounters a sister ship called the *Albatross*. As white and bulky as the white whale himself, the *Albatross* appears to possess secret knowledge of Moby Dick; swinging in close to the *Pequod*, she seems eager to relate all she knows. But then, at the last moment, Time and Nature conspire to drive her off again. Without breaking silence, she drifts away, leaving unfulfilled the implication that, had her captain been permitted to speak, Ahab's quest for understanding of the white whale would quickly have been successful.

Like Melville in this passage, Emily Dickinson writes "A Light exists in Spring" out of premises which are impeccably Emersonian, but which nonetheless move off in a tragic direction. She commences with the notion that Nature can and will communicate. Then she proceeds to demonstrate that, after a fashion, Natural phenomena *do* communicate, *do* make symbolic gestures— but that, far from resolving the mysteries of experience, the communication only serves to confuse the poet and leave her more baffled than before. From first to last, Miss Dickinson never departs from the Emersonian mythos. It is simply that, by the end of the poem, she has shown that the personified forces in Nature can be detriments as well as benefits, and can act to tantalize and frustrate the human personality as well as to sustain it.

To Emily Dickinson, then, time represents the great betrayer. Moving stealthily and with deadly coherence, temporal sequence manages to disrupt stability, to destroy any and all ideas of permanence, and to thwart man's search for the grounds of certitude. In addition to playing an anti-metaphysical role, time is also thought of as imposing the agonies and brutalities of actual experience. Clocks and hours, days, months, and seasons, the images and the increments of time: these are Emily Dickinson's harbingers of woe. As evil, and functioning very much as evil functions in Melville's fiction, they lie constantly in wait for the individual, always holding out to him the potential perils of the next successive moment.

A remarkable poem like "The first Day's Night had come" will illustrate. As we have already seen, the text opens on a strong note of gratitude and hope:

> The first Day's Night had come—
> And grateful that a thing
> So terrible—had been endured—
> I told my Soul to sing—

An ordeal, the precise nature of which is as yet undefined, has subsided, releasing the speaker from a period of great torment. The speaker's first act, during the time of respite, is to re-establish her identity:

> She said her Strings were snapt—
> Her Bow—to Atoms blown—
> And so to mend her—gave me work
> Until another Morn—

For Emily Dickinson's word *Soul*, we may read "self"; and the paired terms of the stanza (*Strings—snapt;*

101

STRAHORN LIBRARY
THE COLLEGE OF IDAHO
Caldwell, Idaho

Bow—Atoms blown) tell us what is happening to the self. Under the impact of suffering, the speaker's personality had collapsed; she became a broken and a ruined thing. Now, however, in the first delicious moments of relief, she will seek to repair the wreckage, so that today's loss of selfhood will, by tomorrow, no longer be evident.

But time, meanwhile, is gathering its forces for a still more ferocious onslaught. Not only is the new day, when it arrives, *as huge/As Yesterdays in pairs;* in two concluding stanzas, the shape of this hugeness becomes sharp and explicit:

> And then—a Day as huge
> As Yesterdays in pairs,
> Unrolled it's horror in my face
> Until it blocked my eyes—
>
> My brain—begun to laugh—
> I mumbled—like a fool—
> And tho' 'tis Years ago—that Day—
> My Brain keeps giggling—still.
>
> And Something's odd—within—
> The person that I was—
> And this One—do not feel the same—
> Could it be Madness—this?

The verb *unrolled* is crucial. It magnifies the sheer brute power of time, making temporality the undoubted deliverer of the poet's "other" self, which is her inarticulate self, her self overwhelmed by madness. Once we have noted that fact, the next step is to trace out the kinship between the drama here and the situation in "A

Light exists in Spring." In "A Light," time-future was portrayed as attacking from without, so that it banished order from a landscape and reduced the observer to a state of bafflement and despair. Now, by contrast, time-future lays on from within, driving order from the precincts of the mind, and reducing the poet to a lunatic's giggle. Underlying these differences, there is an exact correspondence in the degree to which both texts conceive of time as a disruptive force, as a perpetrator of the horrible, and as the destroyer of value and harmony. With only a slight shift in emphasis, Emily Dickinson has made the structure of a descriptive and philosophical poem elucidate equally well a text where the scene is internalized and the events themselves are specifically psychological.

In a preceding chapter, "The first Day's Night" was used to point up Emily Dickinson's sense of the capriciousness and uncertainties in human existence. Looking back now over all her most typical themes, we can see that there have been few, indeed, which did not in some implicit fashion involve an acute dread of time passing. Time was at least tangentially present in portrayals of the "unexpected gift": the gift could not be enjoyed because of the speaker's fear that in another moment it might cease to be. Time figured, from behind the scenes, in Nature's rape of the child: it was in time that the turnabout of the sea from host to molestor occurred. Time was clearly a partner to the depredations in "The Final Inch." On the other hand, it is when temporality *as* temporality becomes her subject that some major changes enter into Emily Dickinson's writing, about which two special comments will have to be made. First, a statement is in order that will bear on the special methods of Miss Dickinson's time poetry. Then a question must be asked concerning differences between the attitudes that Miss Dickinson has introduced into the time poetry, and those attitudes which have appeared in the other areas of her work.

The statement is meant to distinguish Emily Dickinson's material from the poetry of the so-called *ubi-sunt* tradition—a poetry which, fully as much as her own, is rooted in the inexorable facts of change and time. Pondering mutability and seeing (with Heraclitus) that the river one enters can never twice be an identical river, the *ubi-sunt* poet raises a dirge for departed grandeurs. *Where are?* he asks with inconsolable reiteration: *Où sont les neiges d' antan?* Where are the golden ages— and golden ladies? The mood of such a poet is likely to be elegiac and almost blatantly reminiscent. He strikes a deliberately gloomy and sepulchral pose. Generally, his style oozes bathos, and is clotted by all the bitter-sweet devices of a studied melancholia.

There is, however, very little of this nostalgic effect anywhere in Emily Dickinson. The enigma that preoccupies her is far less *where are?* than *what barbarous thing is to be?* It is scarcely ever to the ruined past that she addresses her laments; she speaks them over the onrushing future: over the moment to come, and all the unlovely destinations toward which the new moment promises to drive her. The result is that for the charming and yet flaccid reflections of *ubi-sunt* poetry, Emily Dickinson substitutes tense dramas of disintegration, an atmosphere of hushed foreboding, a sense of the brittleness in all existent forms and of their terrible vulnerability to time's intrusions. Temporality, as she depicts it, is almost never a topic for the backward glance, the fond lingering, the glamorous meditation. Rather, the time theme calls forth a poetry in which the details are crisp and electrifying, while the accompanying emotions are those of pain, shock, and suspense, and the utmost in fear and anguish.

But what are we to make, then, of the failure of irony in the time poems? That is the question with which any analysis of the work must conclude. Clearly, the prevalence of feelings like pain and shock disallows irony. Just as clearly, the ironical countenance has not in fact appeared in the time-and-change texts, but indifference has been almost wholly supplanted by exposure, by the speaker's naked involvement with what she says. Yet merely by glancing at the poetry, do we not find places where the ironical vision could properly be expected to have functioned? If time takes away—we ought to ask —should not the ironical mind derive a modicum of comfort from the thought that temporality might likewise, in the course of time, make restitution? In terms of Emily Dickinson's own principal images, does not the coming of night anticipate the arrival of a new day, as the death of the insects looks ahead to yet another summer, or as the lapse into madness suggests that sanity may come a second time around? Are there not grounds, in sum, for maintaining in the face of time the same double viewpoint—the same careful balance and aloofness—which had spared the poet from other tricks of a tricky world?

One can only reply that, when read with their full symbolic scope in view, the time poems leave little room for the distance and ambivalences required by irony. Immersion in time is, for Emily Dickinson, not simply a matter of contemplating diurnal changes or the ro-

time poems

tating seasons. The true consequence of the immersion
—a consequence consistently expressed through the
symbols of the poetry—is to be reminded of blemishes
on the *moral* landscape. It is to have brought home to
one the facts of death, madness, and incoherence, the
realizations of human finitude and the oppressive silence
of God. And more: it is to perceive that because time
seems to move always in the same direction, there can
be no mitigating the time ceremony, no real chance for
relief or restoration—in short, no way of escape from
the worst conditions that time imposes. Where the situation has become this inflexible, irony must lose its force
as the means of a liberation. The pressures are too great
to allow for detachment. The outcome is invariably so
certain that a belief in clashing possibilities is precluded. What remains is the possibility of one response:
the response of overwhelming despair, which is the
single response of the time poetry.

So, with time and its dark necessities, we reach areas
of her experience about which Emily Dickinson was
frankly and fatally compelled to care. But in lieu of
the ironical mask that she assumed elsewhere, one can
sometimes discern, both in specimens of the poetry and
also in the poet's life, a strange and pathetic substitute.
It takes the form of still another type of pretense, which,
when we consider it biographically, will probably go
farthest toward explaining Miss Dickinson's seclusion.
For whatever the reasons that have been cited or are
yet to be adduced for her decisions of 1858–1859, the
key factor, one suspects, was this: Emily Dickinson
turned indoors on the premise that, once she had got
inside, she could best find release from temporality.
The impulse was absurd, perhaps; yet given the extent

of Miss Dickinson's fears, it is likewise entirely comprehensible. Emily Dickinson would close her eyes on time, so to speak, simply by restricting her everyday outlook to the most stable and familiar of things. She would thrust the four solid walls of her father's house between herself and time's rapacities. Every detail in her life indicates that, following 1859, she was dedicated to nothing less than stopping the clock—to locating a sanctuary where mutability and its horrors could never again intrude.

But even as the gestures were made, she had to see their futility. To shrink from the clock was merely to discover that clocks tick as callously in bedrooms as in the market place. The more Emily Dickinson sought to ignore and evade temporality, the more engulfed she became in the complex mysteries of time. The following poem (notably a very early one) graphically testifies to both halves of her predicament: testifies, first of all, to her delight in the timeless artifice and acknowledges, secondly, her awareness that the artifice and reality are not to be confounded:

> Make me a picture of the sun—
> So I can hang it in my room—
> And make believe I'm getting warm
> When others call it "Day"!
>
> Draw me a Robin—on a stem—
> So I am hearing him, I'll dream,
> And when the Orchards stop their tune—
> Put my pretense away—
>
> Say if it's really warm at noon—
> Whether it's Buttercups—that "skim"—

[handwritten margin notes, left:] 6. Smart as she was she would've known this was impossible

[handwritten margin notes, right:] But that would still not stop or delay time. Why not do everything you can as long as you cannot control the passage of time? Why not ride the ferris wheel? Enjoy the good in between. "new periods of pain"?

107

> Or Butterflies—that "bloom"?
> Then—skip—the frost—upon the lea—
> And skip the Russet—on the tree—
> Let's play those—never come!

Within the *room,* and within the work of art which "decorates" it, time has been arrested. All the least tolerable qualities in experience—cold and darkness, death, decay and fall-winter—these are ruled out here, banished by seclusion (note the complete inwardness of setting) and banished, as well, by an imagination which will permit only pleasant things to exist. But in order for this pretty illusion to be sustained, one must, as the tone of the poem suggests, revert to childhood. Much can be learned, I think, from contrasting this conception of childhood with the one set forth in the child poems that we considered earlier.

In those texts childhood had amounted to a deadly serious pretense, undertaken by the poet so that she might respond with mature criticism to a perilous and otherwise unassailable world. Now, on the other hand, the serious pretense has shrunk to the rather more trivial pastime of "let's play": let's pretend the world is not so bad as it seems, let's withdraw from the world's wretchedness into dream and fantasy and facile "make believe." The difference is immense. If laughter in the other child poems had combined a militant undertone with the childish tinkle, the laughter of "let's play" is the uneasy, self-directed laughter of the escapist, who concedes that actually there is no basis for escape. It is the "hilarity" of one who seeks to smile change out of existence, but discovers that the smile itself is an aspect of change; it is the "jubilation" of one who flees from time into a sanctuary, only to recognize, at the door, that time and change were the first inside.

V ✛

Emily Dickinson's views on time relate her to the darkest side of the Romantic tradition. Within the opposite category, I would, in this respect at least, place writers otherwise as diverse as Blake and Shelley, Wordsworth, Keats and the Emersonians. These figures were uniformly aware of the time problem, for the problem entered very deeply into Romantic psychology. But they resolved the issue successfully, detecting Eternity in a grain of sand or Platonic essences, in the work of art, the Oversoul or the full sweep of human history. Only when Romanticism ebbed to its blackest and bleakest mood did time cease to represent a ladder toward timelessness, and become instead the source of fearful uncertainties: a sign of the chaos in this world, and an insuperable barrier to the next. To this line of thinking, Emily Dickinson's work obviously belongs.

On the basis of the affiliation, let us note once again and briefly the "Emily Dickinson trademark":

> I never saw a Moor—
> I never saw the Sea—
> Yet know I how the Heather looks
> And what a Billow be.
>
> I never spoke with God
> Nor visited in Heaven—
> Yet certain am I of the spot
> As if the Checks were given.

109

Though the manner is certainly Emily Dickinson's, one feels that the matter of the poem is far more typical of Walt Whitman. It was Whitman, in other words, who was able to *know* Eternity—who could know it because he inferred it from the facts of experience, or because he perceived it in a pseudo-mystical vision. But for Miss Dickinson, both these avenues to Godhead were closed. Nothing in her spinning, time-dominated world could serve as a point of departure toward Eternity. Nor, in the poetry we have been examining, is there anywhere a basis for the sort of intuitive knowledge of God which "I never saw a Moor" suggests.

One concludes, therefore, that "I never saw a Moor" and other similar texts were born of one of two impulses. Either they are ironic poems, poems in which the easy act of affirming is itself a kind of ironical device. Or they represent whistlings in the dark: examples of the bold front that occasionally appears when Emily Dickinson tries to persuade herself that some value, really very remote and indefinable, is about to be possessed. But to make "I never saw a Moor" her trademark is clearly to distort Miss Dickinson's entire outlook. The idea that the tickets to Paradise are *given* is not only contradicted by her time sense; it is denied even more forcefully by her studies of death, where the time problem is picked up, re-examined, applied to a new set of circumstances, and made to seem even more insurmountable.

CHAPTER IV

The Aesthetics of Dying

✠
> A Clock stopped—
> Not the Mantel's—

Heidegger, in his brilliant philosophical account of human consciousness, equates man's time sense with the fear of death. He argues that, lacking an awareness of his own mortality, the individual would be a mere observer of time, a passive watcher of clocks and calendars. Through the realization of death, however, time is, in effect, internalized. Man comes to see temporality not as a fact in the public domain, but as a destructive quality which he himself embodies—a force which feeds on his very being and is constantly reminding him of his imminent and total extinction. The relevancy of this existentialist insight to Emily Dickinson should be obvious. With time, as we have seen, Miss Dickinson associates all that the human mind finds most deplorable. Foremost among time's horrors are death, toward which the temporal flow keeps hurrying the individual, and annihilation after death, a dismaying prospect which every action of time appears to confirm.

Thus it is that a number of poems which seem concerned with passing time turn out, in essence, to dramatize an attitude toward death. "This is the land the sunset washes," one such text begins. Another commences, "I'll tell you how the sun rose." In both cases, light functions as a symbol for life: it is an aspect of experience with which the speaker feels securely at home, for it rep-

111

resents to her the tangible, palpable fact of her own existence. But the light is quickly doused by darkness. In the first text, the sun rushes on to be enveloped in the "Western Mystery." The second candidly acknowledges that "how he set—I know not." As light symbolized life, so death is symbolically related to the loss of illumination. The "Western Mystery" is best understood as the eternal riddle of dying. The poet's failure to say how the sun set reflects her failure to see beyond life: her confusion about an action in Nature registers her inability to fathom death or to justify it philosophically.

With death, then, Emily Dickinson was almost uniquely preoccupied. Except perhaps for Melville, no writer of the American nineteenth century looked more habitually than she upon the skull beneath the skin, or was more visibly shaken by the spectacle. To a degree that is morbid and even ghoulish, Miss Dickinson's letters probe for answers among the recently bereaved. How did he die? she demands to know. Was he resigned? What was the look on his face? What were his last words? In the poetry, these same questions either reappear directly—

To know just how He suffered—would be dear
To know if any Human eyes were near . . .

To know if He was patient—part content—
Was dying as He thought—or different—

—or, at best, are transformed into great dramatic utterances. It seems fair to assert that the most gripping of Emily Dickinson's poems are poems centered around the questions of *what is death? why is death?* and *what is it like to die?*

Because the death poetry is so powerful and many-sided, we are justified, I think, in looking to it for more than a single reaction to the subject which it portrays. To say that Emily Dickinson lived in mortal dread of dying is, in a way, true enough. Yet, like all such commonplaces, the statement requires the most vigorous sort of qualification. It is when death is presented as a spectacle —or when the corpse is laid out before her—that Miss Dickinson's speaker is most openly appalled. Then she beholds death as a moral and physical ugliness; baffled by this deformity, she recoils in terror from the sheer complexity of the issues involved. When, by contrast, she thinks of death as a fact about herself—when she sees it as a condition into which she is entering, rather than as the condition of someone else—the speaker's response is likely to be very different. If her terror is still there, it now becomes a terror that is underlain by a strange sense of relief. Almost, she comes to welcome death, to look with perfect equanimity upon the fact of dissolution, to conceive of personal annihilation as a state to be desired.

The result is that within the large body of death poetry, two totally opposed viewpoints often appear side by side. The same set of topics that can give rise to frustration and tension will likewise sometimes serve as the bases for hope and release. Ultimately, I believe, we shall discover that the thought of dying could soothe as well as lacerate Emily Dickinson—and that the certainty of her own death was at once the supreme problem she had to face, but also a kind of psychological outlet, without which her life would have been quite unendurable.

II ✝

In the grimmest and least equivocal of her poems about dying, Emily Dickinson's speakers function as bereaved onlookers who recount the circumstances of some-

113

one else's passing. As in the following example, the poet
and other mourners follow a loved one to the brink of
death; then, left themselves among the living, they seek,
without much success, to interpret the experience they
have watched:

> The last Night that She lived
> It was a Common Night
> Except the Dying—that to Us
> Made Nature different
>
> We noticed smallest things—
> Things overlooked before
> By this great light upon our Minds
> Italicized—as 'twere.
>
> As We went out and in
> Between Her final Room
> And Rooms where Those to be alive
> Tomorrow were, a Blame
>
> That others should exist
> While She must finish quite
> A Jealousy for Her arose
> So nearly infinite—
>
> We waited while She passed—
> It was a narrow time—
> Too jostled were Our Souls to speak
> At length the notice came.
>
> She mentioned and forgot—
> Then lightly as a Reed

Bent to the Water, struggled scarce—
Consented, and was dead—

And We—We placed the Hair—
And drew the Head erect—
And then an awful leisure was
Our faith to regulate—

Clearly, the emphasis in the poem lies with the living.
The point of view is specifically theirs, so that dying and
death are treated throughout as events which the living
perceive. At the end, it is the living who must continue to
act; when the anonymous *She* has become a corpse, the
mourners are still faced with the terrible task of looking
for consolation or purpose in the scene before them.
These facts shape the theme of the poem, making it less
a study of death as such than one of grief and of a crisis
in faith. They likewise help to account for the seemingly
deliberate ugliness out of which the poem has been
wrought.

For the poem that confronts us *is* ugly, about as bar-
barously ugly, indeed, as lyric poetry can be while still
retaining its essentially lyric features. For a little, it
seems worth lingering over some of the sources of this
ugliness. Such a consideration will, in a particularly
dramatic and meaningful way, point up the always subtle relationship between technique and content in Emily
Dickinson's poetry. Moreover, it will allow us to take
another look at Miss Dickinson's style in action, and
thereby to gain a firmer conception of the thought, the
care, and the ingenuity that consistently enter into her
style in general.

To begin with, then, the poem is made ugly by an almost unrelieved barrenness of diction. We notice that only a single sustained image has been introduced; and that one—the figure of the reed bending toward water —comes perilously close to being a cliché. For the rest, the language is severely plain enough to be best characterized as crabbed and guttural. The word choices run steadily in the direction of terms that are not normally thought of as possessing much poetic value: terms like *narrow* and *jostled* and *italicized*. Or the diction abounds with such cumbersome flying buttresses as *at length* in the fifth stanza and *as 'twere* in stanza two. The overall effect of this kind of vocabulary is that of giving the poem a pinched and rather starved quality. There is, from first to last, a striking inconsistency between the emotionalism inherent in the situation being presented, and the dry, spare, prosy diction which permits very little in the way of an overt emotional display.

Complementing the diction, furthermore, are the extraordinarily harsh phrasings that Emily Dickinson has used. Partly, the harshness is a consequence of her twisted syntax, especially of the inversions that appear in the concluding line and all through stanzas two and three. Partly, it derives from the length of the lines she has employed: short, six- or eight-syllable lines, which have a certain terseness about them under any circumstances, and which, when they are end-stopped, quickly come to seem unusually stiff and cramped. But chiefly the harshness of phraseology is conditioned by the fact that the lines are so punctuated that the majority of them must be read as the most formal and laconic of utterances. In stanza six, for example, the dramatic high point of the entire poem is reached. Yet because of the decisive pause that occurs after each terminal word, no one of the lines appears to possess a shred of real feeling:

116

> She mentioned and forgot—
> Then lightly as a Reed
> Bent to the Water, struggled scarce—
> Consented, and was dead—

These are verses which must be *under*read, so to speak —read in such a way that they emerge as blunt, literal statements of fact. Once again, the tonelessness—the sheer, unvaried monotony—of the description seems curiously at odds with the nature of the event described.

Finally, the ugliness of the poem is heightened by what passes for its rhyme scheme. We gradually grow aware that this *is* rhymed poetry, cast to an *abcb* stanzaic pattern. The rhymes involved are not only approximations or half-rhymes; in addition, they are quite as steadfastly unmusical as rhymes can ever become without lapsing into prose altogether. *Night, different; before, 'twere; Room, Blame; quite, infinite; time, came; Reed, dead; erect, regulate:* at the close of each stanza, the reader is arrested by some new combination of clashing sounds. The dissonances could hardly be greater, or more rasping.

Among her critics, as we observed earlier, this is the mode of writing that is often cited as the most annoying fact about Emily Dickinson. There is a widely cultivated truism which says that Miss Dickinson fell into these stylistic habits because, frankly, she knew no better—because, with her faulty ear and sparse verbal resources, she never understood what is demanded by the highest order of poetry. And yet, here in "The last Night," where the gaunt and the grating have reached something of an apotheosis, we have, it seems to me, an ideal place for refuting such assumptions. Far from being the consequence of either inadvertence or naïveté, the ugliness of the poem is a contrived and, what is more, a highly efficient ugliness. It is a technique in perfect consonance with the point of view that it expresses. If we only let them, therefore, the rough edges of Emily Dickinson's style will lead us unerringly to her theme, and will reveal more about what she is saying in the poem than any other approach could possibly show.

For what the style of "The last Night" creates is an atmosphere of rigidly curbed hysteria. The more the text is examined, the more we see that neither is it lacking in emotion nor have the feelings been completely hidden. Instead, the emotions are suppressed: they exist behind clenched teeth, as it were. They are the feelings of one who is engaged in a desperate struggle for self-mastery. They suggest a speaker whose resolve is to maintain control, even in the midst of a response that is overpowering and very nearly uncontrollable. Out of this determination, there proceeds the unfailingly low pitch of the poetry. Where hysteria as hysteria would have to be couched in overwrought expressions, in a language of the incoherent, Emily Dickinson has set for herself an exactly opposite course. Her aim is to portray a dry-eyed grief, a sorrow that will seem all the more poignant for being uttered through the pinched mouth and the carefully ordered speech. She accomplishes her purpose by setting grief to the measures of the spare, inflexible poetic line; by rendering it in the form of tense understatements; by objectifying it, in short, as an emotion which has benumbed the speaker and left her to stumble woodenly through a welter of harsh rhymes and clumsy phrases.

Emily Dickinson's method is shaped by, and it remains beautifully compatible with, her meaning. To be confronted by a corpse is the cruelest, the ugliest, and the most harrowing experience that she can imagine. For one thing, the confrontation exacts from the living their last, pitiful homage to the dead. Whatever their feelings, the living must continue to act; in a kind of stunned agony, they set about placing the hair and drawing the head erect. But, what is far more painful, the living find that the perception of death results in a violent derangement of their own faith. Drawn up before a corpse—brought into the presence of the frozen features and the unbroken silence of the dead—the living glimpse the one philosophical problem which no amount of hope can palliate. They exist in a moment of intense mystery—in the *narrow time,* when every energy is focussed upon solving the unsolveable. All they can see ahead of them is a perpetuation of the mystery. Death has shattered belief; after death, there can come only tomorrow's *awful leisure,* when the ruins of faith will have to be picked up and, if possible, regulated anew.

To behold the dead is Emily Dickinson's ultimate agony, then. And such is the impact of their vision that the living observers sink, necessarily, into a state of dumb despair. They remain sane only if they can compress their feelings into the deadly formal statement— or only if they can counteract their response through the performance of some trivial and threadbare gesture. Hence the style of the "The last Night." If, upon first reading, it struck us that suffering was contradicted by the plainness, the awkwardness, and the inept stumbling of the language, we discover, the second time around, that plainness, awkwardness, and inept stumbling have alike been important aspects of the suffering. Emily Dickinson's style has by no means ruled out emotion;

it has repressed it, rather, and in repressing it provided an emotion of more starkness and intensity than any comparable amount of elegant writing could conceivably have presented.

Using poetic language to this end, Emily Dickinson does, of course, depart sharply from the custom of her contemporaries. Throughout the nineteenth century, the prevailing view was that the more musical the poetry, the greater the emotional fervor it could communicate. Perhaps this idea was challenged by Whitman, in his contemptuous dismissal of the "tinkling piano tunes." It can be argued, however, that when Whitman begins to write most harshly, the emotional content in his work really is dispersed, so that he inadvertently makes a case for the kind of poetry which he intended to belittle. At any rate, among most of the major Romantic and Victorian poets—among the Poes and the Shelleys, the Tennysons and the Swinburnes—the concentration of high feelings was directly related to a regularity, a melodiousness, and a heavily cadenced pattern in the poetic style.

But Emily Dickinson demurred. With her, it was a cardinal principle that the aftermath of a great ordeal might well be feelings of profound formality. She chose to show that if suffering could prompt a shriek, it might likewise, in its most elevated moments, result in a situation where the tongue seems fixed, and the "Nerves sit ceremonious, like Tombs." * In this practice, she struck a note that is surprisingly but distinctively modern. If her exceedingly unlyrical lyrics stand outside

* The line is from her great poem "After great pain, a formal feeling comes." The text will be quoted and discussed in a later chapter.

120

the tradition of nineteenth-century poetics, they are more nearly at home with the poetic tendencies of our own time. We need think only of Eliot, introducing into *Four Quartets* a number of harsh lyric movements, but placing the movements strategically so that their strident qualities bear the greatest emotional burden which the poetry contains.

III ✛

When the quick scrutinize the dead in Emily Dickinson's poetry, the scrutiny gives rise to three different responses. All three tend toward a common center, and are occasionally combined into a single text. But they may also be disentangled in such a way that the separation clarifies still further Miss Dickinson's total conception of dying.

The first response involves the trial of faith that we have already seen dramatized in "The last Night." Contemplating the dead, the living are deserted by any sense they might once have had of an orderly universe. Their souls become *jostled*—that is, crowded by thoughts which question the fitness of things. As, literally, the mourners tread from room to room in the bereaved house, so, symbolically, they are walking to and fro through a maze of doubts and uncertainties. Eventually, a kind of envy of the dead springs up:

> That others should exist
> While She must finish quite
> A Jealousy for Her arose
> So nearly infinite—

At least, in death, the corpse knows—knows whether death leads to anything beyond itself. For the survivors, there is nothing to be seen except a long future of pondering this issue—and of realizing that, so long as one is alive, no real answer is ever likely to be forthcoming.

The second response is directed less to the philosophical riddle than to the physical shape of death. Before being discussed, it had better be illustrated:

'Twas warm—at first—like Us—
Until there crept upon
A Chill—like frost upon a Glass—
Till all the scene—be gone.

The Forehead copied Stone—
The Fingers grew too cold
To ache—and like a Skater's Brook—
The busy eyes—congealed—

It straightened—that was all—
It crowded Cold to Cold—
It multiplied indifference—
As Pride were all it could—

And even when with Cords—
'Twas lowered, like a Freight—
It made no Signal, nor demurred,
But dropped like Adamant.

Grief does not appear this time: the corpse is too much lacking in identity to warrant that; nor are there any metaphysical anxieties. What we are made to feel, however, is a profound sense of the "otherness" of the dead. With an almost naturalistic precision, Emily Dickinson examines the corpse, and shows us that, in its extinction, the dead one has lost every claim to being one of our familiars.

After the distinction between us is announced, it is then elaborated through the simile in lines three and four. As frost overspreads the window glass through which we were once accustomed to see, so death has crept upon a person *Till all the scene—be gone—*or until, in other words, every distinguishing quality that we formerly recognized in the person is blotted out. At this point, life and death are visualized as totally discontinuous states; the cleavage between them is widened by other aspects of the poem—by the repeated use of the impersonal *It* to describe the dead; by a likening of the corpse to such non-human objects as *Stone* or frozen *Brook* or a piece of *Freight;* by the way in which the dead one is reduced to a set of purely mechanical gestures. No longer a unified personality, the corpse becomes various parts of the body (the *Forehead,* the *Fingers,* the *eyes*), which can still act—

> The Forehead copied Stone—

> The Fingers grew too cold

> The busy eyes—congealed—

—but whose actions are now devoid of meaning. Though the gestures all seem to resemble ours—we, too, form expressions, or fix our eyes, or experience cold —it is their difference from our own that is ultimately made to count. Where our movements are continuous, the corpse moves toward one fixed attitude—

> It straightened—that was all—

123

Where our gestures betoken some sort of response, the motions of the corpse denote only a complete lack of responsiveness. The more things the dead one does, the more its indifference is *multiplied,* or accumulated.

Its dissimilarity to ourselves becomes absolute when the corpse is readied for burial. Trussed with ropes and plummeted into the ground, we would have protested —or cried in outrage. Even in these extremities, however, the dead one maintains its separateness:

> It made no Signal, nor demurred,
> But dropped like Adamant.

In Emily Dickinson's terms, then, the result of death is a complete transformation of being. That which was like ourselves, sharing our physical structure, our responses, our mode of behavior, is suddenly and utterly altered. The poet's own reaction is centered around the fact of the alteration. As the onlooker in this poem, she neither weeps over death nor questions its significance. But she shrinks in awe from the total cadaver, from the mystifying loss of humanhood which death has brought.

A third response to death subsumes both the others, and must be inferred from a pattern of imagery in the poetry. The pattern derives from Emily Dickinson's habit of picturing the aftermath of death through the images and activities of a domestic household. Speaking of a "Death in the Opposite House," Miss Dickinson heightens the agony with an account of how "the Neighbors rustle in and out," airing a mattress and awaiting the arrival of the milliner and the undertaker, a "man of the Appalling Trade." She draws upon descriptive touches like an unused thimble, a fly-filled chamber, or a dusty windowpane to suggest that the housewife has

124

fallen into the final "indolence" of death. Or she makes bereavement vivid and concrete by dramatizing it as

> The Sweeping up the Heart
> And putting Love away
> We shall not want to use again
> Until Eternity.

The significance of these household tropes is two-fold. First of all, they reinforce a point made earlier, reminding us again of how in the presence of death, which is chaos, Emily Dickinson's survivors seek to reorder their lives through some tightly disciplined movement, some bare and yet ceremonious act. But the greater importance of the images lies in the way they at once extend and round off Miss Dickinson's portrayals of childhood. If we think of childhood as her principal means of escape—as a stage into which she retreated in order to shut out experience, or to subdue the world by striking back at it—then mature womanhood, a state indicated by the household terms, ought to carry radically opposite associations. Maturity should represent the level of awareness that is imposed upon the poet when retreat of any sort ceases to be possible, and when, therefore, she is forced to look directly and unflinchingly upon tragic necessities. And that, exactly, is the frame of mind which death—death still thought of as an external fact—occasions. Like the perception of time, the perception of the dead is for Emily Dickinson a source of unremitting horror. She must ponder death through completely mature eyes for the simple reason that there is no pretense which can minimize the terrors of the corpse—and no averting of the eyes which will blind one to the dilemmas and uncertainties that the existence of the corpse elicits.

So, viewed in the form of an *objective* condition, death can only unsettle the viewer, arousing her to a sense of loss and grief, or to feelings of absolute futility. This point is attested to by every aspect of Emily Dickinson's style which we have thus far noted: the gauntness of her language, the pinched control in her poetic forms, her use of the images and perspectives of mature womanhood. But the situation changes markedly at just the point where, visualizing death as a *subjective* condition, Miss Dickinson switches the point of view from the living to the dying, and death becomes a fact about the speaker's own person. The fear, it will be wise to re-emphasize, still exists. It is, however, tempered by responses that suggest anticipation and even the presence of something keenly pleasurable. The poetry thus broadens from a single into a double attitude, and style serves as the index to this crucial difference.

Miss Dickinson's intentions in the second category of her death poems may be readily described. She attempts an imaginative construction of her own death: tries, in effect, to catch herself at the very center of the act of dying. As in the time-and-change texts, consequently, the writing stresses a momentous transition; now, however, the transition takes place from within, so that it bridges the period when life starts to drain away to the exact moment when death arrives and the world around her has receded from the speaker. At her most brilliant, Emily Dickinson forges these matters into a poetry that is without parallel in the English language. Certainly it is sharper, more concrete, and better visualized than the death-haunted reveries of Poe, Beddoes, or the so-called graveyard poets. Perhaps it owes a little to Donne—one thinks particularly of "The Relic." But it manages to exceed Donne where the problem of objectifying the death processes themselves is concerned. The ability to find images, actions, and personifications that would transfix death at the very point of striking: this seems an ability that was entirely unique with Emily Dickinson.

One supposes that her most famous, if not necessarily her best, example is "The Chariot":

> Because I could not stop for Death—
> He kindly stopped for me—
> The carriage held but just ourselves
> And Immortality.
>
> We slowly drove—He knew no haste
> And I had put away
> My labor and my leisure too,
> For His Civility—
>
> We passed the School, where Children strove
> At Recess—in the Ring—
> We passed the fields of Gazing Grain—
> We passed the Setting Sun—
>
> Or rather—He passed Us—
> The Dews drew quivering and chill—
> For only Gossamer, my Gown—
> My Tippet—only Tulle—
>
> We paused before a House that seemed
> A swelling of the Ground—

> The Roof was scarcely visible—
> The Cornice—in the Ground—
>
> Since then—'tis Centuries—and yet
> Feels shorter than the Day
> I first surmised the Horses Heads
> Were toward Eternity—

No poem of Emily Dickinson's has been more diligently explicated than this one; and none, it seems to me, remains less well understood. In part, the misreadings are due to an unusually large number of editorial liberties: the early editors muddied Miss Dickinson's intentions by changing important words in the third and fifth stanzas and by dropping stanza four altogether. In the main, though, our misunderstanding of "The Chariot" derives from our failure to see that it is a thoroughly tricky poem, which invites either of two quite different readings, but which can perhaps be read most successfully when the two have been yoked together into a single, all-encompassing theme. It is with the alternatives and the grounds for their fusion that we must be concerned; and probably we can get at them best by taking advantage of the narrative situation which the poem presents.

For "The Chariot" does rest upon a narrative basis —that is, involves characters, an episode, a plot-line of sorts—and the narrative, in turn, has certain conventional literary associations. Up to the door, there come riding not one but two callers: observe that the carriage is occupied by both Death *and* Immortality. Presumably they dally for a little, then presently they ride off with the Lady-Poet into the sunset. Without the slightest strain, an assignation of this kind can be related to the tradition of nineteenth-century "courtly love," a tradition which Emily Dickinson might have known at first hand or through direct observation, but which, in all likelihood, she knew best because of the celebration of its subtleties in the sentimental novels of the late eighteenth and nineteenth centuries. In the novel, it is often the tender, solicitous lover who comes to fetch his Lady for a carriage spin. If we think of Miss Dickinson's Death in this role—conceive of him as the courtly, the well-mannered suitor—then a pattern of meaning begins which can be extended through the entire poem. Words like *kindness* and *civility* can, for instance, be accepted at face value. They mean that Death comes as a gentleman, motivated by honorable intentions, and concerned only with carrying the Lady to her bridal rooms in Heaven. By the same token, the leisurely pace taken by Death bespeaks a tact and a consideration for human feelings, both of which seem highly admirable. Above all, Death-as-lover affixes the part played by Immortality. This silent partner on the drive must be visualized as nothing less than a chaperone. Saying nothing, but always sternly ensconced on a rear seat, Immortality sanctifies the relationship between Death and Lady, keeps the relationship beyond reproach, ensures that the journey into darkness will have a respectable ending. Immortality's function, when we stop to think about it, could hardly be more proper, therefore—or more strictly orthodox.

But in the novel, "courtly love" was not always this innocent a pastime; nor did the "courtly love" relationship invariably develop along such sanguine lines. From Richardson to Mrs. Southworth, it was sometimes the cunning seducer who came calling, and who whisked

129

the Lady away quite against her will. If Emily Dickinson's personification is seen in this guise, a re-evaluation of the whole drama becomes necessary. Death is no longer to be thought of as a kindness; he is someone depraved and malevolent. In the slow, deliberate pacing of his journey, we perhaps glimpse the arrogance of Death, his bland disrespect for human wishes. Certainly the flimsiness of the Lady's apparel—

> For only Gossamer, my Gown—
> My Tippet—only Tulle—

—can only recall us to how vulnerable humankind is when Death attacks. But the greatest change is reserved for Immortality, who, in the second reading of "The Chariot," abruptly ceases to chaperone, and becomes, instead, party to a wicked fraud. As Death now violates, so Immortality now betrays. Both have used the demeanor of courtliness in order to deceive; the victim of both is the helpless human being.

Our reaction to the total poem will hinge ultimately upon how we have interpreted these narrative details. Regardless of which version seems preferable, the journey itself deserves detailed analysis. As the expedition proceeds, the Lady-Poet is leaving life; it disappears behind her like a receding landscape. Emily Dickinson's style, from the third through the sixth stanzas, masterfully demonstrates how differing qualities of language can be used to suggest modes of being which are wholly separate from one another. Consider the language in lines five to twelve. It emphasizes four qualities: light (the sun imagery), warmth and vitality (the children and *the fields of Gazing Grain*), and incessant motion (*drove, strove,* the repeated *passed*). More significantly still, this is a hard and crisply pictorial language; the schoolyard, the fields, and the sunset are all made to loom up off the page with the exactitude of sharp little etchings. Commencing with line thirteen, however, a change occurs. Here darkness (the sun is gone), cold (*the Dews drew quivering and chill*), and stasis (*we paused*) become evident. The writing as a whole seems gradually to be overspread by vagueness. Though the individual images in lines nineteen and twenty are still clear enough—

> The Roof was scarcely visible—
> The Cornice—in the Ground—

—the picture into which the images fit remains blurred and indefinite, refuses to come into focus.

Emily Dickinson's aim, of course, is to record the passage from life, where everything is tangible and hence easily apprehended, to the "otherness" of death, a realm in which shapes necessarily become obscure and mysterious and can no longer be readily seen. Partly, she manages the transition by shifting from light to darkness, from warmth to cold, from motion to rest. In addition to these rather commonplace techniques, she achieves her effect through juxtaposing a precise and pictorial diction with a language that is left deliberately opaque and fuzzy. This gradual merging of the familiar into the strange, the known into the unimaginable, constitutes one of the supremely great moments in her poetry.

But what, aside from the grave, is the destination of the chariot? Are the horses pointed beyond anything more than the house in the ground? Emily Dickinson specifically declines to say. The word with which she ends the text is *Eternity*—in this context a strikingly ambiguous word, one that can grow meaningful only in the light of our response to the narrative situation. Provided we saw Death as the gallant lover and Immortality as a protector, we will presume that dying represented a benefit, and that the Lady-Poet was borne by her escorts to an Eternity of immortal life. Provided we saw Death as seducer and Immortality as his partner in crime, however, we must infer a vastly different outcome, supposing that the Lady was raped of life, and afterward abandoned to the earth and to the void of Eternal nothingness. Between these alternatives, Emily Dickinson pauses indecisively. She first cloaks Death in a form that will provoke two sets of associations; then she leaves open and unresolved the question of which set is really the more applicable to the poem.

Her uncertainty has been vigorously—and, I think, unjustifiably—rebuked by Yvor Winters. Winters sees the conclusion of "The Chariot" as involving a "semiplayful pretence of familiarity with the posthumous experience of eternity," and he declares himself against so hopeless an enterprise. He writes: "In so far as it concentrates on the life that is being left behind, it is wholly successful; in so far as it attempts to experience the death to come, it is fraudulent, however exquisitely, and in this it falls below her finest achievement." And he sums up: "The poem ends in irresolution, in the sense that it ends in a statement that is not offered seriously. . . . It is possible to solve any problem of insoluble experience by retreating a step and defining the boundary at which comprehension ceases, and by then making the necessary moral adjustments to that boundary; this in itself is an experience both final and serious. . . ."

Winters' premises about "The Chariot" are inaccurate. It is not really a poem about the topography of the "undiscovered country." It is, rather, Emily Dickinson's legitimate attempt to imagine the death which she *knows* must come to her and to spell out her responses to this inevitable experience. Furthermore, the irresolution in the text does not derive from the fact that we have crossed a "boundary" and are walking where no mortal has the right or (as yet) the knowledge to tread. Instead, the irresolution comes about because, when Emily Dickinson thinks about her own death—when she seeks to judge it morally—she cannot honestly make up her mind about what her feelings and her attitudes are.

Returning to the poem, we find this psychological ambivalence at every turn. In one sense, the poet is obviously repelled by the prospect of dying. This aversion expresses itself in the idea that Death violates, or in the conception of death as an inexorable journey, or in the stress upon the utter captivity of the human being who travels with Death. But simultaneously with the fears it evokes, the prospect of dying also holds out a definite appeal. This attraction is made manifest not only by the possibility that Death is an ardent lover: the pleasant fellow who brings a pleasing experience. We may glean the attraction as well from other revealing elements of the poem—from the air of constant excitement that accompanies the carriage drive, from the lure of the unknown, from the relaxed nature of the writing, its easy, graceful, almost jaunty tone. One and all, these qualities convert "The Chariot" into an order of poetry signally different from that which we found in "The last Night that She lived." Where style in "The last Night" was uniformly bleak, as cramped and as generally unlovely as the room in which the drama of the poem took place, the method here is far more divided, hinting of delight even as it touches on dread, and making the trip seem somehow enjoyable even as it recounts a journey to the grave. One feels that such divisions reflect the poet's genuine uncertainty concerning the subject which she explores. They suggest that while Emily Dickinson knows what she must think and how she must feel in connection with another's death, about what her own death might signify she has not reached, and perhaps cannot reach, any fixed conclusion.

It may be argued, though, that I have used to illustrate her ambivalence a poem which is not entirely typical of Emily Dickinson. With some accuracy, one could say that while "The Chariot" will stand as her best-known dramatization of personal death, it is by no means the grimmest or the most desolating. Let us turn, therefore, to a darker example. The poem has none of the charm of "The Chariot"; in many ways, indeed, it is as frankly hideous as any account of dying ever written. Yet I submit that beneath the horror, which we see at first, the contradictions of "The Chariot" are likewise to be found in Emily Dickinson's coupling of dying with the fly:

> I heard a Fly buzz—when I died—
> The Stillness in the Room
> Was like the Stillness in the Air—
> Between the Heaves of Storm—
>
> The eyes around—had wrung them dry—
> And Breaths were gathering firm
> For that last Onset—when the King
> Be witnessed—in the Room—

I willed my Keepsakes—Signed away
What portion of me be
Assignable—and then it was
There interposed a Fly—

With Blue—uncertain stumbling Buzz—
Between the light—and me—
And then the Windows failed—and then
I could not see to see—

If a narrative structure offered the best approach to "The
Chariot," the key to this text would appear to lie in
Emily Dickinson's central image. The fly dominates three
of the four stanzas; in stanza two, the one place where
it is not explicitly mentioned, we will perhaps come to
feel its presence the most keenly of all. Consequently,
the questions likeliest to prove provocative are: why
did Miss Dickinson choose the image? how does it operate in the poem? what are the layers of significance it
eventually accumulates?

At its simplest, the image is a purely aesthetic device.
In "The Chariot" Emily Dickinson had specified death
by using a personification that caught him at the very
moment of his onset. Now, she works the other way
around, portraying death not as a force which comes but
as the progressive lapse of life. The fly, active and vital,
is perfectly tailored to her method. So long as the fly's
gyrations can be seen or its noises distract, the poem is
positioned in the everyday world of sense. As the fly
disappears, sense is ebbing with it. When the fly is gone,
the speaker herself has been transported to an ineffable
other-world. The systematic blotting out of the insect

becomes a way of measuring the sort of progression which it would otherwise be impossible to imagine.

A more complex possibility is broached when we go on to think of the fly as feeder upon carrion. This means that, during her last moments alive, the speaker beholds an awful vision of what is to come—glimpses, in the now symbolic activities of the fly, a hint that stink and corruption are death's only legacies. Her perception grows more appalling when it is contrasted with the naïve assumptions of stanza two. There, mourners, gathered round the bedside, are awaiting something akin to a divine revelation. As life passes, they expect a King —a Sign of Beatitude—to appear:

> And Breaths were gathering firm
> For that last Onset—when the King
> Be witnessed—in the Room—

Then the Sign is made, right enough; but it is made to the speaker, and made in the form of the loathsome insect. The point seems unmistakable. With a Lucretian ferocity that outdoes Lucretius, Emily Dickinson reminds us that, for all we can really tell, the fly and the King may be identical. Her image belies any likelihood of immortal life by suggesting that within the precincts of the grave decay will be all and the maggot will take ultimate and absolute dominion.

Yet, if this view opens the way to unqualified despair, do we not find that the fly lends itself to still a third interpretation? At its most demonic—even as the potential destroyer of dead human flesh—the insect continues to represent life. Dipping, buzzing, vibrantly on the move, it remains the only animate object in a poem which moves steadily toward inanimation. Surely it is not ac-

cidental that Emily Dickinson has elected to symbolize
life through the ugly annoyance: that she has located in
an experience connoting the height of disturbance, discomfort, and nastiness an ideal emblem for the world
from which her speaker departs. What the identification
of fly with life requires is a radically different reading
of the poem. It forces us to see that while death may
carry one ineluctably to the fly, still it is no less true that
only through death can the fly be escaped. More forcefully than in "The Chariot" Emily Dickinson has stressed
the gruesomeness of dying. As in "The Chariot," however, she never quite commits herself to the gruesome, for
she keeps entertaining the possibility that with death there
will come a peace and tranquillity that are denied the
individual in every other condition. When the *windows
fail* in line fourteen, the speaker has lost her *Keepsakes:* her entitlements to life and to a continuing identity. But, beyond the fly and safely past the *Heaves of
Storm,* she has also shut out a world with enough unpleasant features to make the leaving of it an experience
that is at least bearable.

If I am correct, then, Emily Dickinson's estimate of
death is shaped by whichever of two points of view she
adopts in her poetry. Identifying with the living, she
sees death as disorder and deprivation and as a philosophical problem that defies adjustment. Placing herself among the dying, however, she falls into a more
mixed reaction—mixed, because the old fears tend to
blend off into outright yearning. The same split is apparent in those of her poems which seek after the hidden ways of Eternity. These texts are all continuations
of the death poetry, in the sense that they push beyond
the fact of death in an effort to define, intellectually and

aesthetically, the state to which death will lead. But what they say and the manner of their conclusions depend upon where the poet stands as she attempts her definitions.

Thus when Emily Dickinson of Amherst looks for Paradise from the standpoint of Amherst, she writes an essentially despairing poetry:

> Their Hight in Heaven comforts not—
> Their Glory—nought to me—
> 'Twas best imperfect—as it was—
> I'm finite—I cant see—
>
> The House of Supposition—
> The Glimmering Frontier that
> Skirts the Acres of Perhaps—
> To Me—shows—insecure—

The orthodox notion that the dead are dwelling in *Glory* provides the speaker with no comfort. All she can see are the vast, vacant distances separating herself from the deceased—and from Godhead. The allegorical landscape of the second stanza represents a savage attack on Christian platitudes (the *House of Supposition* is obviously the church), while, at the same time, it shows that man's knowledge of the Infinite is circumscribed by a frontier so vague and distant that the living intelligence can never hope to cross it. A kind of proto-existentialism runs through the poem; for existence *precedes* essence—and in preceding it appears to veil Eternity with sequence, or to wall Heaven out behind an impenetrable mask of the merely experiential.

But when, by contrast, Emily Dickinson's speakers are

pictured as being contained by Eternity, the poetry is written in a more hopeful vein:

> Our journey had advanced—
> Our feet were almost come
> To that odd Fork in Being's Road—
> Eternity—by Term—
>
> Our pace took sudden awe—
> Our feet—reluctant—led—
> Before—were Cities—but Between—
> The Forest of the Dead—
>
> Retreat—was out of Hope—
> Behind—a Sealed Route—
> Eternity's White Flag—Before—
> And God—at every Gate—

We will not confuse what is said here with the glib facility of "I never saw a Moor." This is a text born of genuine struggle, not a brisk, superficial literary exercise. Nevertheless, the word *is* struggle; and what commands interest is the way the conflict refuses to be reconciled, and demands expression, rather, in a language of thoroughgoing indecisiveness. If the *Forest of the Dead* looms ominously, for instance, then somewhere just beyond the forest, there arises, dimly yet perceptibly, a celestial City. Again, the idea of no retreat may seem frightening; yet fear is, to some degree, offset by the presence of *God—at every Gate.* Ranging imaginatively down a road to the afterlife, Emily Dickinson proceeds with something less than the saint's assurance. But neither are her movements to be characterized as completely unwilling. "Reluctance" and "awe" are underlain by an implied eagerness. As image balances out image or concept is made to match concept, all three emotions—awe, reluctance, *and* eagerness—are yoked together into a mixed, yet inextricably mixed, feeling about the destination ahead.

IV ✛

Almost every day, as Conrad Aiken once said of her, Emily Dickinson must consciously have died a little. And almost every year since the discovery of her poetry, a critic has announced that death was the one subject which could drive Emily Dickinson to an absolutely limitless despair. What, then, shall we make of this fact: that the more personal death becomes in the poetry, the more the poet's despair is qualified—the more her response is divided between despair and desire?

In one way, Freud's analysis of the psychology of death may help. The whole informing principle of a "death wish" involves contradictory impulses that are remarkably similar to Emily Dickinson's. Excessive brooding over death is assumed to reflect one's morbid aversion to the thought of dying; but it also bespeaks the morbid attraction that one feels for the very prospect which has been rejected. Certainly Miss Dickinson would appear to possess, in rare abundance, each classic symptom of the death wish—not only the tendency to brood about death, but likewise the simultaneous fear-and-fascination which prompts the brooding, and in which, again and again, the brooding must always culminate.

Without wishing to disallow the Freudian view, we may still feel that Emily Dickinson's love affair with death is best clarified by a twist peculiar to the poet's own thinking. The twist would be her excruciating time sense, and the extent to which every major dread she experienced was chiefly conditioned by temporality.

Clearly, the fear of time shaped her more despairing conception of death. Change in all forms repelled her; hence death, the ultimate in change, had to strike her as an especially abhorrent prospect. Moreover, she saw time as divesting all worldly events of order and stability. Accordingly, time could only confirm her suspicion that the end of life was to be one further incoherence. When whirl was so deeply engrained into the texture of experience, she had to suppose that no Immortal Estate could possibly exist outside the whirling. It is, one imagines, equally as easy to distinguish the relationship between time and Emily Dickinson's fascination with dying. Death was capable of beckoning and inviting her because, though it might be the final indignity imposed by time, still, paradoxically enough, death also constituted the only real refuge from temporality. To die was, for Emily Dickinson, a matter of gaining immunity. It was to achieve forever the same peace of mind that could be had only fleetingly through the child's pose or through a retreat indoors. Whatever the actual confrontation of death might cost her, therefore, Emily Dickinson could cherish the grave beyond death—could cherish it in despite of herself, no doubt—as the one place safely, securely, and permanently outside the reach of evanescence.

Her taste for death is plainly mirrored in the central circumstances of Emily Dickinson's life. It may be true, as Allen Tate maintains, that "her life was one of the richest and deepest ever lived on this continent"; indeed, since Tate refers to her creative existence, his remark is of course perfectly just. The fact remains, nevertheless,

141

that judged by the light of normal activity or of ordinary, everyday episode, she can scarcely be said to have lived at all. Increasingly after 1860, she was in the world, but not really of it; sequestered behind four walls, she had chosen to enact a kind of living death. If some latent wish for the womb did not motivate her choice—and it may well have done so—then the very least to be assumed is that, within the walls of her father's house, Emily Dickinson was searching for the serenity of the dead, for the fixed and timeless atmosphere of the tomb.

Reviewing her death poems as a group, we discover that the point of view which determines attitude is not simply dependent upon the relationship between living and dying; it derives, as well, from the speaker's involvement with temporality. Where the speaker survives, death leaves her fearfully exposed to time. She must face the business of tomorrow—

> The sweeping up the Heart
> And putting love away

—or of a seemingly endless procession of tomorrows:

> And then an awful leisure was
> Our faith to regulate—

Where death comes to the speaker, however, her voice is extinguished, and, perforce, time and change are likewise halted. As my italics will indicate, either the poetry passes from movement to rest:

> We *paused* before a House

or it closes out the restless world:

142

And then the Windows *failed*—and then
I could not see to see

or it presents a state from which the ordinary ritual of
backward-and-forward has been precluded:

> *Retreat*—was out of Hope—
> Behind—a *Sealed Route*—
> Eternity's White Flag—*Before*—
> And God—*at every Gate*—

The shift from the necessity for continuing, which appears in the first two excerpts, to the promise of utter
cessation, by which the last three are pervaded, tells us
all we need to know about Emily Dickinson's ambivalence toward death. To outlive the spectacle of dying is
to remain painfully aware of all the manifold anxieties
that death provokes. But to be enveloped by death, to
imagine oblivion descending upon one's self—that is to
enter into the presence of stasis, which is the rarest and
the most precious gift that Miss Dickinson can imagine.

Her simultaneous courting and resisting of death supplies another context in which Emily Dickinson's kinship
with Melville ought to be explored. Theirs is a curious
parallel, surely: the world traveller and the shut-in; the
writer of sprawling epics and the composer of a delicate
and almost fragile lyric poetry; the enraged howler at
God's silence and the ironist whose chief weapon against
God was the sly, demure thrust. Yet beneath these undeniable differences, one sees a shared tendency to raise
questions, a shared failure to find the answers, and a
shared tragic outlook through which the failure is dramatized. The cosmic issues that face Melville's protag-
onists strongly resemble the ones that are grappled with

in Miss Dickinson's poetry. Nor are the motives that launch his characters on long, abortive voyages after understanding basically unlike the impulses that sent her upstairs in her fruitless quest for escape. The correspondence does exist, for all its seeming unlikelihood; and it nowhere emerges more forcibly than in the complicated views of death which the two writers reveal.

Fear of death runs through Melville's fiction like a persistent wail. Though perhaps no more than half-consciously introduced, it is a deeply felt part of his early travel books. It becomes explicit in *Mardi*, as the "last riddle that underlieth all the rest." From *Moby Dick* on, it swells to the proportions of a haunting, nagging refrain: a dirge that seems to affect everything in the life of the writer as well as virtually everything he writes. And yet, played off against the fear, there is always an avid hungering for death, which, though it may be handled more covertly, is no less apparent to the reader. This hungering manifests itself in the suicides of Taji and Pierre, in Ahab's determination to destroy himself, in the charm that death exerts for such otherwise diverse characters as Israel Potter, the speaker in "After the Pleasure Party," Claggart, and even Billy Budd. The sheer proliferation of these figures—the regular reappearance of the death-obsessed actor, with his cravings for self-annihilation—suggests the degree to which Melville himself felt the lure of death. In the final analysis, one takes his seekers after extinction to be emblems of that part of Melville's mind which saw that the problems of life were never to be resolved during life, and so sought out death in the hope that, with death, either the answers would come, or else a total obliviousness to the questions.

The situation is exactly duplicated by Emily Dickinson. Like Ishmael, Melville's archetypal survivor, Miss Dickinson, in a surviving role, can lament death's "bitter blanks" and "heartless immensities": can express her repugnance toward dying through the symbolic act of "pausing before coffin warehouses, and bringing up the rear of every funeral [she] meets." But like Ahab, Melville's relentless wooer of death, she can find in the projected image of her own passing an excuse for invoking "darkness," "oblivion," and the "hushed burial." In the poems we have just considered, her invocation is cautiously qualified; it is an acceptance of death that coexists with rejection, and is largely to be felt in an ambiguous poetic style. The acceptance grows more wholehearted, however, in a number of texts where Miss Dickinson is no longer meeting the fact of the corpse head-on, but where, in a mood that is very nearly exultant, she muses over the priceless good fortune of those long dead.

Characteristically, the poetry stresses the confusions of living. All around, there swirl the forces of time and change, inflicting their usual hardships, resulting, as always, in a maximum of bafflement and pain. The dead are out of it. "Safe in their alabaster chambers"; asleep for every Winter to come; citizens of a darkness that permits no knowledge of the dark—the dead have passed beyond the possibility for further shock. If God still terrorizes or Nature is still abusive, the dead no longer know. Emily Dickinson makes their security seem complete, either by defining the advantages of death—

> Suspense—is hostiler than Death—
> Death—thosoever Broad,

Is just Death, and cannot increase—
Suspense—does not conclude—

or through a dramatic conception which visualizes the
dead as

safe in Tombs—
Where Nature's temper cannot reach
And Vengeance—never comes—

V ✠

By her death poems, we are brought to a third general attitude of Emily Dickinson's. The first was irony,
a determination to hold off experience. The second was
a naked involvement with the experiences of time and
change. The third is the sort of ambivalence which the
death poetry, as a whole, displays.

Superficially, the first and third of these responses
may seem similar. Their resemblance is misleading,
however. Writing ironically, Miss Dickinson sought to
neutralize experience by claiming that an event was
neither good nor bad. By contrast, her ambivalences
came about when the same central experience struck
her as being both good *and* bad, and when she was
deeply involved in both extremes of the contradiction.
Emily Dickinson never held herself aloof from death.
She never tried to pretend that death had no power to
affect her. It is simply that, depending upon where she
stood when she thought of death, she could see it as the
greatest of human perils—or as a positive virtue.*

* Another difference between them might have to do with
the degree of consciousness that enters into Miss Dickinson's
ironies, and into her presentation of ambivalent feelings. As an

This divided point of view figures in one other area of her work. When Emily Dickinson writes about love, her subject invites a wide range of responses, varying from the banal to the tragic. At its most exciting, however, her love poetry becomes a poetry of ambivalences. Emily Dickinson imagines herself to be personally involved in a love relationship, and the power of what she says thereafter derives from the fact that this idea at once pleases her and arouses her to a deep sense of loathing.

ironist, she is the highly conscious writer, whose poses and other strategies were deliberately planned and deliberately executed. On the other hand, it is perhaps possible that her response to death commingled the known and consciously understood fear with an urge to die that existed only in her subconscious mind, and was thus revealed in the images, situations, and tonal effects of a wholly unconscious creation. This would bring her feelings more into conformity with Freud's death wish, which is an unconscious drive, never fully apparent to the wisher. It should be added, though, that her life and poetry most often suggest that Emily Dickinson's particular love affair with death was both avowed and explicit.

CHAPTER V

Emily and Him: *The Love Poetry*

⊹ And He—He followed—close behind—

EMILY DICKINSON'S LOVE POETRY has received an acclaim that is all out of keeping with its intrinsic value. The reasons are not difficult to understand. A combination of the maiden lady and the passionate lyric is bound to seem remarkable; no doubt titillated by the possibilities, critics have simply allowed spectacle to warp judgment where this part of Miss Dickinson's work is concerned. Either they have converted the poetry to biographical ends, and have combed it for clues which might help to identify the person—presumably the "married man"—whom Emily was addressing; or, failing to make an identification, they have assumed that some lover must have existed, and have transformed the unhappy affair—the tragic involvement, the blighted hopes, the bitter renunciation, the lonely aftermath—into the basis for the most moving and powerful of Emily's poetic themes.

Over the years, the first of these projects has resulted in a veritable listing of candidates. Indeed, if the hypotheses of *all* her biographers were to be credited, Emily Dickinson would have to be thought of as a libidinous monster, fatally unable to resist any married man who chanced to look her way. Attached to the assorted husbands who have been solemnly associated with her, she would have had scant time for poetry—or for any other productive enterprise. The view that love

149

was central to her art is, in its way, hardly less an exaggeration. What it fails to see is that Miss Dickinson was seldom at her best when she was dealing with the amorous passions. She wrote a handful of lyrics which are genuinely moving and a number of other pieces that have value for their psychological disclosures. In the main, however, her love poetry is thin and brittle and often rather drably unoriginal. To make it bear the chief burden for her tragic outlook is to ignore the fact that, line for line, the love theme was surely Emily Dickinson's weakest: the theme which comes off second best when it is contrasted with any of the other of her dominant motifs.

And yet, there is love poetry. The accounts of separation, frustration, and heartbreak do exist: exist and constitute a sizeable portion of the Emily Dickinson canon. Let us examine some representative selections, therefore, focussing as far as possible squarely upon the poetry, and withholding any suppositions about the scandal that is presumed to lurk behind it. The examination will probably beget no flesh-and-blood lover for Miss Dickinson—male, married, or otherwise. Nor does it promise to turn up the sort of brilliance and insight which are typical of her better writing. But what it may bring to pass are an illumination of the love poems themselves, an explanation for the motives which brought them into being, and a relating of what little does seem of value in them to the rest of the poet's basic outlook. At a time when scandal still obscures the poetry to the point of obfuscation, one feels that such aims have an obvious and a rather decided value.

II ✢

One mark of the somewhat mechanical quality of the love poetry is this: more readily than anything else Emily Dickinson wrote, it tends to fall into neat, self-contained categories. From the standpoint of style and, in some measure, of content, three distinct groupings emerge. We may as well come at once to the grouping in which the texts are by all odds the least rewarding, though not, unhappily, the least numerous. Written in 1858, which was Miss Dickinson's first year as a practicing poet, the following seems a fair choice:

> When Roses cease to bloom, Sir,
> And Violets are done—
> When Bumblebees in solemn flight
> Have passed beyond the Sun—
> The hand that paused to gather
> Upon this Summer's day
> Will idle lie—in Auburn—
> Then take my flowers—pray!

Perhaps the surprising thing is that Emily Dickinson prevented herself from writing in this vein more often. We can be enormously grateful that, even in 1858, she was already finding deeper and more mature notes to strike. Yet the prevailing topics of her poetry—topics given over to death and love, to transiency and loss, to suffering and grief—are all perilously susceptible to just this sort of development. With a shade less skill, a little less taste, Miss Dickinson could easily have committed herself to a lifetime's career of the bitter-sweet strains and melancholy reflections which characterize "When Roses cease to bloom, Sir."

For this is, of course, sentiment, when sentiment is at its stickiest. One assumes that Auburn must be Mt. Auburn Cemetery. On the other hand, place names are not really important. Any graveyard would do as well, for here all is atmosphere, and the atmosphere is all mood and mold and dissolution. The season is fleeting; life is on the wane; the speaker repines. Accordingly, one had better seize summer, flower, and lady while all three of them are still available to be taken. Penned by countless hacks and stuffed into the magazines and gift-books of Emily Dickinson's time, hundreds of poetic effusions were making identically these same points in identically these same flat images and flaccid rhymes. It is in no way unjust to Miss Dickinson to say that "When Roses cease to bloom, Sir" is neither better nor worse than the sentimental tradition of love poetry, which it so consciously and so unpleasantly reflects.

Nor can the poem be explained away solely on the grounds that it was an early exercise. Three years later, in 1861, when Miss Dickinson was no longer a novice, love could still tempt her to exclamation points and bathos:

> Come slowly—Eden!
> Lips unused to Thee—
> Bashful—sip thy Jessamines—
> As the fainting Bee,
>
> Reaching late his flower,
> Round her chamber hums—
> Counts his nectars—
> Enters—and is lost in Balms!

Throughout the ensuing decade, she continued to compose a kind of love poetry in which maidens blush and swains palpitate, in which there are the unfortunate analogies of moon beckoning to wave or river running to sea, and in which the thought is expressed in such abominably lush phrases as these:

> I hide myself within my flower
> That wearing on your breast—
> You, unsuspecting, wear me too—
> And angels know the rest!

> I hide myself—within my flower,
> That fading from your Vase—
> You—unsuspecting—feel for me—
> Almost—a loneliness—

Thus time alone does not purge the poetry of the banal or the precious. But the very pertinacity of these qualities—the way they have of implying that Miss Dickinson was often content to toy with the love theme—gives rise, I think, to a rather intriguing hypothesis.

Certainly Emily Dickinson can be presumed to have known the popular literature of her day. For her, as for virtually any literate person, the widely circulated verse of writers like Longfellow and Bayard Taylor and N. P. Willis would have amounted to standard reading fare. That she easily surpassed these writers—that she knew more, felt more deeply, and had verbal resources far greater than theirs—does not at all mean that she failed to read her contemporaries, or even that her response to what they wrote was anything less than enthusiastic. Moreover, it is at least a likely presumption

153

that, so far as the periodicals and giftbooks were concerned, she again possessed a first-hand acquaintance with their contents. These curious symbols of taste overspread most parlor tables in mid-nineteenth-century America—including, one supposes, the table in the Dickinson parlor at Amherst.

Consequently, our hypothesis might run like this: by 1860, if not before, Emily Dickinson had begun to take herself seriously as a practicing poet. However much she might eventually come to resist the prospect of publication, she revelled in the idea of being a writer, as her earliest letters to Thomas Wentworth Higginson, sent in 1862, clearly indicate. Is it possible, then, that from time to time she ground out a set of love lyrics, for no better reason than her belief that this was the accepted thing—the conventional thing—for poets of the age to do? Knowing the sentimental tradition of love poetry, exposed to it on every side, perhaps attracted to what passed for its charm, certainly recognizing its popular appeal—did she simply choose to copy out of the tradition her own portrayals of loss and loneliness, of suffering maidens and unrequited affections? Conceived of as one part of Miss Dickinson's attempt to regard herself as the fully creative spirit, this possibility would be altogether credible. If we could accept it as true, it would clear up two major mysteries. It would account for the meagerness of the love lyrics, allowing us to understand why so many of them are uniquely clogged with clichés and centered around the stock response. More broadly still, it would account for the very existence of the lyrics, for we would have to see them not as manifestations of the poet's private heartbreak, but as examples of a contrived passion, a passion that the poet borrowed from an eminently public literary convention.

But one advances the hypothesis with the realization that it will have to be discarded or, if not abandoned entirely, at all events sharply qualified. Much of the time it works, since the poetry, much of the time, is sufficiently stereotyped to make it seem relevant. When the worst models of triteness are taken away, however, a substantial number of texts remain which decline to be read as artificial examples of a stalely artificial tradition. Their difference from "When Roses cease to bloom, Sir" is not so much a matter of theme: actually what they say is often similar; but it is a difference in poetic technique. For the redolence of decaying flowers, there is now substituted a more austere imagery, an air of genuine desolation, withal the same intense and dramatic style that is characteristic of many of Miss Dickinson's broodings over death. The attitudes set forth in the poems no longer impress one as having been lifted from another source; instead, they bespeak a sorrow and an anxiety that could hardly be anything except profoundly personal.

Hence while a theory of derivation can—and almost unquestionably does—explain Miss Dickinson's more maudlin love poems, quite another sort of question is evoked by those of greater power. Nothing in their content requires that we speculate about whom Emily Dickinson loved; that is not the drift at all. What this second category of poems does force us to ponder, however, is why she had so desperate a fear of all emotional involvements: why the very idea of an intimate relationship unnerved her, and caused her to retreat in the same tremulous haste with which she shrank from death and mutability.

III ✢

One feels that a principal answer lies in the fact that many of her more successful love poems simply represent extensions of Emily Dickinson's time theme—extensions which transfer that theme from a metaphysical into a more explicitly human realm. Heretofore, our development of Miss Dickinson's obsession with flux has emphasized the philosophical side to the problem. Wherever she has looked, we have seen the poet encountering a relentless temporality which snubs out the intimate and the loved. Her constant lament has been that no aspect of experience will stay fixed, that nothing is willing to endure. She has been consistently appalled by how seasons, life, states of mind—and the values which seasons, life, and states of mind symbolize—are all claimed equally by the processes of disintegration. Seeking to explain these problems, Miss Dickinson has found her solution in a reworking of the philosophy of Heraclitus. Behind the flowing, she has glimpsed the terrible elusiveness of God: an elusiveness so galling and intolerable to the human sensibility that it seems born of outright hatred. The view she has most frequently presented is that of the individual plagued by change and time, because he is somehow conspired against by Divine and Natural forces which somehow loathe him.

Any realistic consideration of the poetry must conclude that this was her subject of surpassing greatness. Emily Dickinson was at her best, in other words, when the scope of her writing was cosmic rather than social, and when she was pitting man against the universe rather than picturing him in relationships with other human beings. Insofar as she did contemplate human society, Miss Dickinson's reactions to it were inevitably rooted in and nurtured by the same old dread of evanescence. What she had to see about human attachments was that they, like all other forms of experience, would necessarily be fleeting. No sooner would the attachments be founded than they would grow vulnerable to the destructive capacities of time and change. Perhaps death would intervene. Perhaps the figures in the relationship would be separated by the sudden, the unanticipated turn of events. Perhaps the emotions themselves might somehow be transmuted. But, regardless of the cause, any sense of rapport between people was invariably foredoomed. From the moment of its establishment, the kinship would march steadily toward some type of dissolution.

Visualizing personal ties in this light, Emily Dickinson was compelled to regard them as essentially disastrous. That is the important point. It makes no difference really what kind of relationship she wrote about, and certainly it is of no moment whether or not she had specific relationships in mind. Love, conceived of in any form or in any degree, was bound to frighten her, simply because the precariousness of love made it a thoroughly frightening experience. Even the prospect of being emotionally committed to someone else would seem calamitous to Miss Dickinson, because the potential involvement would have a way of reminding her of "finalities" and of the "Calvary of woe" which finalities always imposed.

It seems self-evident that this attitude figured in the strange letter-writing habits which accompanied her seclusion. That she increasingly preferred to correspond with friends rather than to see them directly is attributable to the fact that the letter kept impersonal and at arm's length those relationships into which she dared not enter too fully. Furthermore, the occasional cruelties which have been remarked in her correspondence are all parts of the same campaign. The barbs, the wry mockeries, the excursions into a slashing or occult wit: these must be understood as Emily Dickinson's defensive tactics. They were ways in which this unusually responsive person was able to suppress the responses that could disappoint and hurt her—indeed, that threatened to destroy her utterly—if she expressed them without restraint. In the better love poems, the fears that begot the letters come to play a vital role in Emily Dickinson's method. Her writing quickens from platitude into tragic insight when, as in the following text, the love relationship itself is kept secondary to the thought of love's impermanence:

> There came a Day at Summer's full,
> Entirely for me—
> I thought that such were for the Saints,
> Where Resurrections—be—
>
> The Sun, as common, went abroad,
> The flowers, accustomed, blew,
> As if no soul the solstice passed
> That maketh all things new—
>
> The time was scarce profaned, by speech—
> The symbol of a word

Was needless, as at Sacrament,
The Wardrobe—of our Lord—

Each was to each The Sealed Church,
Permitted to commune this—time—
Lest we too awkward show
At Supper of the Lamb.

The Hours slid fast—as Hours will,
Clutched tight, by greedy hands—
So faces on two Decks, look back,
Bound to opposing lands—

And so when all the time had leaked,
Without external sound
We bound the Other's Crucifix—
We gave no other bond—

Sufficient troth, that we shall rise—
Deposed—at length, the Grave—
To that new Marriage,
Justified—through Calvaries of Love—

We should note initially some superficial parallels
with "When Roses cease to bloom, Sir." As before, a
summer's day symbolizes the high point of the relationship. Once again, the day wanes and with its passing
the relationship deteriorates. But at this point the correspondences cease. The murky, manufactured atmosphere of Mt. Auburn has been displaced here by a
drama of separation so intensely painful that the terms
of the crucifixion seem wholly warranted. Over against
the lady's coy warnings, this poem abounds in a metic-

ulous and distinctively original phraseology: in phrases like the sliding hours, or leaking time (with its suggestion of a slow, yet ineluctable process), or the clutching, bereft hands. In a word, the difference would appear to be this: that in "When Roses cease to bloom, Sir," Emily Dickinson was actually writing about something called love, and time, for once, remained an incidental matter. Now, by contrast, she has turned to time's corrosive effects upon a relationship, and with this as her topic a brilliant poem emerges.

For the text has at least a touch of brilliance—but it is brilliance which derives less from the "episode" recounted than from the images and sensations of a dreadful mobility. Whom the speaker has lost seems totally unimportant; it could be anyone. No identity has been specified, and none is needed. What stands forth with tragic clarity, however, is the speaker's awareness of how passing time has caused her destitution. Clearly time has divided the "lovers": the extraordinary details in lines seventeen and twenty-one tell us that much. But the fact of the separation is made still worse by what appears to be the deliberate trickery—the element of a cruel deceitfulness—in time's behavior.

Thus in the four opening stanzas, time permits a false resurrection. It seems to stand still, to suspend the solstice "that maketh all things new." By ceasing to operate, temporality gives every indication of wishing to stabilize the relationship. But then the false resurrection results in a true crucifixion. With stanzas five and six, the sense we had before of a fixed and eternal moment is suddenly ended. Time now rolls mercilessly on, driving the "lovers" apart, dissolving their relationship, and giving rise to the Dantesque image of

So faces on two Decks, look back,
Bound to opposing lands—

Not only does this trick of time's render doubtful and
unlikely the prospect of an ultimate resurrection into
timelessness, which is hoped for in the concluding
stanza. The trick allows us to see that Emily Dickinson's
concern throughout the poem has been not with a love
affair, but with transiency, the transiency which under-
mines, weakens, and disrupts all human ties. She has
written of deprivation, to be sure. It is, however, a deprivation that involves the speaker's loss *to* temporality
far more than it does her loss *of* a particular individual.*

By and large, the situation is the same all through
Emily Dickinson's second category of love poems, a
grouping which should include such successful pieces
as "If you were coming in the fall"; "I live with him,
I see his face"; "You left me, Sire, two legacies"; "I
had the glory—that will do"; "What if I say I shall not

* It will clarify my interpretation of "There came a day" if
we note that the poem is surprisingly similar to "A light exists
in spring," which was analyzed in Chapter III. Here, as there,
light is the symbol for personal fullfillment, of course; we
should expect that of Emily Dickinson. The interesting thing,
though, is that both poems quickly arrive at a point where the
light appears to halt—to have arrested itself—in order to
guarantee fulfillment. Then, just as the speaker reaches out
to take her prize, time intervenes; and the sliding hours or
leaking time here are clearly akin to the stepping off of
horizons and reporting away of noons in the other poem.

These parallels of imagery and structure indicate just how
conscious Emily Dickinson could be of time passing when she
wrote of the love relationship.

wait"; " 'Twas a long Parting—but the time/For Inter-
view—had Come." The first two poems, for example,
again show the speaker contemplating some other person from across the great distances that time has placed
between them. With the next two, the focus shifts
slightly, so that the speaker reflects, from the standpoint
of the present, upon a past relationship which had invited and claimed her, but then failed to endure. In the
last two, the speaker's struggle is one of looking beyond
the love that time has ruined to a vision of love as an
immortal principle. Convinced now that all earthly kin-
ships must perish, she yearns for a "distant heaven"
where human attachments can be everlasting and "flesh-
less lovers" will need to abide no further separations.
In a way, of course, all these emphases tend to resemble the pattern of a traditional love poetry: the
poetry of Shakespeare or Donne or even Elizabeth Barrett Browning. But there is likewise a difference. Where
Shakespeare, Donne, and Mrs. Browning ordinarily provide two centers of interest—provide a sharp sense of
time, but also a sharp sense of the loved one (tech-
nically, the "person addressed") whom time bears away
—Miss Dickinson's habit is to subordinate the loved one
to mutability. The figures whom she addresses remain
vague "you's" and "he's," disembodied personages
who are without much substance or identity. It is the
time problem alone that preoccupies Emily Dickinson;
the failure of a relationship to stand still, rather than
the relationship as such, that really affords her pain.

To say then that the poems necessarily reflect her own
ill-fated involvement is to indulge in an argument that
seems largely groundless. Actually, among the texts
considered, there is not one which gives the clear-cut im-

pression that Emily Dickinson has referred to a special person or is recalling a particular episode. Despite the prevalence of guessing games on the subject, furthermore, one finds in the writing very little to suggest melodrama. No haughty dismissals of unsuitable young men appear; nor are there hints of tearful farewells, proffered to middle-aged men, inconveniently married. Most revealingly of all, these are poems that continue to grapple with exactly the same dilemmas which have been characteristic of Miss Dickinson's work as a whole. Dread of change; the wish to avoid commitments which will magnify the fact of change; the sense that no event can be enjoyed because, in another moment, it may cease to be; the countering realization that commitments are inescapable and events must be borne—these are the springs of Emily Dickinson's art, the elements of her tragic vision of life, the informing themes in virtually all her mature poetry. Set down in the love lyrics, they are matters which go far toward explaining her response to love and toward explicating most of the individual texts that are worth the bother of exegesis.

Most of them, yet not all. So far, one notable feature of the love poems has been their complete lack of erotic detail. Whether sodden with gift-book sentimentalities or kept alive by the symptoms of mutability, the texts have contained little of the passionate and nothing whatsoever that has seemed openly sensual. Even if the "you's" and the "he's" were somehow made identifiable, they could be friends or relatives quite as plausibly as partners in a more amorous relationship. But this is not always the case. In what might be designated a third area of the poetry, Emily Dickinson turns with a vengeance to the erotic; she writes, and often with

163

astonishing candor, about the nuances of courtship, marriage, and love-making. And from this line of interest, needless to say, the legend of her thwarted romance has grown apace. Persuaded that the nuptials of the poetry were born of the poet's wish fantasies, critics have invited us to behold an Emily Dickinson who celebrates in verse the love, the wedding, the housewife's role—in brief, all those physical and emotional fulfillments—which she found tabooed in actuality. Generally, her lover-bridegroom-husband has been specified as the Reverend Charles Wadsworth.

But a close inspection of the poetry will perhaps leave us somewhat skeptical. True, the "loved one" now exists, a figure who is indisputably masculine and whose relations with the speaker are, in some sense, sexual. In presenting him, however, the poems also betray an undercurrent of something that seems decidedly ominous. Far too often to be either chance or coincidence, the "loved one" arrives on the scene to alarm as well as to delight; his actions threaten even as they gratify; and the possibilities he extends are always somehow double-edged, so that love shades off into pursuit, betrothal can easily become seduction, marriage itself is a prospect that dismays. As in the poems about death, therefore, a marked ambivalence occurs when Emily Dickinson seems to imagine herself *actively* participating in the events which she describes. (In what I have referred to as the second category of love lyrics, the poet is more nearly a *passive observer*, of course; she does not really imagine herself to be a part of a situation; she broods over time, just as, in the first group of poems about dying, the speaker did not die herself, but observed death in some form, or watched for its onset.)

164

We can fathom the ambiguity, it seems to me, only if we are willing to track it down a route that leads in a totally opposite direction from the forbidden love affair. In other words, it will not be Charles Wadsworth who best explains Emily Dickinson's portrayals of the male lover. It will be a matter that is a good deal more realistic, though, admittedly, one that is less easy to spell out. Specifically, the explanation will come from the three-fold decision which shaped Miss Dickinson's life: her withdrawal from the world, the habits of her hermitage, and, above all, the spinster's role which was a necessary part of the reclusiveness she chose.

IV ✝

An admiration for what she wrote may tempt one to pass over lightly the fact of Emily Dickinson's neuroticism. The "bow" (to borrow Edmund Wilson's term) was so versatile and frequently so unerring that even many of the out-and-out biographers have tended to play down the motivating "wound," seeing it as interesting perhaps, but not really as a problem of much significance. This is a great mistake, surely. Writing as the most private of private poets, talking constantly to herself, engaged perpetually in telling herself how to live, creating for an audience of one, which was herself —Emily Dickinson inevitably left traces of her personality on every worthwhile poem she composed. Hoping to comprehend the poetry, we shall not only have to take the personality in the bargain; we shall need to acknowledge that it could give rise to behavior which was absurd at best and, at its worst, something that must have been waspish, distraught, and often downright intolerable.

Consider Emily Dickinson, then, at the age of forty or thereabouts, dressing all in white by now and flitting with her nosegay and childish gestures from room to room. Or think of her speaking through a screen, peering down at callers from a second-floor landing, refusing to inscribe in her own hand the envelopes for a voluminous correspondence. By each of these actions she brands herself as the very prototype of the eccentric maiden lady—cracked beyond a doubt, but also, in all likelihood, a figure much given to imaginary fears and to the practice of strange little meannesses. Her conduct approaches caricature. It so nearly resembles something out of a bad novel that, were it not for the evidence of contemporaries, one could assume that a bad novelist had actually invented the whole business.

Many of the motives that drove her indoors have already been specified. On the one hand, Emily Dickinson used concealment as the means of defying an unfriendly universe. That was the positive side of her seclusion, the side which resulted in poetry. In a more negative way, however, she also sought to eliminate, simply by locking them out of her life, certain aspects of experience which seemed too full of menace to be met directly. In connection with this instinct for hiding from her enemies, one last thesis about Miss Dickinson must now be elaborated. It is that, at least half-consciously, she stood in dread of everything masculine, so that one of the bogies she fled from was nothing less than the awful and the implacable idea of *him*.

The chief difficulty in drawing this inference is, undoubtedly, the initial difficulty of getting it said. It will resist belief at first glance, not because the idea seems unconventional, but—quite the contrary—because it is

far too basic to the folklore of the old maid, far too
much the substance of the tired joke about spinsters who
look beneath their beds or ward off "assaults" from behind their closed doors. And yet, once the point is made
about our spinster, there, to confirm it, are all the
quirks that dominated the last thirty years of Emily
Dickinson's life. There are her childish primness and
dislike of exposure, for instance, both so transparently
parts of an attempt to deny the fact of her sexuality. Or
her white dress and protective screen: each a perfect
emblem with which to flaunt her innocence, and each
the perfect symbolic barrier against any wicked attacks.
Or simply her retreat itself, an act of self-immolation
that was guaranteed to place her beyond any necessity
for physical contacts. These without exception are acts
that strongly imply a pathological loathing of the other
sex; or they could imply this, at any rate, if the basis
for such an attitude were anywhere discoverable in
Emily Dickinson's background. And that, as it happens,
is a discovery rather easily come by. To understand
how her conception of *him* might have originated, all
we need do is reflect on the fact that the few men with
whom Emily Dickinson was associated—the few for
whom she honestly cared—greeted her approach with
one set response: they seemed habitually bent on failing
her.

Her father failed Emily Dickinson. She worshipped
the man, as her letters again and again reveal. Austere
and forbidding as he was, Edward Dickinson proved
quite incapable of returning the affection, and his aloofness hurt her deeply. Then her brother failed Emily
Dickinson. Into her relationships with him she poured
all the warmth and fervor her father had rebuffed.

167

why would marriage fail her?

Austin Dickinson responded by marrying, and the bitterness that Emily sometimes displayed toward both him and his wife suggests that she never quite forgave either one. When she timidly submitted her poetry, a masculine critic failed Emily Dickinson. Not only was she more intelligent than a reader like Thomas Wentworth Higginson; she had a keen awareness of her superiority. Nevertheless, Higginson chided, condescended, and reproved; and against his comments Emily was never able to muster an adequate defense. Finally, and primarily, God failed Emily Dickinson. From Him, she asked only for certitude. She wanted the grounds for belief, especially for belief in immortality. But Emily Dickinson's God remained withdrawn and silent. Eventually, one suspects, He struck her as being very like her father.

These slights may or may not have been objectively real. But the point is that Emily Dickinson took them to be true. Existing nowhere else perhaps, they existed in her mind as realities, a fact which is attested to by the circumstances of her life, by many an acid aside in her correspondence, and by the attitudes in her poetry. Reading from the same sources, we can put together a likely guess concerning how the slights affected Miss Dickinson and what her responses to them must have been.

At bottom, probably, she felt envy. It may well have been her conviction that had she only been created a man and given man's capacity to control and dominate, the difference would have simplified her life, by making for far less strain in her dealings with the cosmos. The envy expressed itself, however, in the form of subtle, perhaps not quite consciously realized, antagonisms. Emily Dickinson could turn to men; she could call them "Master" (her term for an unidentified correspondent of the late 1850's and later for Higginson), and find their outlook far more congenial than that of the "Soft—Cherubic . . . Gentlewomen" whom she scorned:

> What Soft—Cherubic Creatures—
> These Gentlewomen are—
> One would as soon assault a Plush
> Or violate a Star— *

But repeatedly wounded in the turning, she had to resent even as she admired. The image of man, which experience confirmed in her mind, was the image of a figure at once strong and dangerous: strong because he mastered, and dangerous because he used this mastery in order to reject and injure. Accordingly, her total view of masculinity had to be compounded of awe and bitterness, of reverence and fear, all struggling together in one uneasy emotional amalgam. This conflict of feel-

---

* It will be helpful at this point to mention the two distinct tones of Emily Dickinson's correspondence. When men are addressed, her style is likely to be grand and philosophical and, increasingly over the years, oracular and profound. This would be the case from the "Master letters," through the correspondence with Higginson and Samuel Bowles, down to the highly mannered "love letters" which she wrote to Judge Otis Lord in the 1870's. But her women correspondents elicit something quite different: a chatty style that grows cloying (the word "Dear" is a fixture) and, ultimately, somewhat patronizing. The only exceptions to this generalization would be Sue Dickinson, her sister-in-law, and the author, Helen Hunt Jackson. And these two, as we shall see later, were regarded by Miss Dickinson as "free spirits," as imposing in their way as men were imposing.

ings is a prime explanation for her mannerisms in seclusion—and it is likewise a driving force throughout her poetry. For it is in the poetry that Emily Dickinson gives herself away completely. Her resentment of man erupts; and in poem after poem masculinity is equated with power, and power becomes the right to imperil or destroy a weaker being.

This describes exactly a motif in the child-poems, a motif which casts the child's molester as a *masculine* sea and the corrupter of the little maid's faith as a specifically *masculine* God. The pattern is repeated in some of Emily Dickinson's descriptions of Nature; for here maidenly flowers are scourged by a *male* frost, the lady poet herself is routed by a *masculine* snake, the *masculinity* of a destructive wind is emphasized—

> He threw a menace at the Earth—
> A Menace at the sky . . .

—and the sun who spurns the morning is, of course, the *male* betrayer of her wronged innocence. We see the situation once again in a poem of psychological horror, where the Goblin holds a helpless poet in *his Paws*, and in those time poems where time's tyrannies are conveyed through masculine images. And we witness it, finally, in the death poetry, where the presentation of Death as a male rogue—

> Because I could not stop for Death
> He kindly stopped for me

—must, by now, seem no inadvertence, but part of a continuing and consistent design.

For the implications are clear, surely. These are texts that develop Emily Dickinson's favorite theme: the

170

theme of the ruthless world, drawn up in all its terrifying array before a helpless individual. Victimizer
and victim are joined in the foreground of the poetry.
Aggressions from without beat in upon the spectator
until the spectator weakens and is vanquished. To this
conventional pattern of her work, it now becomes evident that Miss Dickinson has all along been adding a
last complication. Though her victims take many forms
and though her victimizers represent many different
aspects of experience, one unfailing generalization keeps
the two groups separate. The violated are feminine
figures. The aggressors are virtually certain to be male.
With astonishing regularity, Emily Dickinson sees cosmic depredations as depredations practiced by one sex
upon the other.

This notion of things, a notion so steadily refracted
through the rest of her writing, strips all mystery from
Emily Dickinson's third group of love poems. Obviously the poems are made what they are by fear. The
entry of the male lover into Miss Dickinson's imaginary
world has not really been motivated by desire—at least
not by desire in any normal or healthy sense—nor does
the entry bring consolations. The male lover arises, instead, as a figure out of nightmare. As the following
poem (one usually classified a love poem) indicates,
the demands he makes and the ordeals he imposes were
as trying as anything his creator could visualize:

> He fumbles at your Soul
> As Players at the Keys
> Before they drop full Music on—
> He stuns you by degrees—
> Prepares your brittle Nature

171

For the Etherial Blow
By fainter Hammers—further heard—
Then nearer—Then so slow
Your Breath—has time to straighten—
Your Brain—to bubble Cool—
Deals—One—imperial—Thunderbolt
That scalps your Naked Soul—

When Winds take Forests in their Paws—
The Universe—is still—

His exact *persona* is a bit difficult to determine. He could be a human lover. He might represent Nature personified. Or, in terms of the adjective *imperial*, it becomes possible to think of him as God. Whatever his identity in the poem, one need be in little doubt about the nature of his actions. They are revealed through a series of strong, increasingly brutal verbs. Fumbling at first, then stunning, and finally preparing, delivering, and scalping, he emerges as a Male Marauder, bent on a deed that possesses all the force and savagery of sexual assault.

Over against his strength and insistence, we find the speaker's abjectness. Where he is intensely physical, she remains fragile, as her *brittle Nature* suggests, and is characterized by the delicate or perhaps openly spiritual qualities of her *Naked Soul*. Where he acts, it is her passivity that is emphasized: she is the keys to his player, the target for his hammers, the stillness to his thunderbolt—and, in the strikingly erotic analogy, the forest to his paws. Hence the kinship between them can only be that of a supinely violated person to the relentless violator. And the pulsating rhythms of lines seven through twelve make it plain what the violation itself consists of. To say that these lines merely imply intercourse is to miss the point, for actually they go much further. There is an orgiastic quality about them which converts the whole poem into something monstrous and almost obscene. It is a poem which has masculine lechery for its subject, and one which seems based, in the last analysis, upon nothing more mild than the fear of impending rape.*

Admittedly, it is an extreme example. On only one other occasion, an occasion to be examined in due time, do Emily Dickinson's fears of sexual attack show through quite this baldly. And yet, better disciplined though they are, it is precisely the same fears which permeate her poems on marriage. For all the values that have been attached to it, Emily Dickinson's typical and ideal marriage relationship is hardly more tranquil than the relationship in the poem before us. Nor, ultimately, is its presentation much less distraught.

The happier side to her nuptial poetry has been explored with the greatest acumen by Richard Chase. Seeing Emily Dickinson as a poet much concerned with

---

* Once again it is worth comparing a love poem with one of Emily Dickinson's accounts of Nature—this time with "There's a certain slant of light," which was discussed in Chapter I. Both poems present the passive speaker who is set upon and quickly overwhelmed by an active force in her surroundings. Both attribute to the violator a kind of regal quality: as *He* deals "One—imperial—Thunderbolt," so the light sends an "imperial affliction." Both demonstrate that the violator exists without a shred of compassion, without a particle of interest in the feelings of the victim. In short, through both vocabulary and attitude, Emily Dickinson transfers to *him* the same brutal features which she discerned in the natural order.

social hierarchies, Chase has argued that she associates marriage with the conferral of "caste" or "status" upon the feminine partner. The idea of wedlock, he contends, not only delights and exalts Miss Dickinson's speakers, not only fills them with ecstasy and exultation; in addition, marriage elevates them socially, so that through the marriage ceremony the bride is transformed from commoner to queenship, or is raised from an unprivileged girl to the richer and more complex prerogatives of womanhood. There is no challenging the partial correctness of this view. The key words *exalt, raise*, and *Queen* are drawn directly from Miss Dickinson's own lyric accounts of marriage. It is always perfectly apparent that the imagined ceremony was, for her, synonymous with social change. To be reminded that the change is invariably upward in the social scale, we need only consider these three excerpts, taken from three different marriage poems:

> I'm "wife"—I've finished that—
> That other state—
> I'm Czar—I'm "Woman" now—
>
> . . .
>
> She rose to His Requirement—droppt
> The Playthings of Her Life
> To take the honorable Work
> Of Woman, and of Wife—
>
> . . .
>
> I'm ceded—I've stopped being Their's—
> The name They dropped upon my face
> With water, in the country church
> Is finished using, now,
> And They can put it with my Dolls,

My childhood, and the string of spools,
I've finished threading—too—

Yet the Chase-thesis is partial: partial, because it
reads simplicity and straightforwardness into what is a
highly paradoxical attitude. Emily Dickinson makes it
clear that marriage can be a beneficial experience. But
for every benefit that she mentions, she also cites some
attendant risk—specifically, some diminution of the
feminine self—which marriage necessitates. Her diffi-
dence is partly to be heard in certain equivocal words
she uses: in the verb *ceded,* for example, with its hint
of a forced renunciation; in the ominous lingering over
His Requirement; in the listing of girlish virtues which
are everywhere sacrificed to wedlock. Chiefly, however,
the reserve she feels is embodied in curiously involuted
themes. To be baptised in marriage is to gain prestige,
certainly. On the other hand, the baptism requires a
putting away of the *spools* and *Dolls* of childhood; and,
as we have noted earlier, the loss of the child's outlook
is, for Emily Dickinson, tantamount to standing defenseless before the worst evils in experience. Similarly,
the Czar's role is not one of unqualified bliss, but it
consists of a nostalgic recollection of *that other state*—
presumably the state of maidenly innocence—left behind. If the wife has risen to *His Requirement,* then, in
two succeeding stanzas, we find the gloomy suggestion
that this rise has really been in preparation for a subsequent fall:

If aught She missed in Her new Day,
Of Amplitude, or Awe—
Or first Prospective—or the Gold
In using, wore away,

> It lay unmentioned, as the Sea
> Develope Pearl, and Weed,
> But only to Himself—be known
> The Fathoms they abide—

Though her latter-day disillusionments remain secert and unenumerated, they are made no less real by being hidden, and no less meaningful to the total poem.

Far from expressing simple jubilation, then, Emily Dickinson's marriage poetry is a poetry of ambivalences. Its tensions are gain at the price of loss, or security achieved at the expense of a new anxiety. The contrarieties can be reconciled only when we see that, side by side in the same text, Emily Dickinson conceives of marriage in two fundamentally different ways: marriage as state, and marriage as condition. It is the state that appeals. The state of matrimony has a ceremonial value for the poet, the air about it of something regal and holy to which she can freely commit herself. Moreover, she sees it as a distinctively heavenly state, so that it remains sexless, bodiless, and with no definite sense of the spouse. In order to imagine the state, Miss Dickinson has to reflect as well upon the actual conditions of marriage. By the very nature of her topic, she is brought to an awareness of love as experience, and to a recognition that the ceremony must have its physical sequel. These are the matters that evoke her doubts. Once a bridegroom has been admitted, wedlock loses all its charm, all its honorific status for Emily Dickinson. She can think of marriage only in terms that suggest force and submission, the relinquishment of feminine virtue, and the vicissitudes to come. Either her ecstasy is tempered, as it is in the ambiguous passages just noted. Or her agitations break directly into the foreground, as in the text which touches on the facts of marriage, and which opens with the gruesome image and the sharp, crackling finality of

> He put the Belt around my life—
> I heard the Buckle snap—

All we need do is get accustomed to the idea, and we discover that Emily Dickinson's dread of generalized masculinity plays a vital, not to say obsessive, role throughout her poetry. When the relationship between him and her is transferred to Nature, his rapaciousness is thinly disguised in the coy and yet somehow prurient question of

> Did the Harebell loose her girdle
> To the lover Bee,
> Would the Bee the Harebell *hallow*
> Much as formerly?

And certainly the phallic symbol will not be overlooked in a poem where her heartbreak is not a result of "clubs" or "stones," but is caused by

> A Whip so small you could not see it

which lashed

> the Magic Creature
> 'Til it fell. . . .

But for what is at once the weirdest and the least euphemistical portrait of him, we must examine a poem which has lately crept into the anthologies, but about which, so far as I know, commentators have had virtually nothing to say. It consists of bizarre events that take place "In Winter, in my Room":

In Winter, in my Room
I came upon a Worm
Pink, lank and warm.
But as he was a Worm
And Worms presume,
Not quite with him at home—
Secured him by a string
To something neighboring,
And went along.

A Trifle afterward
A thing occurred,
I'd not believe it if I heard—
But state with creeping blood—
A Snake, with mottles rare,
Surveyed my chamber floor,
In feature as the Worm before,
But ringed with power.
The very string with which
I tied him—too—
When he was mean and new,
That string was there—

I shrank—"How fair you are"
Propitiation's claw—
"Afraid," he hissed
"Of me?
"No cordiality?"
He fathomed me—

Then to a rhythm *slim*
Secreted in his form,

As patterns swim,
Projected him

That time I flew,
Both eyes his way,
Lest he pursue—
Nor ever ceased to run
Till in a distant town,
Towns on from mine
I sat me down—
This was a dream

The poem puts us off, I suppose, because its narrative details seem incredible. We are prepared to believe in an Emily Dickinson who spent her mature years wailing the loss of some departed lover—that fits nicely with our conception of what a genteel Victorian maiden-lady should have been up to. But an Emily Dickinson whose seclusion was haunted by sex fantasies is another matter entirely. At the thought of her even visualizing sexual experiences, much less being able to express them poetically, our proprieties are offended, our imaginations boggle.

And yet, if the point of view propounded here is correct, this is exactly what must be believed. It has to be assumed that physical violation was much more on Emily Dickinson's mind than courtship; it has to be concluded that the "man" in her life was much more the imaginary man who laid constant siege to her virginity than the apocryphal married man whom she is supposed to have rejected. Hence there is nothing surprising about the foray of the worm. *Pink, lank and warm,* the

179

worm signifies the male sex organ—and as such he em- ✓
bodies one of the principal dangers which a perpetually
watchful Emily Dickinson beheld in the perpetually
dangerous world around her. Nor should the images
suggestive of sexual intercourse amaze us. Not only do
the expanding *worm* and the invaded *room* make articulate what were for the poet ever-present possibilities;
we have seen comparable figures previously, have seen
them in the *pearl* that filled the little maid's *shoe,* in
the *Goblin* that toyed coolly with a *hem,* or in *his* ham-
mering blows against her innocence and purity. In brief,
"In Winter, in my Room" simply brings to the surface
what has been a latent (and constant) idea in much of
Miss Dickinson's work. The situation itself is by no
means extraordinary. But what may very well astonish
is the complex of emotions to which the situation gives
rise.

Obviously, the basic emotion is fear. In the presence
of her visitor, the speaker passes from the mild un-
easiness of the first two stanzas, to the charged anxiety
that accompanies the dialogue in stanza three, to the
outright flight with which the poem ends. Her behavior
is, in fact, a wiser, a more perceptive, and a more knowing version of the child's conduct in "By the Sea." For
as the male-ocean sent the little maid scurrying to a
"Solid Town," so here, with the worm-become-snake
behind her, the speaker turns for refuge to a

> distant town,
> Towns on from mine

Underlying this dread of sexuality, however, we detect
a very different response. After all, the worm-snake is
not slimy and not disgusting; he is treated throughout

as a splendid object, first wonderfully warm, then beautifully patterned, and always *ringed with power.* Furthermore, he is never portrayed as the worm of death: specifically, he is *not* Poe's "Conqueror Worm"; but we are made to see him, instead, as active and vital, capable of marvelous changes that take place from within himself. By his sheer strength and animation, the speaker is aroused to a profound awe. Especially in stanza two, her tone is that of undisguised wonder, as she lingers over an event which can only be interpreted as the miracle of tumescence. If the worm shocks his hostess, he likewise excites a sense of marvel that is no less real than her fear, and equally as great.

Directed toward a single experience, then, fear and admiration commingle in the poem. Between them, these reactions help to explain the string, which, next to the worm-snake, is Emily Dickinson's most fascinating image. In one sense, plainly, the string simply constitutes the flimsy defense of womanhood. So slight and tenuous as scarcely to be a weapon at all, the string draws attention to the speaker's weaknesses, heightens the fact of her vulnerability, and thereby makes the worm's invasion seem all the more corrupt and criminal. In another sense, however, the string surely reflects the admiration which the speaker feels. *Not quite . . . at home* with her caller, the speaker is not quite willing to relinquish him, either: she is far too much impressed for that. Thinking of it now as a kind of collar with which one seeks to domesticate the strange animal, we can see in the string, and in her uses of it, the speaker's attempt to claim (or to capture) for herself all those novel properties in him which she finds most enviable. But at still a third level, do we not discover that the

181

string functions as a device for retaliation? Let us note how and when it appears. Initially placed on the worm *when he was mean and new,* the string is left in place until the worm expands and projects—or until, in other words, we are compelled to visualize this collar as something that binds, constricts, and results in discomfort. While I do not claim that Emily Dickinson's motives were altogether conscious, in some half-conscious way, I believe, she has employed the string in order to pay off her score against an old enemy. Symbolically, she is punishing man: punishing him for being the possessor of everything which she craves and resents, punishing him for his hypocrisies (for his deceptively sweet voice of propitiation), and punishing him, as well, for all his multiple crimes against herself.

Does a poem such as "In Winter, in my Room" reflect some actual experience, some incident, half censored from the conscious mind, that perhaps belonged to Emily Dickinson's childhood or adolescence? Or does it, as the concluding line indicates, loom up out of nightmare, one in which desire and hatred have merged into a terrifying surrealism? About this issue, it seems likely, we shall never know for sure. But about the degree of self-revelation in the text, regardless of where its details may have originated, there can be little controversy. In winter, which is the poet's season of despair, man, compressed to his sexual aspects, invades the poet's chamber, which is her only haven, and forces her outside, which is the worst possibility she can imagine. This concatenation of time, place, and situation is instructive. It means that in any listing of Emily Dickinson's particular foes, death, time, exposure, and the dark seasons will have to be joined by the compulsive idea of *him*. Like the others—like death, time, exposure, and the dark seasons—*he* could intrude without knocking upon the poet's privacy. *He* fathomed her; *he* drove her into the open. *He* stands, in a word, as the last of the great forces in experience from which Emily Dickinson was powerless to hide, and against which her irony of indifference was of no value whatsoever.

V ✢

paradox pg. 167 says she worshipped her Father.

With whom was Emily Dickinson in love? With no one, I imagine. She loved no one except herself, upon whom she doted with a completely morbid fascination —and nothing except the ideal and the quite unrealizable vision she had of a timeless, changeless order of things. What have persistently been called her "love poems" are explicable on grounds that have little to do with the statement of honest passion. Either the loved ones she addresses are stock figures, modelled on a literary convention which Miss Dickinson apparently found attractive. Or they are despoilers, born of Miss Dickinson's sense that Man was unjust, and reflecting her wish to catch and transfix Him in His meanness. For the rest, the love poetry amounts to a generalized treatment of time's effects upon all the human attachments. The real tragedy of Emily Dickinson's so-called "love life" is not that she withdrew from an affair which it was morally impossible to consummate. It is, rather, that she withdrew from love and life themselves. Her tragedy was the neurosis which forced her to see only a decaying skull beneath every human relationship. It was the warped conception which caused her to confuse love with rape, and which made her confound sexual experiences with the gross and the revolting.

183

But if we cannot designate a lover for her, there is perhaps, at this point, a way of saying *what* Emily Dickinson might have loved. In the Houghton Library at Harvard, certain of her personal effects have been collected into a memorial room. There they stand, walled in by glass so thick that no particle of dust ever threatens to soil their immaculateness. Protected from climate, humidity, human touch, and human breath, they seem likely to last at least forever. And this is what Emily Dickinson would have adored. She would have marvelled at this scene, as at Paradise. On the other hand, she was spared sentimentality—and probably madness—by a certain wryness of wit, by the habit she had of perceiving that even ecstasy and agony can have their humor. One fancies, therefore, that in the midst of this librarians' monument to hygiene, Emily Dickinson would not be altogether insensitive to the joke.

CHAPTER VI

Some Versions of the Self

> I am afraid to own a Body—
> I am afraid to own a Soul—

As a poet of the Romantic tradition, Emily Dickinson was acutely concerned with what Emerson had called the "me" and the "not me": with relations between the self and the self's external surroundings. The fact that she was an inverted Emersonian in no way vitiated this preoccupation. It simply meant that instead of seeing the "me" as succored and sheltered by the "not me," she beheld the self's world as full of forces by which the self was threatened, set upon, thwarted, and regularly defeated. This has been the case in each of the poems, and each of the poetic themes, which we have so far examined.

But, again in conformity to her Romantic heritage, Miss Dickinson was also interested in portraying the self in its own unique terms. Of her nearly 1,700 poems, no fewer than a fifth start out with the pronoun "I" or the contractions "I've," "I'm," and "I'd." While a good many of these texts go on to link the "I" to something objective, still the "I" alone—the sheer fact and the sheer mystery of selfhood—exercised an enduring fascination. Emily Dickinson could analyze the self with a precision that borders on the clinical and the microscopic. Some of her finest poems take shape when she chooses to de-emphasize the world without, and to write, frequently with little or no reference to external causes,

185

of the quirks, the oddities, and the nightmarish patterns of behavior which were, for her, the characteristics of the world within.

As she delineates the self, Miss Dickinson tends to divide the human being into three distinct parts. The three overlap, to some extent; and they all converge toward a common center, which is their capacity for deep feeling. Nevertheless, in explicating the poems of selfhood, it will be helpful to keep the three parts separate. In an ascending order of value and importance, then, they appear in the poetry as the *physical* self, the self as *mental* being, and the self as a *spiritual* entity.

II ✠

By the physical self, Emily Dickinson can mean the body as a whole, some specific part of the body (in particular, the lungs, the limbs, and the face), or one or more of the five senses. All of these are important to her poetic strategy, largely because it is through physical manifestations that she is often able to dramatize the effects of suffering. The pain which she presents (and, for that matter, the pleasure, which is usually an absence or a remission of pain) does not normally originate in the body. It strikes first and most forcibly at the mind or the spirit. On the other hand, the body does of course respond. It acts as a sensitive and overt register of the disturbances within, and thereby it allows suffering to be gauged or the progress of pain to be measured.

Miss Dickinson's accounts of the physical responses are frequently not very original. In some of the more personal death poems, for instance, she can do no better than evoke standard images like "chill dews" upon the face or a bedimmed eye to suggest the speaker's awe of dying. Again, she shows that a combination of fear and anguish can cause the living form to "straighten"; that it can paralyze the nerves and sinews; and that it can produce the jelly-like quivering of "zero at the bone." Or, in still another death poem, she has the speaker watch in horrified fascination while, one by one, her physical parts succumb. In curiously Eliot-like phraseology, the cold and numbness inch upward from feet to knees to forehead. Then the process of envelopment is finished; and in the last moment of consciousness, with her paralyzed form laid out before her, the speaker recognizes that

> It's dying that I'm doing—
> But I'm not afraid to know.

These examples do not rise above the humdrum. But there is a marked improvement when Emily Dickinson sets out to demonstrate how periods of stress can force from the body some idiosyncratic response—some instance or pattern of physical conduct so weird and atypical that they would never have occurred under ordinary circumstances. A classic case would be "After great pain, a formal feeling comes," a poem in which the aftermath of crisis causes the normally palpitating heart to grow *stiff*, the normally alert nerves to become *deadened*, and the normally active and purposed feet to *go round a wooden way*. The same promising situation is, if anything, made even more dramatic in the following poem, where the crisis is immediate, and where we have the sense that the body has been placed directly in the path of its onslaught:

> It was not Death, for I stood up,
> And all the Dead, lie down—

187

It was not Night, for all the Bells
Put out their Tongues, for Noon.

It was not Frost, for on my Flesh
I felt Siroccos—crawl—
Nor Fire—for just my Marble feet
Could keep a chancel, cool—

And yet, it tasted, like them all,
The Figures I have seen
Set orderly, for Burial,
Reminded me, of mine—

As if my life were shaven,
And fitted to a frame,
And could not breathe without a key,
And 'twas like Midnight, some—

When everything that ticked—has stopped—
And Space stares all around—
Or Grisly frosts—first Autumn morns,
Repeal the Beating Ground—

But, most, like Chaos—Stopless—Cool—
Without a Chance, or Spar—
Or even a Report of Land—
To justify—Despair.

From beginning to end, the poem is an attempt at definition. Some force, always imperfectly understood by her, holds the speaker in its grasp. What—or who— is the assailant? Explicitly through the eight opening lines and by implication thereafter, the speaker offers and promptly discards a number of possible answers. Each alternative has to be rejected, because, even as it occurs to her, she finds that it is entirely out of keeping with her physical reactions.

It is not death into which she has lapsed, for the dead are recumbent and her body remains upright. Nor is she asleep, because sleep stifles the senses and she is entirely alert to the ringing of the bells and to the look of noon. It is not the coldness of stupor, for she feels great waves of heat crawling oppressively across her flesh. By the same token, it is not an other-worldly torment—a punishment taking place in hell—because the coldness of her *Marble feet* is a distinctively this-worldly sensation. The result of these dismissals is to give us a surprisingly lucid account of the *it* which still remains vague and baffling. If we cannot yet say what *it* is, we at least possess an increasingly clear notion of what *it* is not. Solely on the basis of bodily responses, it is proved to be a naturalistic (rather than a supernaturalistic) affliction, an agony of the living rather than of the dead, a waking bad dream as opposed to the nightmare that comes in sleep.

The atmosphere of the first two stanzas derives from the speaker's almost preternatural awareness of herself as a body, a mélange of physical discomforts. This same effect is now intensified by the trio of important events that take place in the seven succeeding lines. To begin with, our attention is switched to a new physical sensation, the actual taste of terror, the introduction of pain and fear onto the tongue. Then, in a particularly brilliant stroke, the poem uses another physical detail to distinguish between what the speaker would like to fancy about herself and her true situation. In her mind's eye

189

she persists in seeing herself as dead, for her rigid body reminds her of *Figures . . . Set orderly, for Burial.* Simultaneously, the physical eye records a totally different impression. It perceives that she is not dead at all, but that it is the living, responsive body, and not the corpse, which has been *shaven,/And fitted to a frame.* By this paradox of a *rigor mortis* in life (or of an effigy that is still animate), we are made ready for the revelation in line fifteen. Breathing would obviously have become a purely mechanical function if the speaker were stupefied or asleep, just as it would have no relevancy at all if she had died. Hence the significance to the fact that she needs a *key* to breathe—or, in other words, that she is actively and consciously experiencing suffocation. The experience is yet another way of pointing out that, whatever has beset the speaker, her malady is a sickness of the living, the conscious, and the wakeful.

In the next five lines, the technique of exploring the mystery undergoes a marked change. The negative constructions drop out at this point; and, for the first time, an attempt is made to define the speaker's difficulties through analogies that are external to her own being. These comparisons make a two-fold contribution. First, they force us to back up and reinvestigate the earlier statements in the poem. For though the speaker has shown conclusively that she is not dead or sleeping or entranced, it now becomes evident that her condition is like the eternal blackness of death, just as it resembles the staring and transfixed horror of nightmare, and just as it is akin to the cold, throbless state of trance. In their stress upon rigidity and stasis, furthermore, the analogies disclose Emily Dickinson's intention. She has sought to dramatize what the psychologist would call a period of the profoundest depression. Her speaker's physical condition—the immobility and prostration she is made to feel, the sense we have that she is both bowed beneath and walled in by a set of unrelenting pressures—is directly attributable to her psychological disorder. The speaker exists in a kind of psychically induced vacuum, one so oppressive that it has brought every normal physical activity to a halt, and yet so intensely real that it leaves the sufferer fearfully sensitive to each of her psychosomatic symptoms.

It is the idea of existing in a vacuum which shapes the concluding stanza. Sleep, stupor, and death all imply their opposites. Accordingly, if the speaker were in one of these states, a *Chance* might yet be open to her, the *Chance* of being awakened, or aroused, or resurrected. As it is, however, her situation admits to no future possibility except the infinite continuation of itself. Her *Chaos is Stopless*—interminable, without recognizable limits. She is like one on a vast sea of pain and disorder, to whom the means of rescue are neither visible, like a *Spar,* nor even imaginable, as a *Report of Land* would be. *Despair* is ruled out, because, as the last line puts it, there are no hopes, no expectations of change or remission, through which a feeling of despair could be justified.

Though "It was not Death" turns out to be grounded in a psychic disturbance, it is the presentation of physical details that determines the method of the poem, keeps it going, and makes of it an extraordinarily interesting performance. Besides telling us where the speaker is at all times and revealing, ultimately, the cause of her situation, the portrait of the physical self involves two

191

other matters that deserve comment. It makes us aware of a struggle that is going on constantly in the speaker's mind. As her many references indicate, the speaker hungers for unconsciousness, for some form of oblivion which would blot out her knowledge of suffering. Release is denied her, however, by the body, which, in its refusal to go under, keeps returning the speaker to the realities and distresses of the present moment. In much the same way, the itemizing of the physical enters into the structure of the poem. Where the subject is *Stopless Chaos,* the descriptions might easily have veered toward the fragmentary and the chaotic. But this is prevented by the systematic analysis of physical behavior. Through orderly transitions from one sensory response to the next and through her use of the body as a basis for actually unifying chaos, Emily Dickinson gives to "It was not Death" a surprising and altogether satisfying firmness of organization.

All in all, it is probably her most successful venture in this direction. One or two other poems may match it; but, for the rest, her treatments of the purely physical are prone to disappoint. Either they settle into clichés, such as the ones we noted earlier, or they remain striking but no more than incidental parts of a total poem, as when a *panting ankle* and *omen of the bone* are used to express the nearness of danger and then dropped. Or they take the form of an interesting and yet essentially unapproachable text like the following:

> I breathed enough to take the Trick—
> And now, removed from Air—
> I simulate the Breath, so well—
> That One, to be quite sure—

The lungs are stirless—must descend—
Among the Cunning Cells—
And touch the Pantomime—himself—
How numb, the Bellows feels!

This is not without a certain fascination. The picture of the lungs, once accustomed to air but now empty and deflated, is as signal an oddity as Emily Dickinson ever composed. No better example of her proto-surrealism exists than the figure of the observant *One,* winding down through the interior of the body, checking on its operations as if it were a machine, and pausing at length before the stirless *Bellows.* What we cannot visualize and hence can never hope to explain, however, are the motivating circumstances, the experiences that have brought the body to its present straits. Perhaps they parallel the ones in "It was not Death," which would mean that the speaker is once again choked with fear, or that her breathing has been made constricted and difficult by the weight of a great depression. But one is unable to say for sure. The poem is sufficiently cryptic to make possible other readings, ranging from an account of "life" in the grave to a description of the sort of "spiritualized breathing" that Miss Dickinson may have associated with immortality. It is, in fact, too cryptic to be anything more than a tease and a curiosity.

Between them, "It was not Death" and "I breathed enough" suggest why the physical self is rarely a great subject for Emily Dickinson. Without some underlying cause to warrant it, the conduct of the body is likely to seem merely eccentric and more or less inexplicable. On the other hand, even when the cause is specified, it remains the important thing, so that physical details simply

193

serve as ways through which the cause can be defined, discussed, interpreted, and structured. In itself, therefore, the body is little more than a bundle of reflexes. Played upon constantly, it has no real capacity for dramatic actions. This is what sets it apart from the mind and spirit in Miss Dickinson's poetry, and keeps it the least interesting part of the total self.

III ✠

Romantic literature is, as everyone has heard, a literature that can be fully as much preoccupied with the man within as with the man, or the world, without. A concern for the individual sensibility not only led Romantic writers to turn inward in order to preempt thoughts and feelings for their subject matter; it also caused them to search for means of expression through which peculiarities of the inner self could be communicated objectively. Students of American Romanticism have long been aware of these tendencies, so that they have made the psychological methods of Poe and Hawthorne a commonplace, and the interest in mental behavior shared by Melville, Whitman, and even Emerson seem hardly less evident. As far as one can determine, however, the psychic explorations of Emily Dickinson have, as a group, gone largely unnoticed.

The result has been to omit from critical consideration some of the most fascinating psychological poems written in the nineteenth century. Miss Dickinson is seldom consistently better than when she has conducted us into the theater of the mind, and made us spectators at the several forms of drama in which the mental self engages. Her various poems on this topic have an unfailing interest, and, at their best, a particular brilliance of theme

and method. Read as a group, furthermore, the poems
coalesce into what might properly be called a theory of
human psychology. Like so many of Miss Dickinson's
basic ideas, it is a theory based upon the contrast between a remote ideal and the harsher facts of the situation.

Ideally, she says, the human mind would be a smoothly
functioning organism. Order, stability, and the power
to keep both itself and its relations with reality perfectly
harmonious: these should be the prime attributes of the
mind at work. The thought processes to which the mind
gives rise ought, in a favorite word, to be *seamless: seamless*, in the sense that they flow easily and continuously
from idea to idea, making all the correct transitions
along the way and establishing all the proper associations. But there is no need to state the ideal apart from
the poet's own terms; for using *mind* and *brain* inter-
changeably as is a habit, she has summed it up in the
text that begins

> The Brain within its Groove
> Runs evenly—and true—

In actual practice, however, the mind is by no means as
sheltered or as efficient as these lines imply. A despoiler
of its order—something the poem just referred to goes
on to call a *swerving Splinter*—can suddenly emerge to
dislodge the mind from its groove and to interrupt the
continuities in thought. Then, panicked and demoralized,
the brain must struggle to recover its lost stride, or it
will totter into madness. Thus it is upon the flimsiest of
foundations that Emily Dickinson's ideal of the rational
rests. Running *evenly and true,* the mental self also runs
along the edge of disaster. Once it falls, the damage it

195

sustains is all but irreparable. It is, as the quoted poem concludes, no less difficult to heal a break in thought than it would be

> To put a Current back—
> When Floods have slit the Hills—
> And scooped a Turnpike for Themselves—
> And trodden out the Mills—

What forces can so jar the mind that they loosen it from its rational moorings and threaten it with outright obliteration? The first, from Emily Dickinson's standpoint, is the demolishing blow, or the moment of inescapable truth, which come from the world outside. We have already seen, for example, how an externally imposed shock can cause the brain to *mumble* and giggle *like a fool;* and we have observed that anguish and mental stress can be the results of a sense of time, a thought of Nature's hostility, an awareness of the proximity of the male lover, and so on. The poetry telling us this has, however, been generally less concerned with psychological states as such than with their causes. To grasp the full toll which experience can exact of the mental self, we need to consider a poem like the following:

> I never hear that one is dead
> Without the chance of Life
> Afresh annihilating me
> That mightiest Belief,
>
> Too mighty for the Daily mind
> That tilling its abyss,
> Had Madness, had it once or twice
> The yawning Consciousness,

Beliefs are Bandaged, like the Tongue
When Terror were it told
In any Tone commensurate
Would strike us instant Dead

I do not know the man so bold
He dare in lonely place
That awful stranger Consciousness
Deliberately face—

The only objective detail here is the report, in line one, of someone's death. It serves as the speaker's point of departure, as her excuse for indulging in a meditation about herself. Having once given the news, therefore, she turns inward to spell out the effects of the information upon her mind.

Chance may be thought of as implying risk or hazard. But why should the report of another's death recall the speaker to the risks and the hazards of her being alive? Why, in other words, is it not the "chance of death" that annihilates her? The answer is, of course, that it is to the living alone that the devastating idea of death can come. This is the *mightiest Belief:* the realization by those still alive that death is, their recognition that even in the midst of life they are also dying. And it is a belief which the *mind,* in its everyday routine, must at all costs be spared from entertaining. Only by *tilling its abyss*—that is, only by cultivating those simple, prosaic thoughts which will keep it blind to the deepest, darkest truth it knows—can the mind stay sane. If it were to look directly upon the fact of existence and upon the attendant fact of its ultimate demise, the mental self would invite the same frantic despair, to which, in un-

197

wary moments, it has already once or twice before succumbed.

In the third stanza, the necessity for protecting the mind is worked up through a related physical experience. The tongue, through which the mind expresses itself, sometimes requires bandaging, in order that it will not admit aloud truths too terrible to be heard. Just so with the thoughts that stand behind expression. The worst of them must be controlled and subdued, and so kept from stirring into active knowledge, for the mental self has limits of endurance beyond which it may not safely go. As the generalized last stanza argues, no man is so bold that he can carry with him for long the awful, active consciousness of his own existence, and the corollary awareness of his own mortality.

The poem, then, has been invested with a surprisingly existentialist theme. In terms that Heidegger would later employ, it has to do with the sense of non-being by which the being are overwhelmed, in those moments when they dare to contemplate themselves as selves. Presenting her material from within, Emily Dickinson asserts that the mind, to hold off lunacy, must bury deep in an abyss of forgetfulness the realization of self, the thought *I am, therefore I am to die*. All the while the assertion is made, the possibility of ever acting upon it is being negated, of course. For the conditions which the poem seeks to thrust away do not, in fact, cease to operate. Reports of death will still come in. The mind is still there to hear the news. As for the mind's shutting out its knowledge—the folly of this is suggested by the folly of tilling an abyss, an abyss being, surely, the least tillable part of any terrain. Hence, with especially trenchant irony, Miss Dickinson has demonstrated the utter futility of trying to conquer fear, or of attempting to forestall a fear-inspired madness. She writes of how the mind must be sheltered from calamity, and shows in the process just how exposed to the calamitous the mental self actually is.

The second threat to mental serenity is more insidious than the first, if only because it needs no external initiation and can strike, at any time, from within. It derives from Miss Dickinson's sense that the mind is not a unity, after all, but a broken wholeness, one that has somehow been divided into two opposed parts. The parts are in perpetual conflict with each other. As their strife is spelled out, a remarkable thing occurs. Emily Dickinson brings to her poetry an instinctive (if highly unwilling) awareness of what, since she wrote, have become the most melancholy findings of modern psychology.

Her favorite metaphor for the mind is a house image.* Seen from above the ground, the house rises as a carefully groomed, well appointed, and stately and beautiful mansion. Beneath the visible surface, however, there nestles what one poem calls

> the deepest cellar
> That ever Mason laid—

Not only is this cellar, like the abyss, a place where the

* As it was for the early Freud, whose initial descriptions of the mind often posited a group of rooms, separated by a door at which the censor stands. In the next three poems I quote or quote from, it will be noted how Emily Dickinson's images of the *cellar* or of underground *corridors* approximate Freud's topography of the unconscious, where the "seething excitations" exist below and are hidden, as a cellar is below and hidden.

unpleasant truth of death is stored; for Emily Dickinson it is likewise the place of the Furies. Memory inhabits the cellar; though this should not be so, though every instinct cries out against the propriety of such a thing, memory can arise to accuse the self—to show it dark deeds which the self never knowingly perpetrated, to present it with an array of dark thoughts and drives which the self never knowingly entertained. By a deliberate act of will, the cellar can normally be kept closed off, and its contents hidden. Nevertheless, even when it seems farthest away, it invokes the injunction

> Look to it by it's Fathoms
> Ourselves be not pursued—

Allowed to draw in close, furthermore, the cellar can make its concealed demonisms a part of everyday experience. It yawns abruptly open and spills into consciousness the shapes and images of a waking nightmare.

Miss Dickinson's least effective poems on this subject are merely descriptive. "One need not be a Chamber —to be Haunted—," she writes,

> One need not be a House—
> The Brain has Corridors—surpassing
> Material Place—

Then, in succeeding stanzas, the speaker takes us on a tour through the underground world of the mind. We are shown, from various angles, the speaker meeting an inner-self, who is far more unsettling than *External Ghost* would be, and far more deadly than an external *Assassin.* Though the poem has some interest for its presentation of the ominous and suggestively depraved *Alter Ego*—and though it will bear comparison with Hawthorne's essay-sketch on "The Haunted Mind"—it is not, internally, a very successful performance. For one thing, neither the images nor the moments of confrontation are graphic enough to sustain our interest. For another, the poem as a whole is marred by curious uncertainties in tone. The confrontations of self by self may be "horrible" and "alarming"; but, as the last stanza suggests, they can also trail off into a kind of jocular peek-a-boo:

> The Body—borrows a Revolver—
> He bolts the Door—
> O'erlooking a superior spectre—
> Or More—

If this is Emily Dickinson's attempt to master fear with laughter, it is one of her few such efforts that do not come off.

But the lapses do not appear when the same situation is dramatized:

> Remorse—is Memory—awake—
> Her Parties all astir—
> A Presence of Departed Acts—
> At window—and at Door—
>
> Its Past—set down before the Soul
> And lighted with a Match—
> Persual—to facilitate—
> And help Belief to stretch—
>
> Remorse is cureless—the Disease
> Not even God—can heal—
> For 'tis His institution—and
> The Adequate of Hell—

201

A veil lifts, and up from the slumbering depths of memory and into the light of consciousness there well—what? The obvious answer is guilt feelings, a sense of shame concerning something out of the hitherto forgotten past. But the obvious answer may presently need to be qualified. For note how the difficulty of defining guilt is enhanced by a remarkable contrast that is first made in the opening stanza and then continues to exist in other ways throughout the poem. It is, initially, a contrast between the connotations of *Parties* in line two and the possibilities raised by *Presence* in the succeeding line.

Parties has a legalistic ring, about it the air of logic, of reasonableness, and of some form of duly constituted authority. We are reminded of parties in a contract, or of parties at a court of law. Either suggestion seems relevant, since the guilty past may be thought of as coming to collect its just debt of penance from the conscious self, or as arriving, like a plaintiff, to impose upon the conscious self those censures and reprisals which are a plaintiff's due. But *Presence,* by contrast, is both a much more ambiguous term and, in context, a term indicative of the illogical, the unreasonable, and the downright oppressive. What crowds up to the *Door* and *window* of consciousness and peers in is not a claimant, demanding proper redress. It is a haunting and bewildering spook, another of Emily Dickinson's "goblins," suddenly aroused now to create a vision of all that is ugliest and least knowable in human experience.

The same distinction is drawn in another way in stanza two, where the *Soul*—here pictured as a symbol of the conscious mind—is forced to read and adjudge the supposed iniquities of the past. Insofar as the *Soul* engages in *Perusal,* the evidence it reads may shock and dismay; but, as the highly formal term suggests, it is also an evidence which can be studied, pondered, assimilated, and even, in some measure, found credible. With the necessity for *stretching Belief*, however, the poem takes a radically different turn. It becomes a drama of sheer incredulousness—an act of self-recognition in which, paradoxically enough, the self is able to feel no real kinship or sense of identity with the things it is nonetheless made to recognize. The impenetrable mystery of the situation is summed up yet a third time in the reference to a *cureless . . . Disease* with which the poem ends. Guilt, Emily Dickinson says, can be known only as a rare sickness is known: known in terms of undeniable symptoms and of the undeniable pain they bring. On the other hand, the fundamental nature of guilt lies beyond all comprehension. Hence no cure is possible, because without grasping the cause of the affliction—that is, without understanding why we are made to feel guilty—we can devise neither treatment nor antidote through which the affliction might be removed.

To linger over these matters is not simply to draw attention to the deliberate ambiguities in the poem; it is also a way of getting at the poem's theme. Though the ostensible subject is guilt and though the immediate source of the guilt seems to be a remembered past, the real issue, one feels, is the issue of what guilt means and why feelings of guilt are allowed to accost the individual. Obviously, Emily Dickinson is in no position to accept the theological explanation, which would make man's sense of guilt the mark of his unlikeness to God and a way through which God may eventually seek to save him. We observe that the God of this poem, far from bespeaking either righteousness or concern, has much in common with the malign and somewhat dimwitted Deity of Thomas Hardy: He is a God who originally invented suffering (*For 'tis His institution*), but who is now as powerless to call His inventions off as He is to use them to any intelligent end (*Not even God—can heal*). Nor is she able to think of guilt as a purely psychic phenomenon. She is too much the Emersonian innocent to hold with Hawthorne that an awareness of sin ought to be everyman's heritage, just as she is too fully committed to the rational ideal to believe, as Poe did, that guilt is the result of something irrational in man. Having rejected these approaches, she is no better prepared to take advantage of the only remaining alternative: a doctrine of personal and conscious responsibility for guilt. Faced by the record of her own corruptions, Miss Dickinson's speaker begins by trying to stretch belief around the offenses—and, failing in that, ends by believing that she herself has been offended. She perceives the darkness within as radically alien to her own being, and as a cause not for shame really, but for unremitting wonder. Her response to the accusations of the past is not "I see these things, and I suffer because I am guilty of them." It is, rather, "I see these things, but I suffer because they seem fraudulent and misleading and totally unrelated to the essential me."

Caught between the mystery without and the mystery within, the mind, in Emily Dickinson's poetry, knows neither serenity nor solitude. When it tries to run "evenly and true" in connection with experience, experience jolts it with the news that *one is dead*. When it tries to draw upon itself for consolation, the mind is shown a vision of evil of which it has no conscious remembrance, but the responsibility for which it is somehow made to bear. There can be no peace of mind, consequently, and little real sense of the primacy of thought. Either the mind is engaged in grappling with its enemies; or the enemies triumph, and a noisy submergence of the rational into the irrational ensues:

> I felt a Cleaving in my Mind—
> As if my Brain had split—
> I tried to match it—Seam by Seam—
> But could not make them fit.
>
> The thought behind, I strove to join
> Unto the thought before—
> But Sequence ravelled out of Sound
> Like Balls—upon a Floor.

Once the shock has worn off—the grinding violence, the shattering into fragments of a former unity—we may note how the conditions of this poem have all been prepared for by the other accounts of the mental self. The *Cleaving* here is, for instance, closely akin to the *yawning Consciousness* that loomed and beckoned in "I never hear that one is dead." Both alike suggest the sudden division in thought, the abrupt rending of the usual powers of cognition, the great, gaping hole of madness into which a mind, so afflicted, must descend. So, too, have we seen this disjunctness—this same array of broken connections—before. They were present in "Remorse is memory astir," where the speaker's past and present seemed to her to have come so unjoined that she could not, without difficulty, envision herself as a single, continuing identity.

But the aim of "I felt a Cleaving" is to present the mind in its last extremity, and to do this through three stages which build toward a climax. The crackup is first portrayed through the short, sharp, explosive, and (in context) highly destructive verbals of the beginning. Next, it is set forth imagistically, as thought is likened to a fabric which comes apart at the seams and then remains too torn and ragged to be repaired. The climax comes with the different but related image that ends the poem. What the speaker attempts at this point is the recovery of *Sequence,* by which she means the reassembling of order, system, coherence, identity. As she reaches outward, however, sequence becomes a collection of *Balls*—presumably balls of yarn out of which the fabric of thought is woven. With each new groping for them, the balls scatter across the floor of the mind, unravelling a bit more of themselves as they go and keeping their actual substance always just out of reach. The harder one struggles to pick them up, the farther away the balls roll. The effect is one of utter frustration and, very quickly, of absolute chaos. To paraphrase Donne—or rather to bring Donne's account of disorder into the mind—*'tis all in peeces, all coherence gone.* Order, relation, design, and pattern have all come unwound past any hope of restoration.

At the end of the poem, we arrive at a state that is always potential in Emily Dickinson's poetry of the mind. We have reached what might be termed the communicable limits of madness. With her rational faculties fallen apart and strewn out before her, the speaker is as obviously unequipped for further communication as she is for the renewal of thought. *Her* utterances must cease now, though the *poet* can, of course, return to the same topic on another occasion.*

* And does so: consider the analysis of "I felt a funeral in my brain" in Chapter VII.

When Emily Dickinson writes of mental aberration —when she concedes that the mind has *had Madness, had it once or twice*—one is prepared to believe that her interest in the subject is more than strictly aesthetic. There is considerable evidence that at least once or twice during her life Miss Dickinson came close to the sort of mental crisis which her poetry describes. The first time was in 1862, when, as she afterward wrote Higginson, there was "a terror—since September—I could tell to none. . . ." Again, a few years before her death, one hears her confiding in a letter: "I saw a great darkness coming and knew no more till late at night. I woke to find Austin and Vinnie and a strange physician bending over me, and supposed I was dying . . . all was so kind and hallowed. I had fainted and lain unconscious. . . . The doctor calls it 'revenge of nerves'; but who but death has wronged them?" Both these incidents have the sound of complete nervous exhaustion and perhaps even of a brush with crackup.

Moreover, certain of the poems strike one as having been written when her mental turbulence was too great to be controlled. A distinction will later be made between a kind of poem in which the honesty of emotions has resulted in a nearly flawless technique, and a kind in which technique is flawed because the emotions themselves seem fraudulent and superficial. But for a type of poetry that fits neither category and yet is disturbingly evident in the collected works, consider the following:

> A Day! Help! Help! Another Day!
> Your prayers, oh Passer By!
> From such a common ball as this

Might date a Victory!
From marshallings as simple
The flags of nations swang.
Steady—my soul: What issues
Upon thine arrow hang!

No one would deny authenticity here; the appeal for help is at once real, passionate, immediately intense. But what does the poem mean? The *common ball*, for instance: is it, as one supposes, a *cannon* ball, the ammunition of the soul which the soul will presently fire off as a last desperate gambit and mark of spiritualized derring-do? If so, why does the ball become, in the last line, an *arrow?* What, for that matter, is the significance of *Victory*, the reason for invoking aid from a *Passer By*, and the point to choosing this particular day for an assertion of selfhood? Unless I am mistaken, the answers are unobtainable. They are overlain by a poem that is too distraught to be expressive—a poem put together on the outskirts of sanity, and at a time when the poet's sense of sequence had ravelled perilously close to the breaking point.

Thus a clear connection can be discerned between Emily Dickinson's accounts of mental turmoil and her own periodic turbulence of mind. "Split lives," as she remarked in a letter, "never 'get well.'" While the splitting itself could produce only collapse and incoherence, still from the memory of such a cleavage,* there appear to have sprung her poems about crackup, as well as those poems in which multiple identities are

---

* Or from the sense that it might come back; once she had known the symptoms of a breakdown, Miss Dickinson must have lived in dread of their recurrence.

presented, and the ones that "rescue" the mind from affliction and torment only to leave it clinging, at last, on the very verge of annihilation. The consequence for the writing is that it comes alive with reverberations out of the writer's psychic history. Her poetry of the mental self is made to seem as intimately lived, as directly known and experienced, as any poetry ever written.

IV ✠

The adventures of the soul provide Emily Dickinson with one of her most memorable themes. More often even than the mind, the soul is isolated in her poetry, to be treated as a separate entity, with special properties, special modes of conduct, and a special capacity for dramatic action. In general, Miss Dickinson thinks of the soul in two different senses. First of all, she takes the conventional view and regards the soul as the link between mankind and God. This view, however, turns out to be based much more upon a vain, never-to-be-realized hope than upon actual experience. At key moments God declines the overtures of the spiritual self. His refusal to be at home in the place where He could be most appropriately welcomed gives a particular poignance to the second role which the soul must play.

Of the three parts of the self, the spiritual is the only one to be regularly personified. From poem to poem the Soul is given a feminine form and feminine characteristics, so that she is almost habitually presented in terms of *her* choices, *her* surprises, *her* superior moments, or, as in "The first day's night had come," *her* damaged strings and bow. This stress upon femininity endows the Soul with an aura of delicacy and refinement. Even when

she is in straitened conditions, we are compelled to see
her as the best, noblest, and purest part of the total self.
She thus emerges from the poetry to stand for the utmost in human awareness, for the most intense kind
of human idealism, and for a haughty indifference to
any except the most rarefied and other-worldly of human
pursuits.

Her fastidiousness is set forth on many occasions,
though never with greater elegance than in the following:

> The Soul selects her own Society—
> Then—shuts the Door—
> To her divine Majority—
> Present no more—
>
> Unmoved—she notes the Chariots—pausing—
> At her low Gate—
> Unmoved—an Emperor be kneeling
> Upon her Mat—
>
> I've known her—from an ample nation—
> Choose one—
> Then—close the Valves of her attention—
> Like Stone—

The poem is not about love or friendship, as has sometimes been supposed. It has to do, rather, with the spirit-
ualization of the total self. In other words, what the Soul
chooses is not another person; she selects and takes dominion over all the other aspects of the speaker's identity. These are subordinated to a rigorous inner discipline, with the result that external circumstances, no matter how grand or ostentatious, come to seem meaningless.

210

As the terms indicate, the waiting *Chariots* and the *kneeling Emperor* belong to the secular world, and, in particular, to the pomp and pageantry of life. They can have no appeal for a speaker who has been claimed and refined by spirituality. If the world is here to commune with the speaker, it discovers that she worships only at an inward shrine. She and the Soul have compacted into a *Society* of one, a union which admits to no distractions and no outsiders.

Underlying the entire drama is the conception of the Soul as Queen. Her regal qualities are suggested by the term *divine Majority,* and by the way in which representatives from the world without are made to *present* themselves (as at court) for her favor. The air of royalty is further attested to by such marks of complete self-sufficiency as the key verbs in the poem: *selects, Unmoved, Choose.* The Soul's majestic carriage is summed up in the specific actions she takes: in her summoning *one* subject from an *ample nation;* in the firmness with which she *shuts the Door;* in her decision to *close the Valves of her attention.* The upshot is that we see the spiritual self as girded with a kind of power that is indeed a rarity in Emily Dickinson's writing. By contrast to the responsive body or the shaken mind, the Soul steps forth here as a model of condescension, a truly magnificent figure, who has been cloaked in the trappings of a splendid, stony aloofness. With the Soul's capacity to accept and reject at will, we seem to have come, at long last, upon a part of the human identity that will feel neither pain nor frustration and upon whom there can impinge none of the usual pressures that afflict and determine human existence.

Yet in Emily Dickinson's scheme, not even the Soul

211

is free from life's tragic paradoxes. The retirement of this queenly being into herself is also the basis for her eventual exposure to destitution and disappointment. The apparent security of the Soul only means that her serenity can be challenged, just as her preference for isolation becomes the mark of her unique vulnerability. And precisely because the Soul is the purest and noblest aspect of the self, she is likewise the aspect to be most deeply hurt by impurity, and the one soonest reduced to a shambles by the appearance of anything in her surroundings which implies the ignoble. Hence, while the imperial decrees of "The soul selects" are still echoing, it is next necessary for us to turn to some darker chapters in the history of the spiritual self. We need to see that for all her seeming tranquillity, the Soul continues to feel unsatisfied needs—and that for all her seeming superiority, she occupies a cloister that is fearfully liable to invasion.

If the Soul in "The soul selects" is thought of as a theological or religious being—and certainly her renunciation of the secular would seem to warrant that interpretation—then it is in no way unjust to the poem to suggest that certain basic questions have been left unresolved. Granted that the Soul can turn her back on the mundane, what does she then contemplate? After the valves of her attention have shut out life, what is left for her to focus upon? Emily Dickinson would like to assume that the answer is God. God alone would be a suitable companion to the Soul, a King fit for her Queenliness. In a number of fine poems, of which the following is typical, Miss Dickinson exhorts (or purports to exhort) the spiritual self to be perpetually ready for God's arrival:

The Soul should always stand ajar
That if the Heaven inquire
He will not be obliged to wait
Or shy of troubling Her

Depart, before the Host have slid
The Bolt unto the Door—
To search for the accomplished Guest,
Her Visitor, no more—

Even if it were possible to take the happy view of her
vigil, we would be obliged to note that the Soul has un-
dergone a certain loss of stature now. From the Queen,
who turned away emperors from her gate, she has become a kind of handmaiden (or deferential servant),
waiting at the gate for the Emperor's appearance. But
the point is, of course, that the vigil cannot be put in a
happy light. The text which records it is profoundly
ironic. Like certain of Miss Dickinson's poems examined
earlier, it develops what appear to be pious hopes, and
then it promptly explodes them by offering a covert attack upon all forms of hopefulness.

The ostensible theme might be stated this way: though
God has not yet manifested Himself, it will be to the
Soul, to the spiritual part of the self, that He will eventually come. Accordingly, the Soul should be at pains
to see that nothing prevents His entry. It is incumbent
upon her that she keep the door ajar and the bolt
loosened, and that she perpetually scan the horizon for
a first glimpse of her *accomplished Guest*. Otherwise,
the Guest may presume inhospitality, and pass on to
someone more in tune with heavenly requirements.

These have the ring of orthodox sentiments. But the

213

orthodoxy is undermined by thoughts that keep occurring as we return for a second look. If the Soul is divine, God should not need to pay her a formal call, surely; He should have been present within her from the outset, validating her divinity. Heaven might indeed wish to impose a visitation upon the wayward mind or the recalcitrant body, but hardly upon the Soul, which is the natural habitation of all things heavenly. Furthermore, if God is the *accomplished* (i.e., the omniscient and all-powerful) Being whom the orthodox claim, there is something patently absurd about the possibility of His being put off by shyness or a closed door. God's failure to *inquire* of the Soul must be attributed not to His fears of a rude greeting, but only to the indifference He apparently feels, His complete disinclination for making the visit. Finally, we are reminded that other, less compatible callers have not been so chary about being received in Emily Dickinson's dwelling places, not even when the gates were locked against them. The ability of madness to gain access to the mind and of pain to wrack the body does not comment favorably upon God's habit of standing apart from the spiritual self.

Doubts like these trim away any remaining cheerfulness from the poem; and they make striking inroads, as well, upon the idea of the Soul's autocracy. In place of the crowned, self-contained figure portrayed in "The soul selects" there is now revealed a Soul whose only qualities are unfulfillment, the fixed smile of welcome, and a forlorn hope. Not only is the Soul bereft of what is needed to make her complete; her plight is not helped any by the sense we have that, however long and vigilantly she awaits satiation, she will remain incomplete forever. In effect, Emily Dickinson has shown us the

214

spiritual self as the pitiful watcher. She is pitiful not simply because she is made to watch and to watch unsuccessfully—but pitiful because, in looking for a God who is *accomplished* at staying out of sight, she seems to watch over nothing.*

Worse than mere deprivation can befall the Soul, however. If God chooses never to call, still other potential visitors are always lingering on the threshold. When the moment for entry comes, they neither knock nor kneel; begging no indulgence, they pass inward in the name of conquest. Their aim is to take advantage of just those virtues which are uniquely possessed by the Soul: to besmirch her purity, to break down her proud reserves, to impress upon her heightened awareness the awful fact of their reality. In Emily Dickinson's eyes, such an experience represents another form of the dreaded invasion, another violation of helpless femininity. She deals with it poetically in a text that will match " 'Twas like a maelstrom" and "In Winter, in my Room" for being as macabre as anything in the English language:

* A poem with a similar theme is the one that begins

> The Soul's distinct connection
> With immortality
> Is best disclosed by Danger
> Or quick Calamity—

At first glance, the argument seems to be that in moments of great stress and peril the Soul is rewarded with a vision of her immortal future. The second time around, however, we see that all the Soul really knows are the dangers and calamities, which create a yearning for immortality. Of eternal life itself, the Soul has no knowledge whatsoever; her *distinct connection* is, again, only a forlorn wish.

215

The Soul has Bandaged moments—
When too appalled to stir—
She feels some ghastly Fright come up
And stop to look at her—

Salute her—with long fingers—
Caress her freezing hair—
Sip, Goblin, from the very lips
The Lover—hovered—o'er—
Unworthy, that a thought so mean
Accost a Theme—so—fair

The Soul has moments of Escape—
When bursting all the doors—
She dances like a Bomb, abroad,
And swings upon the Hours,

As do the Bee,—delirious borne—
Long Dungeoned from his Rose—
Touch Liberty—then know no more,
But Noon, and Paradise—

The Soul's retaken moments—
When, Felon, led along,
With shackles on the plumed feet,
And staples, in the Song,

The Horror welcomes her, again,
These, are not brayed of Tongue—

The *Bandaged moments,* to begin with. They mean, perhaps, that the Soul has been wounded and immobilized by her fear of the impending visitation. Or, al-

216

ternatively, the bandages may be taken for a blindfold, and hence to suggest that the impending visitation is too frightful for the Soul to bear looking upon it directly. Both readings are completely in keeping with the drama of the first four lines. Unable to stir, or even to interpret visually, the Soul only *feels* the *ghastly Fright* as it comes up, pauses, and looks at her. Her situation is startlingly akin to that in Poe's horror story "The Pit and the Pendulum," where the narrator, pinioned to one spot, must feel upon his face the scurry of rats which he can neither see nor fend off.

This nightmare is, of course, infinitely more harrowing than the one in Poe. For what registers upon consciousness here is not simply the loathsome physical object; instead, as lines nine and ten tell us, it is the loathsome thought. The Soul is being violated by an idea, and we need only attend to its actions to see that the idea is compounded of all of Emily Dickinson's worst fears about experience. It is the idea of the dark, immoral underside of life which accosts the Soul: note that it is referred to as *Goblin,* a creature of darkness, and that its evil is further intensified by the salute of the long, inhuman fingers. It is the thought of death: note that it causes the hair to freeze. It is the thought of physical molestation: observe how each of its advances, from the first unabashed stare down to the kiss, is almost blatantly erotic. And, above all, it is the thought of God's remoteness: consider how it plants itself moistly upon the *very lips/The Lover* (and obviously the only appropriate lover of the soul would be God) has merely *hovered— o'er.* These are the conceptions that motivate the Soul's anguish, and they explain, as well, the troublesome word *Unworthy* in line nine. What the speaker offers at this

217

point is a moral judgment concerning the relationship between her spiritual self and reality. It is, she says, not fit or worthy of life that life compels the Soul (the fairest part of the individual) to entertain so thoroughly unspiritual a guest as the *thought so mean.* Meanness may be interpreted in two ways. The thought itself is *mean,* in the sense of being cruel and offensive to its hostess. But the full force of *mean* is realized when we see that it relates descriptively to the whole of the external world, a place sufficiently threatening and unwholesome that it permits an idea like this one to occur.

The next two stanzas present a variation of the unexpected-gift motif. The Soul now extricates herself, both from her bandages and her molester. Although, at first look, liberation seems to have procured for her nothing more than a round of sensuous pleasures, a close reading of the symbols, running from line ten to line eighteen, will indicate that a deeper meaning is intended. To *burst all the doors* has the ring about it of casting off every limitation on selfhood. To *dance like a Bomb, abroad* implies that the self, as a free spirit, has mastered life. To *swing upon the Hours* suggests a dominance over time, and, beyond that, an insight into the timelessness of Eternity. In short, the thoughts of the Soul have become worthy, a point which lends special relevance to the bee-analogy in stanza four. As the bee, when he is free to do so, turns instinctively to the rose, his natural dwelling—so the Soul celebrates freedom in ways that are natural and instinctive for her. She, too, experiences *Noon* (Miss Dickinson's recurring symbol for Eternity) and *Paradise,* which is to say that she has those visions which are perfectly commensurate with her divine status.

218

The key word in the drama of escape is the verb *Touch*. With its connotations of the tentative, the only barely grasped, the verb prepares us for the fact that the last moments in the poem are to be the *Soul's retaken moments*. Her return to captivity is set forth in three important transitions: in the decline from free spirit to *Felon*, in the *shackling* of the feet that danced, and in the *stapling down* of the song of praise. It is given an added chill by the word *welcomes*, particularly when we have observed how *welcomes* loops back to complete the effect first suggested by *Salute* in line five. When one is welcomed or saluted, one is in the presence of a familiar, no matter how obnoxious or apparently unsuitable the familiar may be. In its final summation, therefore, the poem manages to suggest that while *Noon* and *Paradise* may be most natural to the Soul, still what she actually knows best is her old enemy-companion, the *ghastly Fright*. With the *Fright*, she is at home; in any other state, she can be no more than a sporadic guest, and, what is worse, a fugitive from her accustomed surroundings. These are the recognitions *not brayed of Tongue*. The thralldom of the human Soul to horror is not a thing to be shouted aloud or boasted about. If it is admitted at all, the topic should be broached only in whispers, in the subdued tones reserved for fear and wonder.

The three distinct movements of "The soul has Bandaged moments" bring together in a single context both the extremes which the Soul may reach. And with the journey from despair to ecstasy and back into a yet bleaker despair before us, Emily Dickinson's total estimate of the spiritual self becomes evident.

For her, it would seem, the possession of a soul is,

SOME VERSIONS OF THE SELF

like the taking of marriage vows, the source of a great
paradox. The fact of ownership is at once a blessing for
the self, and a curse. As a blessing, the Soul is the positive principle which allows one to shut the doors (or to
open them upon vistas of freedom), to close off the
valves of the attention (or to focus them solely upon
Paradisiacal hopes), and (either way) to gain at least
a momentary triumph over the hardships of experience.
Inevitably, such gestures recall us to Miss Dickinson's
personal withdrawal. It is interesting to note that the
white garments which were the symbols of her seclusion can be used to clothe the Soul, when the Soul is most
intensely dedicated:

> Dare you see a Soul *at the White Heat?*
> Then crouch within the door—
> Red—is the fire's common tint—
> But when the vivid Ore
> Has vanquished Flame's conditions,
> It quivers from the Forge
> Without a color, but the light
> Of unanointed Blaze.

The italics, supplied by Emily Dickinson, suggest the
extent to which she could think of her life as a retreat
from the mundane into the realm of pure, ethereal contemplation.

On the other hand, the Soul's virtues transform her
into an almost intolerable burden. Not only does her
craving for God sharpen and magnify the fact of God's
absence from human life; the sovereignty and per-
cipience of the Soul's finest moments make all the more
unbearable those times when she is dragged down from
loftiness, shorn of power, and led, like a felon and like

a friend, back into the domain of the ghastly fright. Thus the full history of the Soul constitutes, in Emily Dickinson's poetry, another decisive step in the degradation of the total self. Carrying the self to heights never equalled by the body, the Soul also plummets the self to even greater depths. If she is given insights never vouchsafed to the mind, the insights are too much sandwiched between horror and horror to be impressive; they are too often intuitions of the hideous to provide the self with more than a fleeting consolation.

V ✞

The vicissitudes of the self permit us to test, once again, the accuracy of applying the term "tragic" to Emily Dickinson.

Certainly she is not a tragic writer in the sense that her work corresponds to any traditional theory of tragedy. One might argue, moreover, that her particular perception of life rules out the tragic. Since she shows the self laboring under the unmanageable—shows the human personality buffeted this way and that by conditions that can be neither prevented nor controlled, conquered nor delayed—does not this mean that she is a poet of the merely pathetic? The answer is that Miss Dickinson is made tragic by her sense of the discrepancy between man's potential glory and the actual horror that contains him. Her tragic view is born of the fact that the human mind struggles to find order—and is disrupted by the disorderly and the chaotic. It comes from the fact that the human Soul is free to seek God—and is confronted, instead, with a vision of the Satanic. It emerges from the fact that the human being hungers to be innocent—and is bowed beneath the inscrutable accusation. It derives, in brief, from the fact that the self has been endowed with qualities which are the marks of its grandeur and high aspirations—and that these are the very qualities through which the self is regularly and systematically debased.

One has the tragic sense of life, says Pascal, when one views man as the impotent mean between allness and nothingness, and this is exactly the way in which the human speakers in Emily Dickinson's work are visualized. It is not simply that defeat makes them tragic; it is also (and more especially) that they were created with the instinctive awareness of what it would have meant to win. Nor is it abuse alone, but rather that the qualities abused seem to represent all that is best and finest in the self. Unlike her flowers and bees and insects dying "pathetic from the grass," Emily Dickinson's human speakers cannot go easily and unwittingly into darkness, for they have seen the light, even though they are powerless to act upon their perception. This is why we call them tragic, and why we designate them as the creations of a profoundly tragic poet.

CHAPTER VII

Emily Dickinson and the Modern Sensibility

✝
> But Sequence ravelled out of Reach
> Like Balls—upon a Floor.

THE MODERNITY OF Emily Dickinson makes for a complicated and somewhat uncertain issue. Her work has commanded the interest of many of the most sophisticated critics of poetry writing in our time. Sooner or later, virtually all of them have seen fit to damn it with a combination of loud praise and the bitter reproach. To Yvor Winters, for instance, Emily Dickinson is one of the great lyric poets of all time. But in the next breath she has become "of all great poets" the one most "lacking in taste." Similarly, R. P. Blackmur praises the occasional power in Miss Dickinson's lyrics, even as he berates her for ignorance, untidiness, and a failure to be objectively in control of poetic language. Allen Tate, while he congratulates Miss Dickinson for being born at the right time for great poetry and for taking advantage of this opportunity, nevertheless laments the looseness and the self-indulgence which he detects in a good deal of what she wrote.

The modern view of Emily Dickinson, then, has been frankly reserved. At least in the hands of the major critics—the theorists whose tastes and preferences have tended to shape our conception of what poetry ought to be—she has come off, if not quite badly, then rather less than well. Yet it seems to me of the utmost significance that these critics, together with certain others who share their position, have consented to deal with Miss Dickinson at all. It is significant because they are the very writers who profess either disdain or indifference toward every other poet of the American nineteenth century. Of the Cambridge poets—Lowell, Holmes, and Longfellow—they simply do not speak. Whitman they ignore—or drag in to exemplify everything wrong with poetry. With Emerson, they associate a perniciousness that is moral as well as aesthetic. It is true, of course, that Allen Tate feels an enthusiasm for Poe. One suspects, however, that among his colleagues this enthusiastic response is widely regarded as one of Mr. Tate's aberrations.

Thus by their willingness to read her closely and even, for that matter, to impose a severe judgment upon her work, the New Critics confirm an important point about Emily Dickinson: they assert that she still has a voice. Despite their reservations, they make it clear that she continues to speak to us, as her American poet-contemporaries ordinarily do not. What are the sources of her appeal? Why is it that she appears to have a unique claim upon the modern sensibility? It is with these questions—questions having to do not with popularity in the conventional sense, but with Miss Dickinson's attractiveness to a highly technical and highly intellectual type of criticism—that this book will next be concerned.

In suggesting answers, I shall go beyond what the other critics have had to say. Moreover, I shall make generalizations about the poetry with which the others would not and probably could not agree. This, obviously, is a minor matter. My aim is not to evaluate the critics' evaluations of Emily Dickinson; nor is it to assess the principles of modern criticism. It is, rather, to seize hold of certain qualities in her work which make Miss Dickinson a modern, in the hopes that thereby still further light can be shed upon her themes, attitudes, and methods.

II ✛

Beyond a doubt, one key to her modernity lies in the peculiar relationship which Emily Dickinson bears to the Emersonian point of view. In its pure form—that is, as a set of hopes and beliefs identifiable with Ralph Waldo Emerson—the point of view has not weathered very well. Whether for personal or doctrinal reasons, the New Critics have felt a strong pull toward the dogmas of Original Sin. Accordingly, they have found little to impress them in Emerson's stress upon human perfection, or in his harping upon the easy access man has to Nature and God, or in his sweeping denials of pain and evil. The case against his blandness has been made many times in the twentieth century, though never more bluntly than by Robert Penn Warren, who insists that "after Emerson had done his work," life, literature, and culture in America were all divested of "tragic possibilities."

Had it been made with reference to Emerson alone, this statement would be incontestably true. Emerson does offend us with the shrillness of his optimism. There is a way he has of dismissing (or simply looking through) realities which, from the standpoint of our own troubled age, makes him seem willfully blind and shallow almost to the point of stupidity. Yet the Warren allegation remains no better than a half-truth, because it falsifies the facts of history. After "Emerson had done his work," there did indeed come into being tragic writers, and the essence of their tragic outlook was largely conditioned by what they had inherited from Emerson. It was the destiny of these writers to separate the Emersonian belief from the Emersonian hope. The results were psychologically painful, no doubt—but they also made for the greatest moments in nineteenth-century American literature. For, whether we recognize it or not, those nineteenth-century texts that most move us today are the texts which commence with the assumptions of Concord still intact—and then proceed to follow those assumptions into the darkest and most dismal crannies of human experience.

Moby Dick is an excellent case in point. When Captain Ahab undertakes his pursuit of the white whale, he acts in the name of perfectly unassailable Emersonian premises. Like Emerson, Ahab is committed to cutting through the "solid seeming wall of Nature." It is his purpose to track down the whale, until, so to speak, he hears a Voice or sees a Sign—and, from this revelation, comes to an understanding of his place in the mysterious cosmos. As one who holds that "all visible objects are but as pasteboard masks," Ahab exactly duplicates Emerson's contention that every experience is symbolic. As one who would pierce the mask, in order (as he says) "to gaze upon God," Ahab is intent upon nothing less than the successful completion of Emerson's own Transcendentalist pilgrimage.

Nor do the Emersonian implications disappear at the height of his tragedy. The debacle that eventually overtakes Ahab never really involves a repudiation of the Emersonian *hope*. It consists, instead, of what might better be called an inversion of the Emersonian *belief*: an inversion which shows that the belief becomes a mockery when it is applied to the actual conditions of living. By Emerson, it had to be assumed that the world was a completely porous place. The world had to be porous, because, that way, it freely admitted man's entry and so guaranteed that his questionings of Nature could never fail. By contrast, Ahab actually tests the texture of experience—and finds, to his amazement, that the world stays dense and closed. Embarking with the idea that Nature will let him in, Ahab succeeds only in wrecking his ship, his crew, and himself upon Nature's impenetrable bulk. The head of the whale, a "dead, blind wall" against which he repeatedly hurls himself, becomes the symbolic measure of Ahab's undoing. The head defines a world where Emersonian yearnings can still be maintained, but where to act upon the yearnings is to be betrayed by Nature, and is to court the disasters that Nature sends when man pursues too closely.

Melville, then, demonstrates how a writer may be tragic simply because he retains one half of the Emersonian outlook. What has been said of him is equally relevant to Emily Dickinson. She is the second major writer of the nineteenth century to discover tragedy in the Emersonian point of view, and to dramatize her insight by combining the old, jubilant expectations with a new and frustrating outcome.

We have already observed how, at their most profound, her views of Nature tend to invert the typically Emersonian view. If she takes pleasure from the beauty of natural forms, if the look of a sunset delights her or

the sound of the summer wind fills her with ecstasy,
Miss Dickinson still recognizes that in its deeper, more
symbolic aspects Nature is an adversary, a creature
who either withholds her meanings or yields them up in
hints which the individual would be better off not discovering. The poet may deplore those who are totally
indifferent to the natural order. But criticism is tempered by the realization that too deep an involvement
can be hurtful:

> But nature is a stranger yet;
> The ones that cite her most
> Have never passed her haunted house,
> Nor simplified her ghost.
>
> To pity those who know her not
> Is helped by the regret
> That those who know her, know her less
> The nearer her they get.

Sometimes this sense of the complex natural enemy
without will shape a poem which is so similar to Emerson—and yet so utterly distinct from him—that it almost has the ring of cruel and conscious parody:

> Alone and in a Circumstance
> Reluctant to be told
> A spider on my reticence
> Assiduously crawled
>
> And so much more at Home than I
> Immediately grew
> I felt myself a visitor
> And hurriedly withdrew

Revisiting my late abode
With articles of claim
I found it quietly assumed
As a Gymnasium
Where Tax asleep and Title off
The inmates of the Air
Perpetual presumption took
As each were special Heir—
If any strike me on the street
I can return the Blow—
If any take my property
According to the Law
The Statute is my learned friend
But what redress can be
For an offense nor here nor there
So not in Equity—
That Larceny of time and mind
The marrow of the Day
By spider, or forbid it Lord
That I should specify.

We can understand without much difficulty the offense of the spider. It is of a kind with other of Emily
Dickinson's externally caused violations. The insect
first imposes itself upon the speaker's *reticence*—her
explicit wish not to be imposed upon. Then, like the
pink worm of another poem, it compounds the injury
by driving her, compromised and defenseless, into the
open.

But the second offense, the one she suffers in lines
nine to sixteen, proves more complicated. The preliminary circumstances seem clear enough. Seeking for the
peace of mind the spider cost her, the speaker returns

to her *late abode* (the symbol of her former privacy and sense of well being), only to find that it has become an exposed and public place (the *Gymnasium*), overrun by forces who feel no moral obligation (they have taken *Title* to the speaker's identity, but pay no *Tax* for this privilege) and whose aims are clearly those of infringement and intimidation. What are we to make of these usurpers? Are we to take them for natural phenomena: for a proliferation of the original spider into a whole horde of insects? Much of the rest of the poem seems designed to show that the *inmates of the Air* are of an order very different from the spider, and that their function is much more alarming and much more dangerous.

A first clue to their identity comes from the words *Air* and *perpetual,* both suggestive of the cosmic offense that is laid on from above and stands outside time. Next, the situation is clarified through the speaker's rather Kafka-like analysis of the law. There are those ordinary transgressions, she says, for which the injured may expect ordinary redress. But the injury being done her is *not in Equity*—that is, not within the compass of ordinary human experience; hence it is neither preventable nor punishable by any of the statutes of man-made jurisprudence. Such an offense could hardly be other than metaphysical—a fact which is conclusively established by the sharp break in ideas that occurs, in the last four lines of the poem, around the word *or.* The spider has left the speaker denuded of values. Literally as the loathsome, crawling insect and symbolically as the archetypal captor, destroyer, and weaver of time's web, it has stripped her of the *marrow of the Day,* of all that sustains her faith in the fitness of things. Behind the spider's act, however, the speaker discerns another thief, a form of larceny so strange and dismaying that she will only hint at its significance, before asking God to prevent her from mentioning it more directly. The presence of prayer in Emily Dickinson's work is normally a signal for some built-in irony, and the irony implicit here is an especially mordant one. When the speaker pleads with God that she not have to specify her second malefactor, she does so in the light of overwhelming evidence that the second malefactor has to be God Himself.

The cardinal principle of Emersonianism is Emerson's assertion that "natural facts are symbols of spiritual facts." A chain of analogies links the world below to the world above, so that by attending to what lies openly before him or hearkening to its intonations, an observer can detect in immediate experience the larger rhythms of the realm of spirit. And this is the principle to which Emily Dickinson has offered her unique revision. From the spider—from the concrete natural fact—her speaker learns the lesson which says that experience freely trespasses upon the self. Thereafter, her vision steadily enlarges, until it seems to her that the trespass cannot really be restricted to the spider, but that it is an offense *nor here nor there,* a transgression of such magnitude that it must be spiritual and must have originated with God. Thus for Miss Dickinson, no less than for Emerson, Nature has been the symbol of spirit. If in developing this notion, she has given us another example of her "dreaded invasion" motif, she does so while remaining entirely faithful to the Emersonian outlook and solely because she has had her speaker look and listen to Nature with just the alertness that Emerson had counselled. Her poem could have been written only in an age which set great store by the correspondences between the natural and the supernatural. Only as a reflection of the age of Emerson does the leap from the spider to the "other" (so oddly reminiscent of Ahab's leap from the whale to the "being" beyond the whale) become comprehensible.

It might be argued, furthermore, that Emily Dickinson subjects the Emersonian doctrine of "compensation" to the same bitter reversal. Compensation itself represents the core of Emerson's moral idealism. It proceeds from the view that the universe is so finely purposed and so harmonious a place that no evil or injustice can possibly accrue to the individual. If an apparent evil does occur, it is explicable in terms of any or all of three different reasons. Either it is a deserved punishment, as when "the thief steals from himself; the swindler swindles himself." Or it is in preparation for some later good, as when "every defeat in one manner is made up in another; every suffering is rewarded." Or it is subsumable under a Total Plan (Emerson's Oversoul, or his "Spiritual Laws") which negates the reality of evil. At all events, it is inconceivable that evil should exist as a concrete fact, an actual and positive principle. The idea repels human intelligence, which, as Emerson says, "refuses limits, and always affirms an Optimism, never a Pessimism."

Let us make no mistake about it: Emily Dickinson looked at life in an identical fashion. That is, she too was conscious of some overlying plan in moral experiences. In addition, she wanted to see identical relationships. In other words, *her* moral idealism would have been satisfied, had she, like Emerson, found grounds to believe that good is the only reality possessed by man. Once again, however, the wish she carried to experience was confounded by the fact. For her, the crucial truth is not that an apparent evil will be offset by the actual good; it is just the opposite of that happy proposition. Miss Dickinson beholds a world in which the momentary and the apparitional thing is good itself, in which the dream of pleasure only enlarges one's susceptibility to suffering, and in which the Total Plan dispenses one misfortune atop another. In her poetry, agony is the price paid for *each ecstatic moment;* men are lost in the very hour of their salvation; an unexpected gift is followed by the certain betrayal; one discovers that if today is bad, tomorrow will be twice as huge and horrible. What we are shown, in short, is a torture-chamber universe, where Emerson's logic is tested by experience and made to seem hopelessly woolly-headed. To his theory that life will always make amends, Emily Dickinson simply adds that the amends appear always to be further pain and further evil. It is a cruel addition, made all the bleaker by our realization that, however different the conclusions they reach, the two writers have had a common starting point.

The idea of Nature's treachery and the sense of the supremacy of evil mark Emily Dickinson as a modern. By the first, she aligns herself spiritually and intellectually with a poet like Frost, whose sardonic qualities have never quite concealed the fact that he too sees existence as a post-Emersonian tragedy. By the second, she gives to her work the sort of systematic precariousness which we associate nowadays with such influential moderns as Kafka and Dostoevski. Irony of history though it is, then, the fact remains that Emily Dickinson

233

learned from her Emersonian legacy just those insights into darkness and despair which have preserved her hold on the twentieth century. But for her most intriguing connection with Emerson, we need to study a single image which the two of them shared.* For that purpose, a consideration of the following poem of Miss Dickinson's is in order:

> I've seen a Dying Eye
> Run round and round a Room—
> In search of Something—as it seemed—
> Then Cloudier become—
>
> And then—obscure with Fog—
> And then—be soldered down
> Without disclosing what it be
> 'Twere blessed to have seen.

First, the poem in its own terms. It has to do with the death of another person, with the preliminaries and then the act of dying which the speaker witnesses and describes. Like all of Emily Dickinson's work in this vein, the poem is ultimately concerned with death as philosophical problem. Both principals, the speaker and the person portrayed, are intent upon *seeing* an explanation. Their eyes behave as they do—roam, wander, and

---

* Actually there are several such images. Emerson, for example, uses the *circle* as a symbol of eternity, of resurrection, and of the eternal fitness of things. By contrast, Miss Dickinson's *circle* describes a destructive movement. It is the maelstrom or the whirlpool which takes one down into the presence of moral disorder. And, as has been pointed out, her maelstroms have much in common with the spinning, ruinous vortex into which all things have collapsed at the end of *Moby Dick*.

234

probe so incessantly—because each individual is looking for the comfort and consolation that only a discovery of meaning might bring.

Read strictly in its own terms, therefore, the poem
is a deeply poignant experience. Its theme is the limitations on human vision; it records the failure of the eyes.
At the end, the eyes of the corpse are soldered shut in
death, while those of the living speaker have glimpsed
nothing that could assuage her loss. It is their common
plight to have gazed upon the knottiest issue in human
experience—and, for all their looking, to have found
the issue completely inexplicable. But the plight grows
still sharper when the failure of the eyes here is contrasted with the function that Emerson assigns to seeing.

For Emerson, seeing and sight, the workings and the
penetrations of the eye, are of the utmost importance.
"Leaving me my eyes," he wrote in *Nature*, ". . . I
feel that nothing can befall me in life,—no disgrace, no
calamity . . . which nature cannot repair." Then, in
the next two sentences of this same essay, Emerson goes
on to develop his most famous metaphor: "Standing on
the bare ground, my head bathed by the blithe air, and
uplifted into infinite space,—all mean egotism van-
ishes. *I become a transparent eyeball;* I am nothing;
I see all; the currents of the Universal Being circulate
through me; I am part or parcel of God." [Italics
added.] There is a confusion about the word *transparent* that I have never seen straightened out. Presumably, though, the quality of being *transparent* relates less to the eyeball itself than to a marvelous alter-
ing of experience which occurs when the eyeball has
been properly focussed. Thought of in this way, the eye
becomes the instrument for translating Emersonian

hopes into Emersonian knowledge. When Emerson wishes to put his happy assumptions to the test, he merely engages in a little selective looking. Thereupon, his chosen field of vision clarifies before him, and grows luminous and meaningful under his steady gaze. Ranging over those facts in experience *which he elects to see,* Emerson finds that none can resist his scrutiny, that if he watches them long enough he will eventually see through the facts into the peace, light, and order of God's throneroom. Accordingly, Emerson remains a cosmic optimist by the simple act of keeping his eyeball open—and by making sure that it always concentrates on the right things.

This triumph of vision is obviously what Emily Dickinson's watchers have been denied. Searching for an explanation of death which *'twere blessed to have seen,* they have looked through eyes that continually register only blankness and disorder. They have watched, only to be reminded that they are destitute of the power to see. Following the method used in analyzing *Nature,* we might add that the words which describe their eyes will apply equally well to the experience which is the object of their perception. Death, for them, remains something opaque: it is *cloudy, obscure with Fog,* an event that seems tightly *soldered down.* Far from looking through death to the lineaments of God, Emily Dickinson's figures see no significance whatsoever.

But dissimilarities at the end of a process should not make us unaware of fundamental likenesses. The point is that the motives of Miss Dickinson's principals— their reasons for looking, or their expectations about the virtues of the look—exactly duplicate Emerson's own motives. As much as he, these figures who watch and discern nothing have set out to probe Infinity, until Infinity becomes manifest. Consequently, their failure represents a failure of the Emersonian method. It is a failure that comes about because, while the hope of seeing meaning still persists, there is no longer an adequate belief to shore up hope. Or, better yet probably, the failure comes about because Emily Dickinson, in contradistinction to Emerson, has explored an aspect of experience which forces her to see all the enormous difficulties that are really involved in seeing.

There is more. A consideration of the eye in one of her poems reminds us that this, more than any other part of the human anatomy, was Emily Dickinson's favorite. Time after time she returns to the look, the gaze, some gesture of the eyeball, and usually the results are even more painful than those we have just observed. In particular, Miss Dickinson portrays the eye in a glazed condition. *The eyes glaze once—and that is Death,* she writes; or she raises the question

> Should the glee—glaze—
> In Death's—stiff—stare—

But even when it is a living organ, the eye still tends to become hooded and shuttered. Before the gruesome spectacle of experience, Emily Dickinson shows us the eyeball assuming a *look of agony,* or transfixed in a kind of frozen horror. She shows the eyes rolling away, helplessly and as if by instinct, from the panorama of terrors upon which they have been made to affix themselves.

These references will surely suggest the recluse to us: the poet who shut herself away, because it got to be easier not to have to look at life directly. Ultimately perhaps we will think of Oedipus, choosing blindness out of a sense that he could no longer bear to scrutinize the wreckage of the world around him. But the most pertinent parallel is still with Emerson.

In Emerson's scheme, the eye stays open, and masters life—masters it by appearing to look, but by keeping very vague and general, nonetheless, what is actually to be seen. Emily Dickinson began at the same starting place. She too hoped to perceive Universal Being, to spell out oracular disclosures with the eye. The difference, though, was that Miss Dickinson had little talent for Emersonian generalization. Even as she hungered to see, she also saw. Out of the difference came the tragic viewpoint which Emersonianism forced upon her. When, according to the fashion of the day, Emily Dickinson brought her eye to bear on life, she found hard, blunt facts, recalling to her that human vision is finite. When, following Emerson's dictum, she essayed to keep the eyeball open, the facts asserted themselves again, too ugly to be easily endured, and compelling her retreat into self-willed sightlessness. It was precisely because she cultivated the eyes of optimism that Emily Dickinson ended up looking through the eyes of doom.

In our time, the eyes of optimism continue to be a genial institution perhaps, but they are hardly a force. Indeed, so easy and facile does the Emersonian way now seem to be that we have a taste for flagellating Emerson's outlook, and we delight in any writer who appears to flagellate it for us. This is the case with Emily Dickinson. There is absolutely no reason to think of her as a willing critic of Emersonianism. She was far too deeply involved for that, and far too reluctant to give up the Emersonian position. Nevertheless, her inversions have the ring of criticism. The paradoxical truth is that she used Emerson's means to pursue Emerson's ends, until she discovered that those ends could have their cruel and tragic opposites. However painful the discovery—whatever it cost her in peace of mind—this inverted "shock of recognition" is among the qualities in Miss Dickinson's work that makes her one of ours.

III ✛

The quality in Romantic poetry which is most often scorned in the twentieth century is the quality of an undisciplined emotionalism. Among the New Critics, it is commonly asserted that the Romantics failed as a group, because, instead of dramatizing emotions, they were content to list and label them, to tick them off, one by one, on their fingers. The Romantics—we are told—do not show us how or why we should feel deeply. Rather, they are content to say to us: "Look! I feel this way! You must feel this way, too!" One supposes that Shelley and Poe are the worst offenders in this respect: poets whose shrieks and posturings have sorely impaired their current reputations. But for purposes of illustration, a poem such as Walt Whitman's well-known address "To a Common Prostitute" comes to mind.

The text abounds in good feelings. Whitman, engaged in his usual hobby of accepting everything, has for the prostitute only the warmest and the most bountiful regard. "Not till the sun excludes you," he boasts,

> do I exclude you
> Not till the waters refuse to glisten for you,

> and the leaves to rustle for you, do my words
> refuse to glisten and rustle for you.

As a moral proposition, this is in no way objectionable. The problem is, however, that except for the reference in the title, the prostitute herself never appears. Not once in the body of the poem are we made to feel her presence, or to see her as a flesh-and-blood human being. The result is a sloppy, windy, unbearably sentimental effusion. Whitman's good feelings are wasted because they have really been addressed to no one—and hence carry no more conviction than would a drunken gesture, flung to the empty air.

As we have seen, Emily Dickinson is capable of writing sentimentally. She too can present bald emotions which seem to have little foundation in fact, or which, at any rate, strike us as being greatly in excess of the facts that she supplies. This would be the case in those of her love poems which betray the influence of magazines and gift books. It would likewise hold true for certain of the philosophical or descriptive texts, wherein Miss Dickinson seeks to conceal, with a thick coating of sanctimony and platitude, the same grave issues that had plagued her elsewhere. Sometimes, to be sure, this latter type of sentiment appears to be a part of the irony—appears a way of poking fun at statements uttered on the surface of the poem. But one cannot invariably depend upon this interpretation. A certain amount of the time, Emily Dickinson wrote off the top of her mind, without bothering to watch or to listen. Finding her in this vein:

> Nature—the Gentlest Mother is,
> Impatient of no Child—
> The feeblest—or the waywardest—

or this one:

> Inebriate of Air—am I—
> And Debauchee of Dew—
> Reeling—thro endless summer days—
> From inns of Molten Blue—

we are not always sure whether on obscure joke is intended, or whether, for the moment, she really means it.

In the main, though, Miss Dickinson's use of the language of emotion was a good deal more painstaking. Typically, her finest poems sprang from the profound sense she had of how the self is preyed upon by outer realities. In most of the texts dealt with in this study, there has been an exact, effective correlation between the tumult of feeling within the speaker and those circumstances beyond her which have brought the tumult into being. We are made to see precisely how and why death and time, man and God and Nature, can occasion such overwhelming responses. Consequently, the responses themselves have seemed rooted in actuality and properly pinned down to some specific reference. Even if we are not always prepared to sympathize with the reactions to life that Emily Dickinson presents, we are still able to accept them as dramatically true. The responses are that plausibly motivated, that adequately engrained in the style and outlook of the poetry.

Furthermore, Miss Dickinson was directly concerned with the problem of communicating an emotion. As one who wrote of suffering in its various forms and stages, she had the liveliest interest in those verbal devices which could be used to render visible and articulate the nebulous and the private inner state. This interest shows up in a number of her excellent poems, including

241

one that many readers would probably think of as her supreme achievement:

> After great pain, a formal feeling comes—
> The Nerves sit ceremonious, like Tombs—
> The stiff Heart questions was it He, that bore,
> And Yesterday, or Centuries before?
>
> The Feet, mechanical, go round—
> A Wooden way
> Of Ground, or Air, or Ought—
> Regardless grown,
> A Quartz contentment, like a stone—
>
> This is the Hour of Lead—
> Remembered, if outlived,
> As Freezing persons, recollect the Snow—
> First—Chill—then Stupor—then the letting go—

There is a difference which separates "After great pain" from the kind of poem cited in the preceding paragraph. It is a difference of location. No attempt is made here to explain why the pain occurred. We are simply told that agony has existed, without any reference to external causes. Thereupon, the text turns to portraying an emotion which comes after the initial shock. Its location, therefore, is completely inward. It seeks to give body to a state of mind: to say, with force and clarity, what a particular feeling is like.

First, the emotion is defined—a *formal feeling*. Normally, no doubt, the idea of formality would suggest the conscious attempt to restrain and control the passions. Here, however, formality bespeaks weariness, emotional depletion: the sort of exhaustion which ensues when one has passed through and beyond passion, and so has no further need for restraint or control. Hence the behavior of the *Nerves*. They are dead (*like Tombs*), because, already played upon past all endurance, they have lost the power to respond. The ceremony they enact is a ceremony of inertness, a ritual based upon pure rote. Arranged in rows, the *Nerves* are like mourners at a funeral, who, having spent their capacity for overt grief, can now do no more than sit in dumb and dry-eyed apathy.

In this stultifying atmosphere, there will naturally be a complete indifference to the usual activities of the world without. So deadened is the *stiff Heart* to anything except a sense of wonder at its own former agony that the *Heart* has lost all touch with sequence and cannot distinguish between *Yesterday* and *Centuries before*. Similarly, the *Feet* still move—but move in a wooden and plodding fashion. They have no awareness of where they tread (*Ground, or Air*); nor are they conscious of the destination, the obligation, the sense of purposed direction, all of which are implied in the synecdoche *Ought*. Lassitude has brought its own contentment, perhaps. But this is a cold, cheerless, quartz-like contentment, a serenity that has no more real feeling about it than does the stone.

What we are seeing, then, is an emotion which is, paradoxically, the absolute absence of emotion. Intense suffering has dehumanized the person described, reducing her to a collection of bodily parts which are no longer being willed into action, but which perform only automatic gestures. The person described has, indeed, plunged into a barely conscious coma; and her comatose qualities are summed up in the phrase *Hour of*

Lead. Not only is *Lead* the heavy metal, and hence ideally suited to connote the dead, drained torpor; it is dull gray in color, and thus perfectly adapted to portraying the all-enveloping twilight, the incapacity for further stimulation, which torpor involves. But *Lead* also suggests coldness—a fact that prepares the way for the thermal imagery of the two concluding lines. *Chill,* I take it, has to do with the pain which was: it relates backward to the keen, sharp time of the actual situation. *Stupor,* in turn, corresponds to the transitional period after pain, when pain could hurt no more and was displaced by lethargy. The *letting go,* with its overtones of a descent, a withdrawal, a dropping away, refers to just that psychological condition of living death which the poem as a whole has described.

The remarkable thing about "After great pain" is this: it provides us with an exact transcription of interior realities. The mind, the nerves, the heart are laid bare; their contents, during a particular period of time, are fully divulged. We are not told about an emotion, or asked to linger over it; we are compelled to see the feeling directly, to lay our hands on its size and shape. Passing from *wooden* to *Quartz* to *stone* to *Lead,* we have the sense of seeing the heaviness within deepen and grow steadily more inflexible. Moving from *Tombs* to *stiff* to *mechanical* to *regardless,* we watch a progression in which the inner self dies, undergoes *rigor mortis,* and is cloaked for burial in a thick shroud of passivity. In effect, we have stood face to face with the time of depression that follows after some nameless and unspecified anxiety.

At her best, Emily Dickinson exercised great care where the communication of feelings was concerned.

Either she used the conventional means of supplying a concrete motive for emotions or she followed the more difficult process of finding descriptive images which would dramatize the emotions in their pure form. At all times, in her most memorable poetry, she undertook to do three things: to embody emotional and psychological states in a hard, specific language; to prevent the states from becoming abstract or ultra-personal; to endow the states, in short, with the life, the substance, the dramatic impact which would make them suitable for objective statement. This preoccupation with the inner world brings us back, in a new way, to a kind of poetry that was considered earlier. This is the poetry which seeks to portray psychological derangement. We have already observed how Miss Dickinson can make the mind a stage, where a mental idiosyncrasy is put on display, or where, in extreme cases, the spectacle becomes madness itself. What I wish to emphasize this time, however, is how certain of these delineations of the mental self are subserved by a particularly brilliant method. It is the method of symbolism: symbolism of a kind and range that establishes Emily Dickinson as an early forerunner of the symbolist movement in modern poetry.

From several possible examples, let us concentrate on the following, which is probably the best of the lot:

> I felt a Funeral, in my Brain,
> And Mourners, to and fro
> Kept treading—treading—till it seemed
> That Sense was breaking through—
>
> And when they all were seated,
> A Service, like a Drum—

245

Kept beating—beating—till I thought
My Mind was going numb—

And then I heard them lift a Box
And creak across my Soul
With those same Boots of Lead again,
Then Space—began to toll,

As all the Heavens were a Bell,
And Being, but an Ear,
And I, and Silence, some strange Race
Wrecked, solitary, here—

And then a Plank in Reason, broke,
And I dropped down, and down—
And hit a World, at every plunge,
And Got through knowing—then—

We will get our bearings most readily if we first attempt to demonstrate what the poem is not. For one thing, it is not meant to be a description of the funeral in any objective or formal sense. Though the funeral exists, it has been internalized, so that it takes place in the *Brain*. Nor is the poem an attempt to imagine the funeral. The introductory verb is *felt*, not imagined or fancied. Nor can it be read successfully as a dream about the funeral. That interpretation is ruled out by the last nine lines, which suggest, not the relief of waking up—not an emergence from the nightmare within—but which are indicative, rather, that the inner processes have somehow been destructive. It is this idea of a total destruction at the climax which pinpoints the real theme of the poem. Obviously, Emily Dickinson has been concerned with the breakup of rational powers, with the onset and triumph of lunacy. In these terms, her use of the funeral becomes clear. The funeral has provided her with a set of symbols, through which the speaker's gradual conquest by madness can be dramatized. For Emily Dickinson, the funeral is the doleful, the shattering, above all the disruptive, ceremony in the world without. Accordingly, she has brought the ceremony into the realm of the mind, where it symbolizes the morbidity, the death, decay and dissolution, of the world within.

Once that point is established, the concrete details of the funeral service may be seen to function like players in a psychological drama. Consider the development of the eight opening lines. Ordinarily, the observances portrayed here would be thought of as among the most intensely formal activities in human experience: the stately procession of pallbearers, or perhaps of mourners, passing before an open casket; the slow, solemn tempo of the funeral service. In this context, of course, these ordinarily formal rituals have been used to suggest the exact opposites of formality. They stand for the first alarming signs of incoherence. Feet and *Drum* alike represent some intolerable pressure—some relentless tattoo—that bears down upon the brain, and against which the brain is increasingly powerless to protect itself. Under the heavy, incessant *treading*, the speaker feels, in line four, that the ordinary patterns and configurations of sense are breaking up. By line eight, her predicament has worsened, for now the uninterrupted *beating* within threatens to paralyze her mind—to render it numb and hence incapable of further thought.

The air of impending madness is then thickened by the references to *Box* and *Boots*. In one sense, both these heavy objects simply add anew to the insufferable weight beneath which the speaker's mind has already commenced to crack. In another, they suggest the rite of burial—but burial from within, so that the mysterious pallbearers are readying the speaker's rational faculties (and not her physical being) for interment. But since the *Boots* (certainly) and the casket (presumably) are made of lead, the images bear still a third function. As in "After great pain," *Lead* introduces the gray swirl, the color of gradual extinction. This time, however, it is not the gray peace of coma that is implied. It is, instead, the gray blur of a mind too blurred by sickness to make the old distinctions or to perceive the old relationships.

Thus far, then, all the action has occurred inside the head. The speaker has listened, in fear and awe, to a cacophany within: to the clashing sounds of her own mental crackup. But now, from lines twelve through sixteen, the theater suddenly widens to include the world outside. From every quarter of her external surroundings, there seems to beat in upon the speaker a medley that exactly corresponds to the medley in her mind. The *Heavens* appear to her to have become a gigantic *Bell*, tolling out a single refrain, which is the fact of the speaker's disorder. She, in turn, fancies herself to be all *Ear*, feverishly attuned to this single sound. In so hallucinatory a countryside, *Silence* is the stranger because, in fact, all is noise—there is no *Silence*. The speaker is equally a solitary outsider, because, even in the throes of derangement, she still has wit enough to see her alienation from every ordinary experience and to recognize that she is being cut off from all the commonplace responses. Though the funeral images seem to disappear from four of these five lines, they have actually been instrumental in keeping us alert to where we are. The images have defined inner symptoms, which are now transferred outward, until the landscape around her becomes a mirror of the speaker's own hysteria.

The images are quickly resumed as the final stanza opens. The *Plank in Reason* (reminding us of the scaffolding across an open grave) stands symbolically for the speaker's only remaining toehold in rationality. Now it breaks, collapses beneath the combined weight of feet, drum, and coffin, which are the symbols of her breakdown. With this last prop demolished, the speaker's wreckage is complete. She must be buried—which is to say, must consummate her journey into madness by spiralling down and down through all the successive stages of unreason. Superficially, her descent resembles the falling away in "After great pain." But there is a vital difference. The "letting go" there amounted to entering a state of trance where all feeling was extinguished. Here, on the other hand, it is the obliteration of reason which falling involves. At the end, the speaker has *Got through knowing:* that is, she has finished with thought, has passed outside the realm of ordinary cognition. If this is true, she has also passed beyond the possibility for orderly and coherent speech —a fact which makes the concluding *then* hardly less than a stroke of genius. *Then* does not really terminate the process which the poem has been describing. Nevertheless, it denotes an absolute breaking point in that it marks off the communicable part of the process from an aftermath which could be expressed only through the shriek, or gibberish, or wild, undifferentiated raving.

"I felt a Funeral" is made the great poem that it is by the particularizing quality of the symbol. In "After great pain," Emily Dickinson had relied upon descriptive words in order to picture a feeling. Now, however, when derangement is her subject, she heightens description into a richly symbolic vocabulary. Through the symbols of death and burial, she has bodied forth the sick and scrambled mind, approaching disintegration. Through her symbolic account of a landscape gone mad, she has given us the exact lineaments of hysteria. Through the funeral images, with their suggestion of a passage from one state to another, she has shown us the divided personality, gradually losing control of its rational self and lapsing into the "other" self of insanity. A few of her symbolic images—the *Bell* and the outsized *Ear* are prime examples—possess the sort of grotesqueness and distortion which might be associated with surrealistic writing. But even if "surrealism" pushes a point unnecessarily, there can be no question but that Miss Dickinson's method confirms her place in an important literary tradition. Quite unwittingly no doubt, yet no less effectively, she has adumbrated in "I felt a Funeral" the principles and techniques of modern symbolist poetry.

Indeed, with the text before us, it is surprising the number of connections that can be drawn between it and other poems which we recognize to be parts of the symbolist experiment. One thinks immediately of Baudelaire's "Spleen," a lyric which sets out to demonstrate the mood of the title, and proceeds to do so with symbolic images that are strikingly akin to Emily Dickinson's:

Quand le ciel bas et lourd pèse comme un couvercle
Sur l'esprit gémissant en proie aux longs ennuis
Et que de l'horizon embrassant tout le cercle
Il nous verse un jour noir plus triste que les nuits;

.   .   .

Des cloches tout à coup sautent avec furie
Et lancent vers le ciel un affreux hurlement,
Ainsi que des esprits errants et sans patrie
Qui se mettent à geindre opiniâtrément.

—Et de longs corbillards, sans tambours ni musique,
Défilent lentement dans mon âme; l'Espoir,
Vaincu, pleure, et l'Angoisse atroce, despotique,
Sur mon crâne incliné plante son drapeau noir.*

Or, at a slightly farther remove, there is Yeats's fine
sonnet, "On a Picture of a Black Centaur by Edmund
Dulac." The aim of the poem, as Edmund Wilson re-

* In the translation of St. John Squire:

> When the low heavy sky weighs like a lid
> Upon the spirit aching for the light
> And all the wide horizon's line is hid
> By a black day sadder than any night;
>
> .   .   .
>
> Suddenly bells leap forth into the air,
> Hurling a hideous uproar to the sky
> As 'twere a band of homeless spirits who fare
> Through the strange heavens, wailing stubbornly.
>
> And hearses, without drum or instrument,
> File slowly through my soul; crushed, sorrowful,
> Weeps Hope, and Grief, fierce and omnipotent,
> Plants his black banner on my drooping skull.

marks, is to convey a special frame of mind. The symbols through which Yeats projects point of view are, again, basically similar to the ones Miss Dickinson employs. His stamping hooves and black woods and "horrible green parrots" are made to bear the same general function that she assigns to treading feet, a tolling bell, and the casket, lowered inside her speaker's mind. But Emily Dickinson's relations with symbolic poetry can be established most forcibly, I think, if we examine a text wherein the images are qualitatively very different from anything she could have devised, but where they nevertheless operate in a way that is identical with hers and are meant to encompass identical ends. Despite its length, therefore, let me quote the opening sequence of T. S. Eliot's "Gerontion":

Here I am, an old man in a dry month,
Being read to by a boy, waiting for rain.
I was neither at the hot gates
Nor fought in the warm rain
Nor knee deep in the salt marsh, heaving a cutlass,
Bitten by flies, fought.
My house is a decayed house,
And the jew squats on the window sill, the owner,
Spawned in some estaminet of Antwerp,
Blistered in Brussels, patched and peeled in London.
The goat coughs at night in the field overhead;
Rocks, moss, stonecrop, iron, merds.
The woman keeps the kitchen, makes tea,
Sneezes at evening, poking the peevish gutter.
                                    I an old man,
A dull head among windy spaces.

252

At first glance, no two samples of poetry could seem much less alike than "I felt a Funeral" and "Gerontion." What can serve as an excuse for joining them: the one so personal, the other so ostensibly objective; the one concerned with a mental landscape, the other oriented in what is apparently an urban slum; the one so evidently symbolic, the other so seemingly pictorial? The answer is that they come together at the most important of all meeting places, that of technique. The poems share a method, and it is a method which will shed as much light on "Gerontion" as upon the Dickinson text.

"Gerontion" is no more the picture of an objective house in an objective city than "I felt a Funeral" is the portrayal of an objective burial in an objective churchyard. The house, like the rite of burial, and the occupants of the house, like those present at the graveside, are symbols. They are symbols of the speaker's consciousness. Throughout these fifteen lines, we are continually being presented with thoughts and emotions: with the futility and desolation that the old man feels; with his sense of being morally and intellectually stagnant; with the despair he experiences as he ponders the outcome of existence. Instead of being mentioned directly or treated discursively, however, the feelings of the old man are embodied in images. His responses are given life, tangibility, and exactness by the concrete symbolic details which express them. The old man's unfought battles are, as their very order indicates, the symbols of his awareness that he has failed to win the battle for self-abnegation. The sick goat and peevish gutter and sneezing woman objectify his sense of being spiritually impotent. The dry month, the absence of rain, the decadent atmosphere of the tenement, all the details in the line that begins "Rocks, moss . . ." —these dramatize the old man's knowledge of his sterile life, his recognition that he has gone beyond salvation, his terror of the death to come. In the later and more or less non-symbolic stages of the poem, the causes of the speaker's despair are shown to be his rejection of Christianity. But so far as this opening movement is concerned, it is the despair itself—the sheer, naked feeling—that occupies the foreground. Eliot has sought to do nothing more than create and keep alive a special state of mind.

Eliot's method for doing so has simply involved an extension of the method in "I felt a Funeral." To be sure, some differences exist. Where Emily Dickinson specifies that we are *in* the brain, Eliot forces us to grasp our location by inference. Where Miss Dickinson's topic is madness, an aberration of mind, Eliot works with the attitude, a mental set that is rational enough, though sorely troubled. But these are superficial differences, beneath which a single underlying pattern is discernible. As Emily Dickinson uses the symbol to make hysteria articulate, so for Eliot the symbol has bodied forth the meditation, has made introspection dramatic. As Miss Dickinson finds in funeral imagery the perfect equivalents for lunacy, so Eliot has discovered in the imagery of the slums the perfect counterparts for a sick and ravaged soul. For both poets, therefore, symbolic language serves to clarify the inner world and to make it expressible. The symbol acts, in both poems, to bring the private condition into the public domain of art.

We have little difficulty in seeing how writers like Baudelaire, Yeats, and Eliot arrived at the symbolist method. For one thing, all three were gifted critics, keenly aware of the Romantic tradition and in full revolt against many of its excesses. Beyond that, all three were eminently public poets. They wrote for publication, which meant that no matter how limited the audience they envisioned, they still had readers in mind with whom they were consciously communicating. Through the symbol, accordingly, they were able to cast off the looseness and the flaccidities of Romanticism and they were able to invent fresh means of communication, by extensive use of the meticulous symbolic-image and of the hard and genuinely evocative symbolic-phrase.

Emily Dickinson's experiments with symbolism are nothing short of miraculous. Writing in seclusion and without any real critical training or knowledge, Miss Dickinson could easily have filled her little booklets with page after page of sentimental gush. The circumstances were right for her to produce a poetry in which swoons succeeded tremors, in which the palpitation was as standard a feature as the exclamation point, and in which emotion became the ultra-personal cry of

> Oh! lift me as a wave, a leaf, a cloud!
> I fall upon the thorns of life! I bleed!

That she usually avoided these extremes is perhaps less a tribute to her artistry than it is a measure of her intense personal suffering. It may be, in other words, that the everyday acuteness of pain caused her search for ways in which pain could be expressed. It may be that by her profound sense of personal instability she was driven to find refuge in the stabilizing force of words. But, regardless of the reasons, Emily Dickinson's precision with the language of feeling is a mark of her continuing greatness. Her tendency to show emotions (rather than to state them) not only rescues her work from the worst defects in the poetry of her time; the tendency is a second quality in her writing which confirms Miss Dickinson as one of ours.

IV ✛

Confusion and *order* are the polarities of Emily Dickinson's world view. They inform her poetry, shape her style, enter into the basic themes to which she repeatedly returns. Out of the conflict between them, there arise the anxieties that overspread her work. And there emerges as well from this conflict her elaborate moral scheme.

Confusion is an observed fact. Or rather it is *the* fact, since confusion is, for Emily Dickinson, the essential condition of every experience. Looking to the world she dwells in, Miss Dickinson perceives a bewildering proliferation of events. Time, change, the physical and mental deterioration of the self: these are her eternal mysteries. The delusive gift, the unlooked-for bereavement, the surprising intrusion, the sudden betrayal, the abrupt looming of a new threat to security: these constitute daily shocks which she has no power to comprehend. Yet, mysterious though they themselves are, the events point to a mystery that is still greater than themselves. So regular is their appearance, so steady the rhythm of suffering which they evoke that they seem the effects of some dim and indecipherable Cause. This is no aimless succession which Emily Dickinson beholds. Rather it is (or at least appears to be) a strangely determined flow. On the surface, all is confusion and mere sequence. But there are constant hints that beneath the surface a Plan exists, a governing principle which the surface of experience simply represents.

Order would come with the discovery of that principle. To find order would be to understand how and why experience works, and what the significance of experience might be. This is Emily Dickinson's dream. Her lifelong quest was to establish coherence in a Humpty-Dumpty world. She wished to reach outside the dense welter of experiences, to grasp their Plan, and thereby to transform mere sequence into an orderly, a predictable, above all, an intelligible pattern. But her wish was balked by the manner in which experience presented itself. Asking for answers, Emily Dickinson had no recourse except to confront the riddle again. With each new confrontation, her craving for order was dashed by the onrush of confusions. In the maze before her, she found veiled clues, but nothing definite to seize hold of. Mobility gave her no fixed starting point, from where the search for coherence could begin.

Thus an irremediable cleavage separates the fact, which is the ambiguous flowing, from the ideal, which is the dream of mastering the flowing intellectually. Faced by the conflict, Emily Dickinson is aroused to philosophical speculation. Why is it—she asks, in effect —that her love of arrangement, her taste for harmony, her commitment to decorum, are left perpetually unfulfilled? Why, when she is consigned to a world that obscures her vision, does she still hunger to see things from the standpoint of Eternity? Why, in a word, has she been created to suffer—and to suffer most acutely because there is never an adequate explanation for the ordeal? By her very need to frame such questions, Emily Dickin-

257

son obviously sets herself apart from the consoling influences of religious dogma. On the other hand, her background, her habits of mind, and her instinctive Emersonianism *were* religious. In proffering trial answers, therefore, she continues to think within a basically religio-metaphysical orientation. Her conjectures are built around the crucial relationship between herself and God.

One conjecture is that she has been made what she is by her own guilt. Her condition is justified by the fact that she is a fallen being in a fallen world. The confusions around her are simply her share of the punishment which God has decreed to all of sinful mankind. She is denied access to God's secrets because, as one infected with human depravity, she has lost the right to understand.

If this is so, life may be thought of as a constant process of purgation. One lives to atone—to purify one's self in the hope that, with purification, the afflictions of the present world will be banished in the hereafter. This hope explains the great store that Emily Dickinson sets by immortality. Theorizing about immortal life, she never sees it in terms that are suggestive of beatitude; nor does she behold it as a state of rapt contemplation. She equates immortality, instead, with the obtaining of insight. *I shall know why—when Time is over,* she assures herself in one poem. The combination of timelessness with knowledge is highly revealing. Safely past the temptations of earth, the poet will have conquered temporality. But she will have conquered it by knowing why. To escape from confusion will amount to discovering what the confusions signified when they were burdensome, ever-present realities.

The possibility that confusion results from personal sin is a possibility that Emily Dickinson only mentions —and immediately rejects. She dismisses it for the simple reason that the idea strikes her as wholly preposterous. She feels no guilt. Contriteness or the vague sense of having been naughty: these are parts of her emotional equipment. The experience of outright depravity, however, is something completely foreign to her. To assume guilt is to raise the unanswerable question: guilty of what? To accept the need for atonement is to broach the equally absurd dilemma: how shall I atone, when I have no clear understanding of what it is that I am atoning for? Consequently, the association of suffering with sin, or of knowledge with redemption, fails for want of plausibility. Deprived of this more or less orthodox solution to the problem, Emily Dickinson has only one remaining alternative to which she can turn. If she is not guilty, then God must be. Since she has done nothing to earn the confusions of life, they must, necessarily, have been imposed upon her by a malicious Jehovah. The thought gives her no pleasure. She resists it with a will, and arrives at it only after she has been driven to a corner where no other explanation will work. Nevertheless, it stands as a recurring idea in a large number of her poems.

To remark, as one critic has done, that her God resembles an aloof Victorian squire is to err in the direction of generosity. Actually, He is considerably less attractive and lovable than this. Miss Dickinson variously describes Him as burglar, swindler, marauder, robber, thief, unfeeling merchant. She sees him as Master of the time-ceremony, approving flux for His creatures, while He Himself enjoys repose, and withholding information from mankind because He is infernally jealous of His own prerogatives. She convicts Him of duplicity, for He is the bestower of clues which invariably mislead, even as He promises an immortality which will, in all likelihood, turn out to be fraudulent. As she makes these allegations, Emily Dickinson seldom casts off the protective devices of irony. She dares not go too far, and her use of the child's pose is nowhere more evident than in her attacks upon Deity. But the carefully arrayed diminutives—the shy appeals to "Papa," the coy apologetics, the wistful yearning for "My Father's house"—never quite conceal her true intentions. Emily Dickinson is explaining her earthly situation by postulating wickedness as a prime condition of the silent Heavens.

The worst of the wickedness is that one must cower defenselessly before it. Secure in her innocence, convinced that she has been deeply wronged, Emily Dickinson would like to vindicate herself by addressing an appeal to some Higher Tribunal. It would be comfort of a sort if she could only cry out against God and rage at God's injustices. But who would hear her plea when the only imaginable Judge is likewise both the Prosecutor and the Executioner? The sheer futility of protesting begets in Emily Dickinson's mind the impression that she is forever being brought to trial on trumped-up charges that she can never hope to fathom, and that she is constantly punished for crimes of whose nature and commitment she is in total ignorance. There is no possible change of venue when one argues a case against the cosmos, a point that Miss Dickinson recognizes in the four following lines, written a year or two before her death:

Of God we ask one favor,
That we may be forgiven—
For what, he is presumed to know—
The Crime, from us, is hidden—

The irony here is so broad that, in effect, the stanza
ceases to be ironical and becomes a slashing and straightforward complaint. God is indicted on three different
counts. First, He is blamed for having devised the
Crime that human beings foolishly—or hypocritically
—presume to be theirs. Secondly, He is blamed for refusing to share with humanity the knowledge that He
possesses. Finally, He is held directly responsible for
the confusions and disorders of earth. If humankind are
anxiety-ridden creatures, plagued by uncertainties and
mystified by their surroundings, these lines make it plain
that the fault for their misery lies with God, and is none
of humankind's own doing.

Emily Dickinson was in no sense a systematic philoso-
pher. Her unresolved metaphysical ponderings were the
results of the determination that she had to know, rather
than of logical thinking or of an active interest in philosophy. One might even add that the ponderings reflect
a mind too vain and petulant to be at ease with the ordinary, inescapable limitations on human knowledge. Miss
Dickinson chose to see through God's eyes; her philosophical poems are protests against all the aspects of
experience—whether natural, human, or divine—which
seemed to interfere with that impossible project. Yet,
for all its naïveté, her philosophical point of view will
bear comparison with (for it represents an amateurish
variation of) the crisis philosophy that has been of influence in our own time. There is more than one trace

of Christian existentialism in the relationship which Emily Dickinson establishes between existence and essence, in her stress upon God's unreliability, and in her conception of man as the pawn and prisoner of obscure cosmic forces.

Too much is made, it seems to me, of the absolute chaos and absurdity which are supposed to characterize the existentialist's vision. The existentialist sees a thoroughly disjointed world, yes; he seems overwhelmed by a veritable clutter of activities, all of which decline being patterned, and from which every shred of significance appears to have been removed. As it confuses, however, experience still has a way of proffering vague hopes. Hemmed in by chaos, the existentialist is haunted by the feeling that order might be realized, provided he took a fresh approach to the problem, or looked at life in a new way, or chose a different perspective from which to survey the world before him. Kierkegaard himself will illustrate this frustration. The attempt to find order— specifically, the struggle to offer rational proofs for God or to deduce God's existence from the facts of experience—is, in Kierkegaard's notorious phrase, an "excellent subject for the comedy of the higher lunacy." But to recognize the folly of the attempt is by no means to be free of making it. None save the foolish deny God outright; and to give up looking for Him is simply to be reminded of His presence all over again. The real heart of the existentialist dilemma is that one perceives meaninglessness everywhere, even as one is prodded to search anew for meaning. Existentialist terror derives from the fact that one must concede the impossibility of the search, even as a struggle to achieve the impossible continues unabated.

Emily Dickinson's relations with experience were expressed through identically these same paradoxes. Her quest for certainty could have been consummated in either of two ways: through an exact knowledge of whatever purpose life possesses, or through the final realization that since all is rush and disorder, there is no purpose and never can be any. But both these fixed views were luxuries that life never permitted her to enjoy. If the flowing of detail might suggest to Emily Dickinson that incoherency had triumphed, still by the manner of the flowing—by the fact of its constancy—she was forever drawn back to the idea that a Plan existed and could ultimately be spelled out. One of her most powerful symbols, as we observed earlier, is the springtime light, which comes, hovers, beckons, and withdraws—but in the act of withdrawal gives promise of a later return. This is the symbol of an essentially existentialist universe, in which experience simultaneously invites and rebuffs, and in which the individual can no more deafen himself to the invitation than he can follow it through to a satisfactory conclusion.

In sensing that she is under perpetual surveillance, furthermore, Emily Dickinson anticipates in her work an important theme of existentialist fiction. In particular, she is likely to remind us of the indignities suffered by Kafka's Joseph K. It is his fate to feel himself the victim of what might be termed cosmic gossip. He is talked about by "somebody," arraigned for trial before unaccountable jurors, set upon by the mysterious occupants of a mysterious castle. His extreme anxiety results not so much from the situations themselves, as from his awareness that while he can never begin to comprehend his adversaries, still, where Joseph K. is concerned, they possess the most complete knowledge, have somehow been supplied with dossiers containing the most intimate kind of information.

It is an anxiety from which Emily Dickinson is rarely free. We noted previously how she suspects that Nature whispers about her, and how, in the presence of Nature's "Haunted House," she represents her identity in the form of a cracked cave, dreadfully exposed and open to invasion. In lines that are still more Kafkaesque, she can say of herself:

> Nature and God—I neither knew
> Yet Both so well knew me
> They startled, like Executors
> Of my identity.

As for Joseph K., the problem of Emily Dickinson's speaker is that of knowing nothing, but of laboring under the realization that she is terribly known. A two-way conversation with God and Nature is out of the question, for both are too vague for definition and far too remote to be reached. But there is no denying them, either. Both are indisputably "out there" someplace, operating as existential menaces, who have the insight to see at a glance and the power to destroy in an instant.

Yet the term "existentialism" is, of course, an importation where Emily Dickinson is concerned. The label fits her predicaments well enough. But unlike Emersonianism, of which she was actively conscious, and unlike symbolism, which she explicitly practiced, the *formal* concepts of existentialism remain so foreign to the concepts in which she might have thought that they have the air of being rather dragged in and made to fit. Hence a better, or perhaps a more indigenous, approach to her plight is needed, and this can be supplied if we look at Miss Dickinson's place in the cultural and literary history of her own locale. New England is a small place which has produced a relatively small amount of first-rate poetry. Nevertheless, region and poetry have this in common: their evolution from the seventeenth to the twentieth century epitomizes almost perfectly the history of human thought over the past three hundred years. Emily Dickinson's dilemmas were, if not determined, then given form and impetus by the fact that she stepped at a particular moment into a particular geographical and intellectual context. Through a look at the context, we can come to terms with the dilemmas afresh, understanding something of their origin as well as the fascination they continue to have for the modern reader.

The first New England poet of any real consequence was Edward Taylor, a minister-physician who lived in the Connecticut valley after 1670, and the great bulk of whose poetry was apparently composed in the years from 1690 until his death in 1720. Taylor was a steadfast Puritan, a devotional poet of some considerable ability, and a writer who aimed to deal poetically with the relationships between the human and the divine. Characteristically, his method involved the presentation of little allegories, compressed to the lyric form. Committed to God as his true subject, but aware that such a topic could not be explored directly, Taylor resorted to exact, one-to-one symbolic equivalents. God is revealed in his poems through the milling process, the minting of coins, the construction of a sewer, the building of a house, the gyrations of a spinning wheel—in short, through some commonplace, earthly activity which has been made to stand for the activities of Godhead.

265

There was no room for confusions in the world which Taylor contemplated. He might indeed protest that his eyes were befoulled with sin, or that his pencil could not limn the immense distances from his threshold to the "bright throne" of God. But these were polite fictions merely. At every turn Taylor was sustained and pacified by Puritan dogma. He had no questions which theology was unprepared to answer. No aspect of his experience could be so strange—or so terrifying—that it refused to be illuminated by the Puritan drama of sin and regeneration. His complete assurance is as evident in the method that Taylor employs as in his themes. He sets forth a universe that is not only serene and basically simple; it is a universe which guarantees the correctness of allegory. Everything it contains is meaningful. Since each event is providential, all events alike may be drawn upon to symbolize Providence. A precise correspondence links here with There: links the seen phenomena in the world below to the hidden (yet perfectly understood) wonders of the realm Above.

Following Taylor, the next great poets of the New England tradition were Emerson and, by intellectual extension, Whitman, a New Englander in point of view if not by geography. Though far more versatile than Taylor, both writers nonetheless shared Taylor's general purpose. They were intent upon displaying life in its spiritual aspects; they aimed to harmonize history with the Eternal. There were key differences, however. Where Taylor had been supported by theology, Emerson and Whitman turned self-consciously away from the church, rejecting creeds and institutions and repudiating the priesthood. Accordingly, they substituted for Taylor's dogma a belief in the private revelation. In place of Taylor's allegory, they devised a loose theory of symbolism, which turned visible phenomena into the very general reflectors of a spiritual essence.

By trusting to the revelation, Emerson and Whitman were able to hold confusions at bay—most of the time. In terms of their symbolic doctrine, they were prepared to keep before them a universe that was fixed and stable —usually. Yet neither was completely free of doubt. If Taylor had said, with the complacency of the orthodox, "As here, so There"— Emerson and Whitman were obliged to repeat the statement with an important qualification, "As here, so There, we hope." Precisely because he looked deeper into life than Emerson ever cared to venture, Whitman knew periods when the hope guttered and flickered out. God is Whitman's Camerado, Nature his familiar, life a subject that he masters with the earnest look. But in the total structure of *Leaves of Grass*, one can still come upon a passage like this:

Me and mine, loose windrows, little corpses,
Froth, snowy white, and bubbles,
(See, from my dead lips the ooze exuding at last,
See, the prismatic colors glistening and rolling,)
Tufts of straw, sands, fragments,
Buoy'd hither from many moods, one contradicting another,
From the storm, the long calm, the darkness, the swell,
Musing, pondering, a breath, a briny tear, a dab of
             liquid or soil,
Up just as much out of fathomless workings fermented
             and thrown,
A limp blossom or two, torn, just as much over waves
             floating, drifted at random,

267

Just as much for us that sobbing dirge of Nature,
Just as much whence we come that blare of the cloud-
trumpets,
We, capricious, brought hither we know not whence,
spread out before you,
You up there walking or sitting,
Whoever you are, we too lie in drifts at your feet.

It is a terrible moment. Doubts have come; and with no
externally imposed dogma to turn to, the religious sensibility can only fall back upon itself. But the self is
without remedy. A personal symbolism has failed, so
that God, the vague "You up there," seems to have
slipped outside experience. The private revelation has
gone dark, so that experience, as far as the eye can tell,
has become a clashing and contradictory, an ugly and
impenetrable chaos. It is the moment of Emersonian
despair.

Emily Dickinson transforms this momentary doubt
into a lifelong agony. Which is to say that she carries
the lapse from a guaranteed security—a preconceived
source of certitude—to its logical end. For her, the
dogma remains quite as unworkable as it is for Emerson or Whitman. Though her vocabulary still includes
such terms as *grace* and *redeem, election* and *salvation,*
the terms turn up in human or natural contexts, never
in connection with divine functions. But no more does
she possess the private revelation. Though fully as convinced as Emerson or Whitman that the world is symbolic, she is never able to determine what nameless, un-
knowable quality it symbolizes. All hope of reconciling
here with There becomes, in her case, the suspicion that
since what can be seen is pervaded by misrule and dis-

order, the unseen There must be a place of pure bedlam —or, worse yet, an absolute inferno. What happens in Miss Dickinson's poetry is simply this: the unity, which was inherent in Taylor's theology and which Emerson and Whitman wrested from experience by not looking too closely, collapses under a genuinely tragic gaze. Left with only the self, and unable to force the self to believe, Emily Dickinson, from poem to poem, explores a situation in which the older religious and philosophical orders, with the values they guaranteed, are dissolving into nothingness. Her vision is, basically, the vision of modern man, as, certainly, it is the vision recorded in a great deal of modern poetry.

For a sequel can be written. After Emily Dickinson, two of the major poets of the twentieth century have been New Englanders: Frost obviously, and Eliot, who, as he himself acknowledges, retains the New England temperament despite his expatriation. Both have inherited pretty much the world-view that Emily Dickinson propounded, and each has written out of the view, making it central to his own poetic themes.

For Frost, the trick has lain in sealing up every conceivable chink in such an ironic armor as Emily Dickinson wore. As aware as she that life has the power to terrify, Frost has sought the means of parrying fear— and found them in the quip, the jest, the wry grin, the sardonic countenance. He has substituted for Miss Dickinson's policy of not crying until it hurts too much what seems the steadfast determination never to feel pain and not to cry at all. And yet the tears do break through. One can find them in a run-of-the-mill piece like "Bereft" (which reads like a lesser version of Miss Dickinson's "To my quick ear the leaves conferred"), or in such texts of undoubted greatness as "Once by the Pacific," "Neither Out Far Nor In Deep," and the sonnet called "Design." These are tragedy-ridden poems, poems which, as Lionel Trilling has said, can chill and startle by the very ferocity of the universe they portray. The bleakness which overspreads them stems from a world view that differs in no broad particular from that maintained by Emily Dickinson. If Frost seems more serene than she, if he employs her strategy of retreat somewhat more successfully, he still has moments of feeling (as she did) that God glares malignly over his shoulder, that Nature conspires against him, and that wherever he looks the avenues of withdrawal seem utterly blocked off.

Eliot, by contrast, has made no attempt to shut out the issues. "The sea is all about us," he laments, meaning, as Emily Dickinson had meant, that man is adrift on a flood of moral and intellectual uncertainties. Time for Eliot, though less the personified demon than it had been in Emily Dickinson's poetry, is no less the source of confusion and disorder:

> Time and the bell have buried the day
> The black cloud carries the sun away . . .

But if Eliot sees the problems, he has also asserted the positive solution. As the poet of strong moral rigor, he counsels a return to dogma, a reacceptance of the Christian Word and the Christian institution, a submission of the believing self to Godhead. The road to Little Gidding (the road not taken by either Miss Dickinson or Frost) becomes Eliot's way to salvation. Immensely difficult to follow, the road never by-passes Emily Dickinson's countryside: it passes straight through her land of doubts, and calls the traveller's attention to every tragic enigma that she encountered. But it does pass through. For the darkness in which Miss Dickinson ended, Eliot substitutes the moment of faith, when prayer is possible, when the chapel is reached, when the possibility of the Timeless Moment can be realized, and when, after long and desperate struggles with the self, the self believes, and

> all shall be well
> And all manner of thing shall be well. . . .

Emily Dickinson stands, therefore, at a crucial turning in the history of the religious-poetic sensibility. Behind her stretch the old, outmoded systems, arguing in their placid way that life is merely a finite enactment of the Infinite. Before her lies a situation in which the Infinite seems to have disappeared—or in which, if Infinity can be demonstrated at all, the demonstration is a result of long and arduous effort. In her poetry the easy way breaks up, and the difficult way begins to crystallize. By the very questions she asks, the transition from the one to the other is made necessary. Emily Dickinson is one of those writers who cause us to see, with renewed understanding, the literature that comes both before and after them. She remains one of ours, because her attitudes break with "theirs," and continue to shape —in fact, continue to be our own.*

---

* Residence in Hartford is not always enough to make one a New Englander, of course; and there are not many other grounds upon which Wallace Stevens could be called a specifically New England poet. In his philosophical poetry, nevertheless, Stevens often seems to fit the pattern we have been examining. Consider the agitations of the woman in "Sunday Morning":

> She says, "I am content when wakened birds,
> Before they fly, test the reality
> Of misty fields, by their sweet questionings;
> But when the birds are gone, and their warm fields
> Return no more, where, then, is paradise?"

And she continues in another place:

> "But in contentment I still feel
> The need of some imperishable bliss."

Clearly, these are Emily Dickinson's agitations. They reflect her craving for order, for Paradise, and for an endless continuation of the spring-summer radiance.

To allay the woman's fears, Stevens can only urge a kind of aesthetic hedonism. He insists that since she is but the creature of an hour, she should exploit the hour fully, by living a life devoted to beauty, to sensory pleasures, and to a passionate use of the imagination. His suggestions would have little appeal for Emily Dickinson, with her New England conscience and her tendency to withdraw from life. But the point is that the suggestions are made in response to Emily Dickinson's world view. Like Frost's irony and Eliot's Christian submission, Stevens' hedonism is an attempt to repair the shattered, ruined world that one finds in Miss Dickinson's poetry.

The Clock, the Father, and the Child

··
⁙ Pain—has an element of Blank
··

F EAR IS THE DOMINANT EMOTION in Emily Dickinson's poetry. It is her constant subject, as well as
the underlying motive for most of her stylistic habits.
Miss Dickinson was, in every important respect, the poet
of dread, regardless of whether she expressed the dread
openly or struggled to conceal it in one or another of
her ironic poses.

The sources of her fear, at least the major ones, have
been sketched out. They range in kind from trivial
events, like the ticking of a clock or the arrival of a letter, to sweeping philosophical issues, like the problem
of time or the mysteries of death. They could excite a
physical distress (the touch of a stranger's hand), or
a distress that is moral (the question of one's own guilt),
or a psychological anguish (the suspicion of approaching madness), or an intellectual torment (the apparent
meaninglessness of life). The sources cut across all the
broad categories of experience, for they involve alike
the difficulties in human relationships, the apparent an-
tipathies of Nature, and the ambiguous silence maintained by God. A further extension of the list would be
tiresome—and really quite pointless. The plain truth is
that everything and anything was capable of arousing
Emily Dickinson to the most acute trepidations. To re-
phrase a point made much earlier, she was the poet of
dread because she knew no aspect of existence which did

273

not, sooner or later, strike her as being fundamentally dreadful.

Can we say why this was so? Can we, in other words, explain Emily Dickinson's psychic behavior? Can we hope to say, with some clarity and exactness, what it was in her psychological conditioning that made her the agitated, the almost preternaturally responsive, the easily overwhelmed person whom she turned out to be? Knowing what rendered her anxious—and when, and how often—can we possibly come to terms with the sense of anxiety itself?

These questions are not beyond resolution. By way of trying to answer them, though, we shall next have to take one step backward from the poetry, in order to look as directly as possible into the mind of the poet. This undertaking involves two grave difficulties which may as well be stated at the outset.

To begin with, there is the problem of just how much of this particular mind can be scanned. In one way, obviously, Emily Dickinson's life invites psychological speculations. It was so strange an existence that she led—one so much dedicated to a practice of the eccentric and the perverse—that the wish to locate in it some sort of specific neurotic pattern is virtually inescapable. And yet, at the same time, no life could possibly be more opaque than hers. Intimate glimpses of her in her day-to-day routine are rare, and usually not very helpful. Moreover, in those innumerable letters that she sent to friends and relatives, Miss Dickinson tended to keep the door as tightly closed upon herself as ever it was closed in the upstairs bedroom. When personal revelations do appear to slip through, one supposes them to be an inadvertence, or one is made doubtful of their meaning by the crabbed and highly guarded style in which they are couched. Hence the basis which her life provides for psychological speculations is, to say the least, limited. Attempting to turn up evidence, the critic soon recognizes that he must work largely at the level of inference, and that he had better proceed tentatively and provisionally, and with the utmost in tact and patience. He feels constrained to announce before he begins that any conclusion he may reach will fall considerably short of proof, that it could conceivably be wrong, and that however well it may seem to square with the facts of the poetry, it is perhaps only one of several other conclusions which would square almost as well.

If the life allows for little access to the poet's mind, the only alternative route lies through the poetry. And while this is the way that we must, for the most part, take, still the very taking of it presents us with a second difficulty. It involves us in what appears to be a marked change of both perspective and method.

Heretofore we have been claiming for Emily Dickinson's work a truly universal significance. The claim has been validated by repeated appeals to her themes and language: to what she said and how she said it. Now, however, if we turn the work to biographical ends, we seem to replace a concern for the universal aspects of the poetry with an interest in the poetry only as a repository for certain of the poet's thoughts and feelings— including, no doubt, some thoughts and feelings which she never entertained knowingly. We seem on the verge of shifting away from the consciously created tragic design, and of focussing, instead, upon personal disclosures which the poet made unconsciously about herself in particular texts. And certainly we are moving from a kind of criticism where an appeal to the given is always possible to a critical endeavor in which the given, slight at best, is much less demonstrable, much less visibly and publicly *there*. All these enterprises are hazardous, if only because, on the face of it, they have the look of terminating an interest in strictly literary matters, and of leading toward a guessing-game which may appear essentially irrelevant and even, perhaps, a little frivolous.

And yet, the risks and reservations notwithstanding, the undertaking before us is, I feel, worthwhile, and one to be conducted in the name of a serious point and purpose. It is true, of course, that there is only one ultimately significant fact about Emily Dickinson of Amherst. By her poems alone, she has the power to command our interest and attention, and to arouse our curiosity and sense of wonder. Behind the poems, however, there does still stand the specific imagination—the particular attitudes and habits of mind—which brought them into being. These poems, which front so consistently upon a fearful world, do not exist in a vacuum. They are reflections of the fear-ridden countenance that Emily Dickinson turned outward to meet her world. They are the manifestations of a face afraid. To understand at least a little about those features of fear would be to discover a last vital fact not simply concerning Emily Dickinson (that, by itself, *would* be frivolous), but concerning her art. Already we know that the art was tragic, and that the particular vision it expresses was often determined by the artist's cultural and historical affiliations. If, turning inward, we could now effect a psychic reconstruction that would be plausible and even halfway accurate, this would mean illuminating the art in yet another fashion. We would know why it was tragic, and why the post-Emersonian mode was especially congenial to the artist. We would know not just the patterns of her poetry, but also the compulsions that drove Emily Dickinson to choose the patterns, and kept her developing and sustaining them throughout her creative life.

II ✛

Oddly enough, we may begin with a remark of Emily Dickinson's that Thomas Wentworth Higginson happened to record. I say this is odd, because for years Higginson has been portrayed as the obtuse friend and critic, as one too steeped in both the social and the literary amenities to have any real conception of Emily Dickinson's value. And of course the allegations are correct. Glib and facile, Higginson craved sweet rhymes and platitudes in poetry: he ventured to suggest that Miss Dickinson's verse would be better off if it sounded more like the work of Alice Lowell. And yet, by a strange inadvertence, he also stumbled upon a truth. Without at all knowing what he had, Higginson once held in his hands a key to Emily Dickinson's personality. What is more, he did us the inestimable favor of setting it down on paper.

He did not actually visit the Dickinson home in Amherst until the summer of 1870, nearly a decade after the beginnings of his correspondence with Emily. Once there, he reacted with shock and amusement to much of what he found: the blue and white robed maiden lady, speaking with sybilline inflections; the father of the house, a "thin, dry and speechless" man; the air of constant tension, which, as he said, "drained my nerve power so much." Twice during his brief stay, Higginson sent back to his wife, in Boston, long letters, relaying some of the quirks and oddities he had discovered. On August 17, 1870, he included, among other things Emily Dickinson had said to him, the following comment (or perhaps it is a paraphrased comment): "I never knew how to tell time by the clock till I was fifteen. My father thought he had taught me, but I did not understand and I was afraid to say I did not and afraid to ask anyone else lest he should know."

There is no reason to disbelieve this remarkable story. Certainly Higginson would not have made it up. He found so much that was genuinely astonishing in the Dickinson parlor that he had scant need to fabricate. Nor does it strike one as a story of Emily's own concocting. By 1870 she had unquestionably learned to see through one part of Higginson: that is, she saw his literary judgments for what they were. On the other hand, he remained her friend, a confidant of long standing, whom she was just now meeting face to face. Pained by what must have been his obvious bafflement—or embarrassed probably by his obvious reserve—Emily Dickinson was, one suspects, attempting to tell him a truth. In ways that may not have been totally apparent to her (and that were all too plainly missed by him) she was setting forth memories of childhood, in order to render herself accountable before a person whose understanding she needed and desperately wanted to possess.*

---

* The air of a "confession" is accentuated by other of Emily Dickinson's "sayings" which Higginson quoted in his two letters:

"Women talk; men are silent. That is why I dread women."

"My father only reads on Sunday. He reads *lonely* and *rigorous* books."

For the story is not of course the trivial and silly anecdote that Higginson took it to be. It has a significance that is almost immeasurable. In the first place, it bespeaks, as one concrete example, a long and troubled childhood. Like the visible part of an iceberg, it arises to suggest an immense world beneath: in this case, the world of parental tyrannies, of a little girl who suffered silently and stubbornly, of a father-daughter relationship which was always strained, always difficult, and, for the daughter, bound to have destructive aftereffects. But the really electrifying quality of the story derives from what might be called its constituent images. As one reads and returns, they fall into place: a trio of images that Emily Dickinson is able to recall over the stretch of thirty or thirty-five years—the images of clock, of father, and of child. Suddenly one realizes that these are not images confined to a single childhood incident. Far from it: They are the very images that outlasted Emily Dickinson's childhood, that were linked inextricably to her mature thinking, and that became eventually the bases for her greatest poetic themes.

The clock. This was the enigma. It constituted a problem which the little Emily Dickinson was told to master, and could not. It offered a riddle which she felt the pressing need to understand, only understanding would not come. For a long while, therefore, the clock repre-

"Could you tell me what home is?"

"I never had a mother. I suppose a mother is one to whom you hurry when you are troubled."

Clearly, these are all meaningful revelations: the sorts of disclosures which a naturally shy person would make only if the need to explain herself were greater than the pain of explaining.

sented her special mystery. It registered something of the most profound importance; Father had said so. But what it registered—and how it did this—were matters that, try as she would, the little Emily was unable to grasp.

And then, when the clock has been comprehended, that which the clock measures remains a dark unknown. Time now becomes Emily Dickinson's foil. Into temporality she reads all the threats that the clock had once posed; onto temporality she projects all the troubled responses that the clock had formerly evoked. Like the clock, time ought to be simple, but it resists simplifying. It must be explained (peace of mind and even sanity depend upon that), yet no explanations are available. For Emily Dickinson, time represents the starting point toward any understanding of life. But how time works —and why—are matters that Miss Dickinson is fatally unable to grasp.

By her early experiences with the clock, Emily Dickinson's attention was drawn in a special and even a unique way to the mysteries to time. Out of this experience, I believe, there ultimately developed her neurotic obsession with temporality, which is the chief obsession of her poetry.

The father. He was the giver of the riddle. He introduced Emily Dickinson to the clock, but failed to tell her how it functioned. He was also supreme master in a father-dominated household. Accordingly, he should have been obeyed. One should have been able to draw closer to him, simply by following his precepts. But how could one obey, or draw close, when one had not understood? Almost, it seemed, the father put one off deliberately. By the process of confusion, he set an impossible task, just as he resisted the obedience which he likewise demanded, and defied the relationship which he appeared to have invited.

Emily Dickinson's God the Father comes to behave in exactly this same manner. God makes her a creature of time, imposes upon her the double riddle of the temporal flow and the inevitability of death. But then God withdraws, leaving behind no key with which she might unlock these puzzles. Moments come when God seems on the verge of explaining Himself. Invariably, though, His answers are vague and muddled; Emily Dickinson sees them as token gestures which only tantalize her, and make her search more difficult. And worse still can be alleged of God. As Supreme Authority in the universe, He exacts obedience; and, according to His prophets, He speaks in a language of love. But how can one obey when one has no knowledge of the rules? Or how can love exist, when one has been separated from God by the barrier of time that God devises? To a mature Emily Dickinson, it appears that God has put her off, just as her father had done. He sets up problems which defy solution, and invites her approach, only to turn away.

As the human father knew the secret of the clock, so God knows the secret of time. But neither tells—and both are masculine. It would appear, then, that maleness is to be identified with special privileges. Men have the power, the insight, and the capacity to rule experience which are denied to feminine beings. And the denial occurs because men guard their knowledge so jealously, because they resort to willful obfuscation in order to keep the secret theirs. Thus for the mature Emily Dickinson, it becomes necessary to take two distinct attitudes toward the Father, who is, by now, Edward Dickinson, God the Father, and man in the most general sense. There is her envy of the privilege he possesses. But there is also her bitter resentment at the fact of his possession.

Because of her long and complex relations with her father (relations of which the clock story is but one graphic indication), Emily Dickinson came to see Supreme Authority as a figure whose properties were masculinity, aloofness, the deliberate wish to confuse, and a tendency to join the invitation and the rejection into a single ambiguous gesture. Out of these relations, I believe, there emerged the warped notions of God and man, the morbid idea of a masculine Nature, the deep distrust of love and marriage, and the neurotic spinsterisms, all of which are among the ubiquitous features of Emily Dickinson's later life and poetry.

The child. Despite its rigors, childhood was, in one way, Emily Dickinson's peaceful period. It was the period before time was: the era before the beginnings of sequence. And since Emily Dickinson could not read a clock until she was fifteen, her childhood remained timeless to an extraordinary degree. Ever afterward, therefore, childhood must seem to the adult Emily Dickinson to be the blessed state. It is the state to which she looks back with nostalgia as her later years grow more and more unbearable. The point has already been made that when she retreated into her father's house, Miss Dickinson was seeking to escape temporal processes. We can now see even more explicitly, however, that she was intent upon reinhabiting the place where clocks were meaningless, and upon living over and over again her first fifteen years, when time had stood still.

282

In another sense, childhood was the time for showing up one's elders. When Emily Dickinson misunderstood her father's lesson, she did not merely draw attention to her own stupidity; she demonstrated, as well, that her father's teachings could be less than perfect. Repeating the episode thirty years later to Higginson, she still manages to convey the same impression: *Father thought he taught me:* Poor father; in his smug self-assurance, he never suspected that I might decline to learn. Thus for the adult Emily Dickinson, childhood comes to be identified with the practice of a subterfuge. What the child accomplished long ago, the mature poet can continue to do. She can re-enact a triumph over authority, any time she cloaks her true self with the guilelessness and the wide-eyed innocence of childhood.

Because of her own early years (and, once again, the clock story is no more than one illustration of what her early years were like), Emily Dickinson recollected childhood as a troubled time, but also as a period of peace and security. Out of this recollection, I believe, there emerge two last concepts which will fit the mode of adult behavior we have been assembling. There is the retreat backward into childhood, which is the crucial fact about Emily Dickinson's seclusion. And there is the symbolic assumption of the child's outlook, which is the most effective of her ironic strategies.

III ✛

In a way, we have been acting as the analyst does. We have before us a set of neurotic symptoms, openly displayed in the poetry of Emily Dickinson. Then a childhood episode comes to light. It is one of a kind with many others, no doubt; reading from it, while we simultaneously remain alert to what it suggests about the *whole course* of Emily Dickinson's formative years, we see that it helps to explain the symptoms, that it clarifies both the reasons for their existence and the particular form they took. From a strictly Freudian point of view, we should not be surprised that Miss Dickinson recalls the episode so vividly or tells it without restraint. It may be that she feels no inhibitions, since she has no notion of the full significance of what she is saying. Or (in a more likely alternative) it may well be that she speaks freely, painful though this is, because the episode is addressed to a friend, whose compassion she greatly needs. Higginson misses the point; but we, as more attentive and sympathetically disposed listeners, need not do so. We perhaps are in a position to see the truth—gleaning it, ironically, from a story that comes to us without reserve, because it was never at all intended for our ears.

We may as well concede that what we have done involves certain risks, although the vital connections—the relationships between an early event and later poetic themes—seem almost too definite to be denied outright. But the next conjecture I wish to make must push us still further into the realm of guesswork. This time, we may begin with a poem. It has already been quoted and discussed as a startling example of self-revelation. Now, however, I shall italicize, for special emphasis, seven key lines:

> In Winter, in my Room
> I came upon a Worm
> Pink, lank and warm.
> But as he was a Worm
> And Worms presume,

Not quite with him at home—
Secured him by a string
To something neighboring,
And went along.

A Trifle afterward
A thing occurred,
I'd not believe it if I heard—
But state with creeping blood—
A Snake, with mottles rare,
Surveyed my chamber floor,
In feature as the Worm before,
But ringed with power.
The very string with which
I tied him—too—
When he was mean and new,
That string was there—

I shrank—"How fair you are"
Propitiation's claw—
"Afraid," he hissed
"Of me?
"No cordiality?"
He fathomed me—

Then to a rhythm *slim*
Secreted in his form,
As patterns swim,
Projected him

That time I flew,
Both eyes his way,
Lest he pursue—

Nor ever ceased to run
Till in a distant town,
Towns on from mine
I sat me down—
This was a dream

The more obvious comments were made earlier. The poem appears to be an out-and-out sex fantasy. It betrays Emily Dickinson's simultaneous fear of and contempt for masculinity. It shows her mingled horror and awe at the fact of tumescence, her dread of sexual violation, and her wish to cower and to punish through the same central image. Consider again, however, the appearance of the string, so carefully planted in lines seven to nine, and so carefully repeated in lines eighteen to twenty-one. If, in one sense, the string suggests the flimsy defenses of womanhood and, in another, becomes the means of woman's subtle revenge, still this is not to rule out of the poem the more ordinary uses of a piece of string. In its most conventional role, string is that which binds, or secures, or makes fast. Far from being irrelevant, this is a point that may bring us very close indeed to the true intentions of the text. It may just be, in other words, that a string is placed around the *pink, lank Worm* because the worm is a gathering symbol for something that Emily Dickinson unconsciously wishes to secure for herself—something that she secretly admires, and so unconsciously desires to possess.

According to Freud, feelings of penis-envy are among the most common of the infantile experiences. The feelings spring from a little girl's awareness of the difference between her body and that of the male child. Out of the recognition, there comes the little girl's sense of having been deprived and made destitute. Something marvelous has been denied her—or stolen from her. As a result, she is not only different; she is actually less than a complete being. She envies the possession of an object which is as rare and novel as the penis, and obviously as important as the penis is.

We may note in passing how the circumstances of Emily Dickinson's early life were right for some such experience as the one summarized here. After all, she had a brother, less than two years older than herself, from whom, as a child, she might easily have made the discovery that Freud holds to be crucial. But, be that as it may, a more meaningful point to be suggested is this: that in the case of Emily Dickinson, the envious response to maleness seems to have lingered into maturity, and to have remained, in the mind of the mature woman, a central idea, a compulsive and a driving force.

There can be little real question but what the mature Emily Dickinson explicitly envied masculinity. Her poems indicate this, as we have observed over and over again. And so too do such random (yet revealing) biographical facts as her condescension toward her mother, her life-long cultivation of "strong" and "important" men (her father, Higginson, the editor Samuel Bowles, Judge Lord, and others), her interesting comment to Higginson that she "dreaded" women's chatter, and her obvious admiration for the emancipated and somewhat mannish Helen Hunt Jackson. Furthermore, without stretching the evidence at all, we can readily detect the basis for her envy. Because certain men had seemed so free to mistreat her, Miss Dickinson imputed to them the possession of a privilege and a prerogative which she

had been denied. Men (or their liberated female counterparts) mastered the same world that dominated her;
they got their poetry into print; they were able to criti-
cize, or to marry, or to set forth canons of taste, or even,
for that matter, simply to leave the house each day, with
no apparent fear of the world outside. However she
looked at the situation—whether as poet, as philos-
opher, or as recluse—it must often have occurred to
Emily Dickinson that the first cruel joke played by life
at her expense was the joke that made her a woman,
that brought her into the world as a lesser being. Hence
the adult Emily Dickinson repeated, in basic outline,
the pattern of destitution-and-envy that Freud describes.
We are not alleging, to be sure, that she was specifically
jealous of man's physical attributes. But we are saying
that she repeats the pattern of jealousy in her longing
for the power and the freedom, the poise and the superiority, which she everywhere associates with masculinity. Her envious feelings have become much more complex, much more diffused, and far less conscious than
they would be for a female child. On the other hand,
the feelings still persist, to be introduced unconsciously
into all those poems that have to do with the dominion
of "him," and to appear with unusual directness in a
poem like "In Winter, in my Room."

(Now seems the time to say that the same feelings
make themselves felt in the occasional slips of Miss
Dickinson's correspondence. Sometimes in her letters,
when she is referring to the children of Sue and Austin
Dickinson, she speaks of herself as their *Uncle* Emily.
Again, as is well known, she early adopted the brisk,
unadorned *Dickinson* as the signature for her letters to
Higginson. Consciously, these were among her little

jokes. But who will doubt that, unconsciously, the pre-empting of the masculine title and the masculine sur-name—the surname that somehow allows her to meet Higginson on his own grounds—was her way of as-suming the masculine role which she so deeply coveted?

(Then there is another matter. In the last decade of her life and after a series of misunderstandings with the Dickinsons in the house next door, Emily's relations with her brother Austin gradually worsened. From the hero-worship that she had felt for him earlier, she now comes to think of Austin in terms that portray him as Sue's dominated husband, and as a weak, somewhat vapid personality. Observing the change, Thomas John-son, in his *Emily Dickinson: An Interpretive Biography,* surmises that Austin had disappointed Emily because "an instinctive warmheartedness left [him] without relish for the rough and tumble of politics, and his civic leadership did not extend beyond the perimeter of the village. He lived for and within the college and the town, overseeing the erection of new buildings as his father had done, but adding to the natural beauty of the place by well-planned landscaping. Did he busy him-self with the minutiae of community improvements to sublimate a sense of frustration? Though Emily was the recluse and Austin the person of affairs, one senses that she knew that her accomplishments were substan-tial, but that his never quite matched his capabilities." But I would wish to go one step beyond Mr. Johnson's interpretation. If spite and vexation were the immedi-ate motives for a new view of Austin, do we not see that the new view masks a still larger issue? Austin is weak, a devotee of the trivial; yet by his sex alone he has been assured a dominant role in life. In contrast, Emily is

289

strong, her accomplishments *are* substantial; yet she has been denied the fruits of achievement by the fact of her femininity. One suspects that her real quarrel at this time was less with Austin than with the Fates, who should, by all rights, have made Emily the male member of the Dickinson family.)

These details are at least suggestive. They point to a principal source of Emily Dickinson's anxieties. They help to explain the theme of deprivation—the air of *A loss of something ever felt I*—which is so constantly embedded in her poetry. They certainly illuminate the emotional ferment that occurs whenever the poetry turns to an explicit account of male and female relationships. But the matter that will best explicate her features of fear (and thus her work) is a side issue of Miss Dickinson's envy of maleness. Or, rather, it is to be thought of as a consequence of this envy.

If we assume that Emily Dickinson wished she were a man, is it not a likely presumption that she had to be bitterly resentful where her own femininity was concerned? Opening up this line of enquiry, do we not find that there was much for her to be resentful of? Miss Dickinson, after all, was no Helen Hunt Jackson, able, despite her femininity, to deal with life freely and as an equal. She was not even like her sister-in-law Sue, whose charm and strength of mind apparently made her the center of every social gathering in Amherst. But what she was in her womanhood is, when we have paused to think of it for a little, almost painfully evident. Living "at home," responsible (in her own thinking at least) for the welfare of her parents, hedged in by parlor taboos and parlor chit-chat, forced at times to be a practitioner of the dutiful smile and the cheery little missive, dependent for outside stimulation upon those visitors who chose to call on her, and compelled (for whatever reason) to take her tea with them from behind a screen—cast to this part, Emily Dickinson had become nothing less than one of the "plush," "brittle," "cherubic" gentlewomen whom she scorned. It was not only the fact of being feminine that must have appalled her; it was that, as a woman, she epitomized every defect— every humiliating weakness—that she found despicable in femininity. It was that circumstance had made her enact literally the very role, which, of all the roles in her poetry, is the one considered to be the least attractive, the least desirable, and the most debasing.

What this means, surely, is that she also turned inward upon herself a gigantic self-hatred. She had to despise her physical, emotional, and psychic self, precisely because what she was stood in direct antithesis to what she desired to be. And in particular, one supposes, this hatred would center upon any specifically feminine function—upon, for instance, any such special and distinctive mark of femininity as the menses. Psychology has accustomed us to the fact that a woman, disaffected with womanhood, may resent menstruation; it has shown that, however unconsciously she does so, she will be likely to deplore the process as an affront and a burden. This response (continuing to grant our premises about her) might easily have constituted for Emily Dickinson a problem of the most critical kind, and one to which no ready adjustment would seem possible. Eager for masculine liberties and contemptuous of anyone (especially herself) who lacked those liberties, she would be prone indeed to regard as obnoxious and intrusive any process which recalled her to her true sexual nature. It

seems virtually inevitable that she would react antag-
onistically to the function which regularly gave her
away by branding her a woman.

And the antagonism has consequences. For to find
the menses psychologically painful is, according to a
good many recent studies of the subject, to heighten
proportionately their capacity for causing physical
pain.* Hence by the very vigor with which she rejected
her femininity, Emily Dickinson could well have con-
demned herself to a peculiar and exaggerated physical
distress. She could well have transformed menstruation
into a process so grim and terrible that it ruled her life,
and, in ways partially unrecognized by her, came to
color and condition the view that she took of every sort
of experience.

When we have reduced it to a handful of sentences,
what is her most persistent theme? Emily Dickinson
writes of pain: the rhythmical, regular, periodic pattern of pain. Whether the overt topic is God or Nature,
death or love or time or human society or the depredations of the self, Miss Dickinson's speakers are customarily to be found in any one of four related conditions. They are squarely in the midst of agony:

> But, most, like Chaos—Stopless—Cool—
> Without a Chance, or Spar—
> Or even a Report of Land—
> To justify—Despair.

* I am greatly indebted at this point to implications in
Freud; to the views of Marie Bonaparte, Bruno Bettelheim,
and Karl Menninger; and to such psychologically oriented
studies of woman as Simone de Beauvoir's *The Second Sex*
and the *Modern Woman* of Ferdinand Lundberg and Marynia
F. Farnham.

Or they are remembering an agony which is still so near
at hand that they seem to stand in its center:

> 'Twas like a Maelstrom with a notch,
> That nearer, every Day,
> Kept narrowing it's boiling Wheel
> Until the Agony
>
> Toyed coolly with the final inch
> Of your delirious Hem—

Or they are being pushed closer and closer toward the
agony ahead, so that each new moment is, in itself, an
agony of preparation:

> [Pain] has no Future—but itself—
> It's Infinite contain
> It's Past—enlightened to perceive
> New Periods—of Pain.

Or they have emerged from agony, but emerged in full
awareness that the conclusion of this ordeal is also a
preliminary to the next:

> And then—a Day as huge
> As Yesterdays in pairs,
> Unrolled it's horror in my face—
> Until it blocked my eyes—

The vision of Emily Dickinson, therefore, is the vision
of a recurring hell. She writes of a world in which the
only certain thing is process—and the process is a
deadly ritual of physical, mental, moral, emotional,
and spiritual torments. This is her unique subject: the
portrayals of *New Periods—of Pain.* And we need only
look at the subject, and at the way she habitually struc-

tures it, to see that it conforms exactly to the preparation, the fact, the release, and the new preparation which are the basic stages of the menstrual cycle.

But once again a word of caution is in order. Nowhere is it being implied that Emily Dickinson wrote poems directly about the menses. That conclusion would be unsupported by any real evidence; and it would, in all likelihood, be psychologically unfounded. Clearly, Miss Dickinson had to be aware of the problem that we are ascribing to her. She had to be aware, that is, of the pain, the depressions, the anxieties, the tensions, the psychological and physiological accompaniments to menstruation. On the other hand, one must surmise that she was no more conscious of expressing the problem in its own terms than she was prepared to recognize that the real cause of the problem lay only in her mental dissatisfactions. For Emily Dickinson to have written openly about the menses would not only have involved her in a violating of social and moral taboos; much more seriously, it would have committed her to violating the psychological taboo. She would have had to say frankly and explicitly that which the conscious mind would never have permitted her to say. Accordingly, the idea of menstruation enters her poetry by the twin avenues of repression and displacement. The real problem—the actual, but unmentionable pain within—is carefully hidden from view. But the problem erupts anyhow; and it is projected by Emily Dickinson onto pain-giving persecutors who exist in the world without.

She projects it onto her view of the universe—and creates out of it the post-Emersonian universe, a place of the personified bringers of suffering, of the cunning and willful forces who engage perpetually in their cycle of affliction, release, and a new affliction. She projects it onto time, and creates thereby that moving, driving, ruthless, and ceremonial entity that is forever bearing down upon the speaker and carrying her from the moment of despair to the moment of false hope to the moment of the fresh despair. She projects it onto the theme of the dreaded invasion, a theme which shows that while welcome and pleasurable guests (peace, stasis, immortality, the earned bliss, God, the Celestial Bridegroom) never linger on the speaker's threshold, still the speaker's doors and windows are all too vulnerable to the unwelcome, the pain-giving visitation (the periodic trespass of death, doubt, the inexplicable guilt, the undeserved punishment, the wicked male, the ghastly fright). And primarily of course she projects it onto the characterization of her speaker: the helpless, abused, harassed, tormented female; the tremulous feminine figure who shrinks from the blow that falls upon her nonetheless; the forlorn feminine watcher who sees that her unexpected gifts are merely preludes to disaster; the archetypal feminine victim whose body, mind, and soul are regularly set upon by external horrors; the violated feminine sensibility, to whom, at intervals, there comes the pain which threatens, impinges, shatters, destroys, and then withdraws—but passes away only to renew itself for the attack that will be repeated on some all-too-clearly imagined tomorrow.

These are nothing less important than Emily Dickinson's basic conceptions of life. And if the present analysis of their meaning is correct, the conceptions are used to disguise a problem which they constantly suggest, but are never quite allowed to state. They are psychological defense mechanisms, and, as such, they rep-

295

resent a series of substitute expressions. They supplied her with an "innocent vocabulary," through which Emily Dickinson's discussion of Emily Dickinson's periodic torments became a tolerable activity, a permissible enterprise.

And, finally, it is worth observing that the real problem seems to present itself in the trio of images with which this chapter has been concerned. The *clock* is central to Emily Dickinson's poetry, because her own life was time-dominated—was measured out, so to speak, by the repeated passage from one time of pain to the next. The *father* is the ambiguous figure of her poetry, evoking a complex double response, because, while as God the Father He caused the pain she felt in life (and hence was to be hated), still as the human male he stood outside the painful process (and hence was in an enviable position). *Childhood* is the symbolic retreat of her poetry as well as the literal retreat of Miss Dickinson's life, because childhood precedes puberty, and so, aside from unimaginable death and unobtainable maleness, it constituted for Emily Dickinson the only free and unencumbered state: the only state in which the pain could be escaped.

IV ✛

What have our conjectures told us? Not, certainly, why Emily Dickinson was a poet of genius. Depending upon one's preferences, one might like to explain that fact as a miracle of the genes, or as the gift of God. But the point is that neither criticism nor psychology has a way of telling us why Emily Dickinson transformed personal problems into enduring poetry, while another woman, confronted with the same grave issues, might have become an hysteric, a feminist, a lesbian, a religious tractarian, or an aggressive shrew (somewhat, apparently, in the manner of Lavinia Dickinson)—but would, at all events, have written nothing of value.

Provided they seem even reasonably correct, though, the conjectures have not simply turned into a public spectacle the intimate details of a writer's life. Were this what they accomplished, we should only have paid a last, needless indignity to a lady whose chief value was obviously the value of privacy. But much more is involved. In three ways, each of them more crucial than the ones that precede it, our speculations about Emily Dickinson's psychic nature—her psychic wound—will shed their light on what we have already called the one ultimately important fact about Miss Dickinson, which is the complex fact of her art.

They first provide us with a cogent explanation of why she wrote. Plainly, Emily Dickinson wrote poetry in order to gain relief from great personal tensions. Writing became her way of rendering at least halfway intelligible, and hence halfway endurable, a world in which awful things could happen. At a time when the springs of religious faith ran strong, she might have found solace from her hurt in prayer or incantation. Where the springs had dried up, the only solace available to her had to come from the sheer magic of creativity. The freedom to speak the hurt aloud was as necessary to Miss Dickinson as breathing itself. The use of substitute expressions through which the hurt could be transmuted and set down on paper—this, it would appear, was nothing less than her salvation.*

* Note, in this connection, what may well be a bit of relevant chronology. Emily Dickinson became aware of time at the age of fifteen. She began to compose poetry with a kind of frenzy in her late twenties. And by 1875, when she was in her

297

Secondly, our speculations will help explain a good number of the things that she so insistently wrote about. From the childhood experience with which this chapter began, there can be deduced four of Emily Dickinson's lifelong poetic subjects: a special view of childhood, a unique sense of time, a resentment of all authority, and a bafflement occasioned by certain particular authorities that refuse to be faced down. Out of the adult fears and aggressions that we explored next, it is possible to trace an intensification of these concerns and, in addition, Miss Dickinson's poetic fascination with the beleaguered self, her poetic portrayals of love as compromising and hateful, her poetic vision of a menacing universe, and her poetic need to escape the menace, whether through ironic withdrawal or into the sort of complete escape that death promises. In short, the spinster's wounds, as we have reconstructed them, would seem to speak with an almost classic exactness about the themes, conceptions, and responses—and beyond these, the imagery, diction, structure, and drama—of the poet's work. Reading the work against the background of the wounds, one catches the underlying motives that have entered into individual poems. And one detects as well the basis for that unified outlook—that grand, tragic design— into which the individual poems are repeatedly swept up.

But there is yet a third way in which our speculations mid-forties, there was a marked decline in her writing. In other words, the issue that was to be central to her art was first made apparent to her at puberty. Her need to express the issue was greatest during her third and fourth decades, or at the time when her spinsterish prejudices and their consequences were probably most demanding. And the need became progressively less urgent with the onset of the female climacteric.

can be valuable. Once they are made, it is more nearly possible for us to measure the distance between the private anguish and the public statement of anguish, between the tormented woman who was and the poetry of torment that is. This sort of measurement I take to be the last, essential function of literary criticism which has a psychological bias.

The difficulty about such a criticism is that it too often turns out to be reductionist, not in intention perhaps, but in effect. Literary strategies are reduced to their psychic causes; and however the reduction occurs —whether the critic infers the wound from the work, or derives the work from the wound, or (in the manner of the present analysis) tries to work simultaneously in both directions—there is an ever-present danger that the cause will become a matter of more moment than the strategy. But the triumph of autobiography over art is by no means the concluding fact that I would wish to adduce about Emily Dickinson. Just the reverse is true. The supremely significant fact in her case is that (to paraphrase her) she outlived the pain, not literally in the sense of resolving it, but symbolically in the sense of making the hurt universal. Drawing again upon Edmund Wilson's metaphors, we have to remember that if her "bow" was at once the product and the reflector of a "wound," the bow was also a creative principle, with a power and integrity all its own, and with the capacity to reveal both personal sickness and something much greater than the sickness.

There is a poem of Miss Dickinson's which will help to clarify my point:

> A *Wounded* Deer—leaps highest—
> I've heard the Hunter tell—

'Tis but the Ecstasy of *death*—
And then the Brake is still!

The *Smitten* Rock that gushes!
The *trampled* steel that springs!
A Cheek is always redder
Just where the Hectic stings!

Mirth is the Mail of Anguish—
In which it Cautious Arm,
Lest anybody spy the blood
And "you're hurt" exclaim.

Brought together in this group of superb paradoxes are
two actions: the *wound* and the *leap*. The *wound* moti-
vates. Without it, as the italicized words keep suggesting, nothing at all could happen. And yet, consequence
though it is, the resultant *leap* is not simply equal to
the force of the motivation. Looking at the whole event,
we necessarily focus one part of our attention upon the
hurt; to do otherwise would be to miss the point of the
wholeness. But we are also made to see that the leap
has its special grace and beauty, its aesthetic refinement, its own distinctive purity of movement—and that
these qualities represent a transcendence of the hurt,
and even perhaps a kind of triumph over it.

It does no good to hush up Emily Dickinson's sickness. For one thing, the malady within is too clearly indicated by her life and work to be ignored. For another,
suppressing the probable circumstances only deprives
us of one legitimate way of illuminating her poetry. On
the other hand, neither is there much point in citing the
sickness, unless, with the poetry always in view, we note

that the hectic is not merely reproduced there, but that, as in "A wounded Deer," it begets an effect which is far beyond itself. Emily Dickinson's greatness is this: that writing from and of a hurt which is not ours, she also managed to record the hurts we share. Or it is this: that out of the grotesqueness of her private situation, there was wrested the insight she had into man's tragic lot in a tragic world. Born of frustration, her work passes the supreme test which art demands of suffering. The frustrations are important, since, lacking them, Emily Dickinson might never have written a line of verse. What really counts, however, is the aesthetic leap to which the frustrations give rise. By virtue of the leap, Miss Dickinson enjoys, as an artist, the very triumph that life denied her. She ceases to be the agonized maiden lady of Amherst, and becomes, by a profound and moving irony, the poet of the tragic man.

Index of Poems

303

General Index

Aiken, Conrad, 140
Alice in Wonderland, 38
American Transcendentalism
(*see also* Emersonianism),
10–11, 24, 96–97, 258

Baudelaire, Charles, 250–251
Bergson, Henri, 94
Blackmur, R. P., 223
Blake, William, 20, 109
Book of Job, 54–56
Bowles, Samuel, 169n, 287
Browning, Elizabeth Barrett, 5, 162

Chase, Richard, 173–175

Dickinson, Austin, 8, 168, 207, 287, 288, 289–290
Dickinson, Edward, 8, 78n, 167–168, 277–283, 287
Dickinson, Emily, correspondence, 9, 158, 169n, 207, 288–290; seclusion, 8–9, 11–12, 40, 56, 76–78, 83, 106–107, 141, 158, 165–170, 179, 183, 184, 207, 220, 274, 277–279, 283, 290–292, 296

Emersonian legacy, 10–11, 24–27, 28, 39, 97–99; contrasted with Emerson, 80, 81–82, 185, 225, 227–231, 232–233, 234–239, 267, 268; contrasted with Whitman, 80, 94, 97, 267–269; contrasted with Melville, 6–7, 79–80, 100, 112, 143–145, 226–227

poems about immortality, 137–140; poems about marriage, 174–177, 220; poems about time contrasted with *ubi-sunt* poetry, 104–105; poems about guilt, 202–204, 258–261

theme of "the dreaded invasion," 102–103, 129–130, 178–183, 216–220, 228–232; theme of "the momentous transition," 86–93; theme of "the unexpected gift," 47–49, 51–56, 103, 218

ironic style, 56–58, 61–68; surrealistic style, 182, 193, 250; symbolic style, 245–256; two styles of the death poetry, 113, 115–121, 126, 130–131, 133–134, 145

existentialist attitudes, 198, 262–264; masculine personifications, 21–22, 170–171, 176–177, 179–183, 281–282, 286; feminine personifications, 21–22, 170–171, 177, 209, 221
Dickinson, Lavinia, 8, 207, 297

306

ALBERTSON COLLEGE OF IDAHO

PS1541.Z5.G7

The long shadow;Emily Dickinson's tragic

3 5556 00052239 1

DATE DUE

WITHDRAWN

PRINTED IN U.S.A.